Feeling the \

Feeling the Words incorporates a thorough review of essential psychoanalytic concepts, a clear critical history of analytical ideas and an assessment of the contribution neuroscience has to offer.

Mauro Mancia uses numerous detailed clinical examples to demonstrate how insights from neuroscience and infant development research can change how the analyst responds to his or her patient. Major topics such as the transference, the Oedipus complex, the interpretation of dreams and the nature of mental pain are reviewed and refined in the light of these recent developments. The book is divided into three parts, covering:

- Memory and the unconscious
- The dream: between neuroscience and psychoanalysis
- Further reflections on narcissism and other clinical topics

Feeling the Words offers an original perspective on the connection between memory and the unconscious. It will be welcomed by all psychoanalysts interested in investigating new ways of working with patients.

Mauro Mancia is Professor Emeritus of Neurophysiology, University of Milan, Italy and Training Analyst of the Italian Psychoanalytical Society. His interest is in the link between neuroscientific knowledge and psycho-analytic theories of mind and he has written extensively on the subjects of narcissism, dreams, sleep, memory and the unconscious.

THE NEW LIBRARY OF PSYCHOANALYSIS
General Editor Dana Birksted-Breen

The New Library of Psychoanalysis was launched in 1987 in association with the Institute of Psychoanalysis, London. It took over from the International Psychoanalytical Library, which published many of the early translations of the works of Freud and the writings of most of the leading British and Continental psychoanalysts.

The purpose of the New Library of Psychoanalysis is to facilitate a greater and more widespread appreciation of psychoanalysis and to provide a forum for increasing mutual understanding between psychoanalysts and those working in other disciplines such as the social sciences, medicine, philosophy, history, linguistics, literature and the arts. It aims to represent different trends both in British psychoanalysis and in psychoanalysis generally. The New Library of Psychoanalysis is well placed to make available to the English-speaking world psychoanalytic writings from other European countries and to increase the interchange of ideas between British and American psychoanalysts.

The Institute, together with the British Psychoanalytical Society, runs a low-fee psychoanalytic clinic, organizes lectures and scientific events concerned with psychoanalysis and publishes the *International Journal of Psychoanalysis*. It also runs the only UK training course in psychoanalysis that leads to membership of the International Psychoanalytical Association – the body which preserves internationally agreed standards of training, of professional entry, and of professional ethics and practice for psychoanalysis as initiated and developed by Sigmund Freud. Distinguished members of the Institute have included Michael Balint, Wilfred Bion, Ronald Fairbairn, Anna Freud, Ernest Jones, Melanie Klein, John Rickman and Donald Winnicott.

Previous General Editors include David Tuckett, Elizabeth Spillius and Susan Budd. Previous and current Members of the Advisory Board include Christopher Bollas, Ronald Britton, Catalina Bronstein, Donald Campbell, Sara Flanders, Stephen Grosz, John Keene, Eglé Laufer, Juliet Mitchell, Michael Parsons, Rosine Jozef Perelberg, Richard Rusbridger, David Taylor and Mary Target.

ALSO IN THIS SERIES

TITLES IN THE NEW LIBRARY OF PSYCHOANALYSIS TEACHING SERIES

THE NEW LIBRARY OF PSYCHOANALYSIS

General Editor: Dana Birksted-Breen

Feeling the Words

Neuropsychoanalytic Understanding of Memory and the Unconscious

Published in Italian as *Sentire le Parole: Archivi Sonori Della Memoria Implicita e Musicalitá del Transfert*

Mauro Mancia

Translated by Judy Baggott

Routledge
Taylor & Francis Group
LONDON AND NEW YORK

First published in Italian as *Sentire le Parole: Archivi Sonori Della Memoria Implicita e Musicalitá del Transfert* by Bollati Boringhieri Editore
Vittorio Emanuele II, 86-10121 Turin, Italy

Italian language edition © 2004 Bollati Boringhieri Editore srl, Turin

First published 2007 by Routledge
27 Church Road, Hove, East Sussex BN3 2FA

Simultaneously published in the USA and Canada
by Routledge
270 Madison Ave, New York, NY 10016

Routledge is an imprint of the Taylor & Francis Group, an informa business

© 2007 Mauro Mancia
Translation © 2007 Judy Baggott

Typeset in Bembo by
Keystroke, 28 High Street, Tettenhall, Wolverhampton
Printed and bound in Great Britain by
TJ International Ltd, Padstow, Cornwall
Cover design by Sandra Heath

This publication has been produced with paper manufactured to strict environmental standards and with pulp derived from sustainable forests.

British Library Cataloguing in Publication Data
A catalogue record for this book is available from the British Library

Library of Congress Cataloging in Publication Data
Mancia, Mauro.
   [Sentire le parole. English]
   Feeling the words : neuropsychoanalytic understanding of memory and the unconscious / Mauro Mancia ; translated from Italian by Judy Baggott.
      p. cm. – (New library of psychoanalysis)
   Includes bibliographical references and index.
   ISBN 0–415–39096–6 (hbk) – ISBN 0–415–39097–4 (pbk)
   1. Psychoanalysis. 2. Neurosciences. 3. Memory.
   4. Subconsciousness. I. Title.
   BF173.M35656513 2007
   150.19′5–dc22
                              2006028295

ISBN: 978–0–415–39096–5 (hbk)
ISBN: 978–0–415–39097–2 (pbk)

To the composers and musicians of all times
who have taught me to "feel the words"

Contents

Foreword

One hundred and fifty years after Freud's birth, we are in the midst of one of the great epochs in psychoanalysis. On every continent, there seems to be a lively ferment of psychoanalytic ideas and a new freedom to explore again the legacy that we have inherited from Freud. Old issues of loyalty, hegemony, or schism seem to have spent their force. Many of the most creative minds, both in psychoanalysis and in allied disciplines, are devoted now to developing new ways of thinking and applying what we have learned from Freud.

Mauro Mancia has written a remarkably comprehensive book in which he presents a review of major psychoanalytic domains and areas of interest, bringing to bear an extraordinary knowledge of scholarly and scientific contributions from throughout the world. Psychoanalysis has developed on many fronts in many directions and these are part of the knowledge base of this volume. But while Mancia provides an extensive review of essential psychoanalytic concepts, and a clearly presented critical history of analytic ideas, his major interest is in the new perspectives offered by empirical research in infant development and neuroscience. His emphasis is on how the cutting-edge new scientific information available to us today can change and expand the ways in which analysts hear and respond to their patients' productions. He is less interested in presenting us with new theories than in demonstrating to us, through many detailed descriptions of clinical encounters, how analysts' listening capacity and their range of responsiveness is hugely enlarged by this new knowledge.

Mancia reviews major topics such as the transference, the earliest infant–parent relationship, a re-examination of the Oedipus complex, the sources and interpretation of dreams, Klein and Bion, ethology and sleep, the nature of mental pain and more. In each area he not only has new and interesting things to tell us, but also carefully illustrates his ideas with detailed clinical examples, showing a master clinician at work. Mancia is one of the pioneers in helping us to review the corpus of psychoanalytic knowledge, attempting to retain what is best, modify what no longer suits our current state of knowing, and integrating new kinds of knowledge which were not available only a few years ago.

The advances in neuropsychiatry have been startling – so much so that increasingly psychiatrists and researchers tend to talk about what the brain is doing rather than what the person is doing, providing a new mode of Cartesian dualism. Neuroimaging techniques have revealed the extraordinary degree of localization in the brain that corresponds with specific cognitive and affective tasks. Cellular biochemistry has discovered an array of chemical cascades involved in mental activity and together these sciences have begun to map the ways in which memories are laid down and changed – areas of critical interest for psychoanalysis. Eric Kandel was awarded a Nobel Prize for his work on the neurobiology of memory in 2000, and he has carefully related his reductionist scientific strategy to the larger purposes of psychoanalysis (Kandel 2006).

Psychoanalysts have responded in several different ways to the excitement of neurobiology. One group continues to insist that the activities of the brain may be an interesting topic, but it is unrelated to psychoanalysis. For this group, psychoanalysis is interested solely in the unfolding interaction of analyst and analysand in the traditional analytic setting in which the patient's free associations are the focus of the analyst's attention, and the analyst's aim is to provide interpretations that will help to unmask and undo the resistances that hide the conflicts and their neurotic resolutions that date back to childhood experience. In this view events occurring before the age of 3 are not of interest to the psychoanalyst.

Another group of psychoanalysts, at the opposite pole, eagerly embraces these new findings of neuroscience, coining the term neuropsychoanalysis, with the hope that blending analysis and neuroscience will give psychoanalysis the scientific objective and empirical base that has eluded it until now. In this view Freud's project, abandoned for lack of data at that time, can now be successfully resumed and psychoanalysis can join the family of empirical sciences.

I believe that both these positions are misguided. Surely neuroscience and infant observation have alerted us to possibilities that psychoanalysis has previously tended to be unaware of or to ignore. Clearly, we can no longer ignore what neuroscience might teach us about the nature of learning, memory, and forms of unconscious processing, topics at the core of psychoanalysis. Implicit memory, or the unrepressed unconscious, a focus of Mancia's interest, is prominent among these findings. But the effort to create a single field of neuropyschoanalysis implies the notion that we relinquish our focus on the person or the self in favor of crediting the brain as the locus of initiative and action. This seems like too much to give up at this point in our knowledge. Following Freud's lead, we have learned an extraordinary amount about how individuals function in society and about the hermeneutic, narrative base of the self, and it would be premature to abandon this focus at this time.

Mancia takes a third route. He is interested in all that neuroscience has to teach us, but his aim is to use this new knowledge in the service of what we know about attachment, desire, fantasy, pain and terror. As he illustrates in his many vivid clinical examples throughout this volume, the concept of the unrepressed unconscious – implicit memory – is an essential one for him in understanding his patients' lives and their relationship to their analyst. Implicit memory is the name given to the category of memories that have never been verbalized – those procedures or habits that are learned before language acquisition or which encode bodily activities that do not depend on verbal representation for their retention in memory. Using this concept of the unrepressed unconscious, Mancia succeeds in greatly enlarging the domain of the apparent content of free associations and dreams, and also focuses our attention on the music of the transference–countertransference relationship – the ways in which posture, tone of voice, the atmosphere of the analytic setting, are critical to understanding the relationship of patient and analyst and thus ultimately to understanding the patient. Mancia convincingly demonstrates how the earliest preverbal period of patients' lives may lay down relational and affective patterns of response that will enduringly determine the depth and emotional coloring – negative and positive – of relationships throughout adult life. He emphasizes that this domain of implicit memory – unrepressed and yet unconscious, not subject to verbal recall – requires construction on the part of the analyst as well as reconstruction, and is communicated, often without words, in the patient's dreams and in the transference–countertransference interactions of the analytic couple.

Mancia's emphasis on the music (and I might add, the dance) of analysis, highlights aspects of relatedness that are non-conscious, automatic, and are not caught up in inner conflict or instinctual repression. This tremendous expansion of the domain of psychoanalysis opens up new arenas for analytic understanding and intervention. In order to take advantage of these new sources of information, analysts must adopt new attitudes regarding their attention to non-language expressions, mastering the techniques for attending to the silent footprints of habitual early learned forms of relating that are critical in the lives of their adult patients. The dream analyses presented in this volume are vivid and masterful examples of how this is done. The experienced clinician will also be particularly informed by the detailed discussion of transference and reality and the nature of transference-love, that hybrid that is one of the motors of psychoanalytic technique.

Mancia's appreciation of the multileveled nature of psychoanalysis takes him into the realms of philosophy, theater and art and the nature of reality – physical and psychic. Interested not only in neuroscience, Mancia's sophisticated knowledge of the philosophical and artistic underpinnings of psychoanalysis informs this volume. Mancia does not shrink from exploring some of the deepest enduring problems of human thought and feeling. What is happiness, for example? His fascinating discussion links happiness to our fears of death, implicit memories of the blissful moments with the mother before separation interfered, a sense of revelation of the fullness of the human possibility, and the wish for continued ecstasy. As if that were not enough, we are reminded that the wish for enduring happiness constitutes a danger, luring us to believe that we may attain it without self-examination, painful knowledge of one's self and enduring hard work. Much depends on the quality of the infantile experience of pain or satisfaction – experiences that are stored in implicit memory, intermixed with varying degrees of pathological defenses such as splitting, projective identification, denial and false idealizations, all of which provide the background for later misery. The analytic task is (p. 207)

> to help patients manage their negative parts better since these are a source of unhappiness, and to transform their internal figures so these are more tolerant and creative. The problem is not so much to free patients of a neurotic or psychotic symptom but to help them establish a different way of living.

I know of no better statement of the goals of analysis.

This book is notable for being stimulating and comprehensible to both the experienced psychoanalyst clinician as well as to anyone with an interest in the work of Freud and his followers, and the state of psychoanalytic research today.

Arnold Cooper

Reference

Kandel, E.R. (2006). *In Search of Memory: The Emergence of a New Science of Mind*. New York: Norton.

Acknowledgements

My gratitude goes first to my patients, without whose help I would never have acquired the experience I refer to here and who have enriched my emotions and thinking. I have also to thank my pupils and colleagues who, in our various seminars and meetings, have stimulated and fueled my scientific interests and aroused my curiosity. Very special thanks are due to Judy Baggott for her competence in the translation of the book and to Laura Matteini, my valuable assistant, for her skill and patience in searching the literature and setting out this manuscript. I also wish to acknowledge the New Library editor and the readers for their helpful comments, which have lead to a partial reworking of the original Italian book for this English edition.

INTRODUCTION

Beyond Freud:
the twilight of Oedipus and the neurosciences' contribution to psychoanalysis

The twilight of Oedipus

Psychoanalysis was officially born with the "Dora case" (Freud, 1901), but it had been gestating in Freud's mind for a long time before this, when he shifted from identifying himself with Joseph Breuer, a severe guardian of the scientific method so dear to the natural sciences, to Wilhelm Fliess, who showed scant respect for orthodoxy and the scientific method, and was much more interested in his own biological "fantasies". It was Fliess who enabled Freud to think more freely about the mind's functions, detaching them from the brain's functions which served as the naturalistic "guarantee" that Freud felt he needed if he was not to wander too far beyond the borders of the Austrian and German scientists' positivist culture at the end of the nineteenth century (Mancia, 1983, 1985).

The *Project for a Scientific Psychology* (Freud, 1895) marks this change in Freud's thinking, as he tries to explain psychology in neurophysiological terms, proposing a model of the relation between mind and brain. However, he did not publish this because he was convinced that the medical and academic circles of Vienna – unlike Troy! – would never let this explosive Trojan horse through the gates of their university citadel. So he picked up the basic concepts laid out in the *Project* and incorporated them into a new, major oeuvre he was working on, *The Interpretation of Dreams* (Freud, 1900), in which, five years later, he illustrated his concept of the unconscious and the mind's Oedipal functions.

The idea of the unconscious certainly comes from the model described in the *Project*, where it appears as the repression of infantile (sexual) desire in the ψ system which is satisfied in dreams through regression – topical,

1

temporal, or formal – so that the wish can be fulfilled by pushing the gates of perception (the φ system) from within, thus creating a perception with no object, in other words a hallucination. The unconscious was subsequently described "dynamically" in metapsychological writings in 1915 and linked to an active process of repression. In the *Project* model Freud picks up the roots of his definition of the dream, as the hallucinatory satisfaction of a wish repressed in infancy.

Closely tied to the concept of the unconscious is the Oedipus complex, which Freud announced to Fliess in a letter dated 15 October 1897, a few months after the death of his father; it was subsequently defined in further works, as the pivot around which his whole theory of the mind revolved.

The use of the myth of Oedipus in relation to the theory of the mind's development is too important to be left behind without comment. It was triggered by a personal experience which Freud guessed had universal impact. It was also, however, the fruit of the dominant culture in Europe at the end of the nineteenth century, particularly of the Austrian middle class and Jews, with their attachment to the patriarchal family and much less weight given to the woman's maternal role, even though fairly recently the mother's importance in Freud's own education and choice of profession was highlighted (Speziale-Bagliacca, 2002).

All the central European literature of those years was centered on the father–son conflict, from Arthur Schnitzler to Franz Kafka, Otto Weininger and Robert Musil. Together with Freud, these writers found themselves faced at the end of the nineteenth century with a "mirror game" under the constellation of Oedipus (Dalle Luche, 2002).

Arthur Tatossian's *Oedipus in Kakania* (1988) (a word-play on the two Ks of *Kaiserlich* and *Königlich* which stood for the power of the Austro-Hungarian Empire) pans over this period from the point of view of the relationship between psychoanalysis and central European literature. Tatossian notes that we should hardly be surprised that Oedipus was "discovered" in Kakania in 1897. This was the year – a significant coincidence – when Emperor Franz Josef I received a group of Viennese painters, headed by Gustav Klimt, who announced they were rebelling against "academism" (symbolically killing their fathers) and founding the *secession* movement. All this happened a few months before Freud's letter of 15 October 1897 telling Fliess he had "discovered" Oedipus.

At that time the question of identity was becoming acute for the Austrian Jews. They could go for total assimilation, denying their original identity, or neutralize it through socialist ideology, or accentuate it by embracing Zionism. Psychoanalysis could be viewed, at this particular moment in history, as another attempt to sort out the question of the Jewish identity.

The KaKania writers did not take long to show interest in psychoanalysis – they were among the first. The cultured public at the end of the nineteenth century was familiar with the father–son conflict, from Henrik Ibsen's plays and Arthur Schnitzler's works describing a patriarchal world where the mother was constantly overshadowed first by her husband and then by her sons. Schnitzler's family setting was very similar to Kafka's and Musil's. All these authors presented the father figure in a bright light in their writings and diaries, so much so that Tatossian (1988) calls Kafka an "exemplary Oedipus". Kafka, in particular, expresses a "flight" from the father throughout his work, or at any rate takes the son's side against his father. Musil (1957) too in *The Man without Quality* has Ulrich say that any attempt at evasion leads in the end to the father.

Franz Kafka knows the basics of psychoanalysis and in *The Judgment* (*Das Urteil*, 1912) he tells the tale of a son who wanted to take his father's place, and was punished for it. It is inevitable to see the connection with the castration anxiety that Freud suggested was one of the reasons for the Oedipus resolution.

Kafka considered the unconscious something that belonged to the "spiritual world", so it cannot be described, and can only be lived. The disagreement with psychoanalysis peaks when he says the origin of psychogenesis is not individual, and is convinced that man is conditioned by the contingencies of his actual existence. Kafka – says Tatossian (1988) – certainly admits his suffering and his neurosis too, but denies that these mark him individually. They are the bad luck of his generation, meaning the generation of young western Jews, who were not just "four-day Jews", referring to the three Jewish high holidays and Franz Josef's birthday, who could not and did not want to transmit authentic Judaism. Kafka therefore allowed that there was some truth in psychoanalysis but it had to be seen against the background of his generation of Jews. He disagreed with Freud, paraphrasing Wittgenstein's idea that anyone who could only repeat what psychoanalysis said should shut up (Kafka, 1980). Like Kafka, Musil (1957) too found Freud's ideas of causality unacceptable, so from this point of view, both are closer to Wittgenstein (Mancia, 2002).

Kafka's (1975) *Letter to Father* is full of reflections that bring us back to Oedipus. The letters are not full of painful nostalgia, but offer a dual message – apparently contradictory – that the father sends his son, who should emancipate himself following his example, and become an adult, while asking him to be submissive for gratitude and remain a child.

Quite understandably, Deleuze and Guattari (1972) criticize the *Letter to Father*, because of its excessive emphasis on Oedipus, to the point of seeming almost a caricature. As a matter of fact, the incestuous desire for the mother is not at all evident in Kafka's Oedipus, and the basic problem is a question of *power*.

Linked to the question of his neurosis is also the problem of sexuality, which Kafka certainly does not see as a source of pleasure. He talks of sex as a "punishment for the happiness of living together" (Kafka, 1954) and says he feels sick when he walks in front of his parents' bed. In *The Castle* (1926) he describes Agrimensore and Frida, both naked, having intercourse in a puddle of beer on the floor. A revolting scene that is anything but erotic! So all Kafka's writing suggests he is strongly inhibited when it comes to sexuality, as the whole series of his various "fiancées" confirms. In actual fact this abnormal attitude to sexuality is part of a more general personality disorder dominated by persecutory internal parents who he hates, but with incurable affective ambivalence.

In the eyes of an analyst today, the Kafka case seems to go well beyond Oedipus, expressing a poor primary relationship with the mother, which has the effect of shifting the "axis" from the father to the mother, involving both parents and the child's surroundings as he grows up. Quite possibly an early relational trauma, which we know little about, helped create Kafka's personality dominated by a suffering, persecutory part that became pivotal in the figures and situations represented in his writings. There might, on the other hand, have been a major lack of maternal care – with the threat of abandon – that prevented Kafka identifying with his father figure, or possibly his father himself, his absence or inadequacy, failed to help Franz dis-identify or separate himself from his mother. This affective situation was the cause of his neurosis, his difficulty separating himself from the family, but also his hatred and ambivalent feelings about the family.

Defensively, Kafka – and the same holds for Musil (1957) – preferred to acknowledge that the cause of his mental suffering was related more to power than to love or hatred of his parents. Tatossian's (1988) opinion was that Freud had preferred to formulate the questions facing him in terms of libido or love rather than power, and as a corollary attributed the primary role to an incestuous desire for the mother rather than competition with the father. It was fairly natural, therefore, for his interpretation to take more account of the individual and his life story than of society and its history. This privileged viewpoint was probably not based wholly on scientific reasons. We must not forget the complexity of Freud's own family and its multilayer genealogy – to say nothing of the intricate layers of its "geology" – which may even have been necessary for someone to discover the Oedipus complex, at least in the form Freud presented it. The "dissident" analysts, or Kafka and Musil, take a different angle on the question, at least partly because of their own different family backgrounds.

4

It is interesting that in Italy too, branching out first from Trieste, a city heavily influenced by central European literary trends and sensitive to the culture of "Kakania", the Oedipus idea was widely adopted in the literature, especially as a narrative organizer. Italo Svevo (1976), in *La coscienza di Zeno* (*Zeno's Conscience*), uses the father as a metaphor for the inexorable cycle of the generations. Zeno is working through his grief for the loss of his father, who was the object of profound identification and fantasies of prohibition and punishment which became more acute while he was dying (Dalle Luche, 2002). To paraphrase Svevo in this masterpiece:

> Dead! I did not realize he was dead but my heart shrank with the pain of the punishment that he, on his deathbed, had wanted to mete out to me. Crying like a child who has been spanked, I shouted into his ear: "It's not my fault!" . . . They had to drag me away from his room. He was dead and I could no longer prove my innocence!
>
> (Dalle Luche, 2002: 29)

After Svevo, Berto (1964) in *Il male oscuro* (*The Obscure Evil*) was drawn strongly to the Oedipus theory of the mind, and wrote that

> his unconscious knew full well that this father was an abominable creature who stole my mother every day while I was in the midst of my Oedipus crisis: I loved my mother to death and how could I, a little thing, defend myself against that omnipotent dog except by hating him, with the bottomless hatred of a child, who is capable of boundless love or hatred; I wished my father dead a million times over in my mind, so my unconscious is a million times parricidal. I don't know whether that's true; maybe it is if these people who explore the unconscious say so – they must have their reasons – so I have the impression that what I have to do now is get rid of this remorse for my numerous acts of parricide, as much as I can.
>
> (Dalle Luche, 2002: 30)

The life and writing of Pier Paolo Pasolini was certainly influenced by a strong Oedipal situation. He was always hostile towards his father, considering him

> an unfair rival, with whom there was no way of reaching agreement, unless he could completely win over his mother's love, restoring a pre-Oedipal dyad in adult life at the price of sexual dis-identification and compulsive homosexuality, tormented and hidden (from his mother).
>
> (Dalle Luche, 2002: 37)

★ ★ ★

The year 1920 was important in Freud's thinking. The introduction of the dialogue between life and death instincts in determining human mental life seems to have reduced the importance assigned until that time to the Oedipus complex in an individual's development. We do not know why Freud turned onto this path. It might have been because of philosophical considerations linked to the theory of opposites, or to reflections on the drama of the First World War (1914–1918), in which Austria was defeated and the Austro-Hungarian Empire broken up; it might have been inspired by psychosocial ideas (which turned out to be true premonitions) related to the cultural and political climate in Austria and Germany in those years, where preparations for the advent of Nazism already seemed under way. Subsequently, in fact, Freud himself linked the conflict between the life instinct (Eros) and death instinct (Thanatos) to the human events of the moment, and the death instinct was introduced into clinical work: as a cause of negative therapeutic reactions, of an unconscious sense of guilt, and of narcissistic neurosis (in other terms, psychosis).

The second topic of *The Ego and the Id* (1922) enabled Freud to offer an idea of mental function controlled by the Id, out of which came the Ego and the Super-Ego. This latter, drenched with the death instinct, can harm the Ego and cause mental distress. It was perhaps pessimism that gave Freud the idea that the Super-Ego could take on itself the Ego's own ideal, left over from a (narcissistic) identification with the parents. This operation means the Ego ideal suffers the same fate as the Super-Ego, losing the ideal, positive characteristics needed if the interiorized parental figures are to allow smooth management of emotions and efficient thought. Humans will remain under the influence of the severe, punitive Super-Ego without the reassuring, illuminating support of the Ego ideal.

The second topic highlights the unconscious, focusing on the Id. Freud bases himself directly on the metapsychological work of 1915, particularly *Repression* (1915a) and *The Unconscious* (1915b). In these two fundamental works, Freud lays the foundations for defining the unconscious as a "dynamic" product created by repression. He uses the term *primal repression* (possibly referring to a child's earliest experiences with its parents), and *repression proper*, which comes later. Despite their different timing, both are still repression, and Freud seems to believe that the unconscious can originate only from repression, this being an active process of (temporarily) forgetting that can be achieved only through the structures needed for storing experiences in the autobiographic memory.

The 1915 metapsychological work can be seen as confirming and further extending the concepts related to memory that Freud deals with in *Screen Memories* (1899) and in *Remembering, Repeating and Working-Through* (1914b). In the first he talks about repression of certain facts and their shift onto contiguous facts. In the second he refers to recollections stored in the autobiographic memory which the subject under analysis can bring to the surface, in the appropriate circumstances, through free associations and dreams.

At that time Freud certainly had no means of referring to any other form of memory – such as implicit memory, which I shall discuss fully later in this book, but which was not yet known in Freud's days – which extends the concept of the unconscious and considers a possible non-repressive origin, linked to a child's earliest preverbal and presymbolic experiences that cannot be recalled but nevertheless influence the person's affective, cognitive and sexual life even as an adult. This unconscious can return to the surface in the analytical relationship through the transference, as we shall see further on, and can be represented in dreams.

In actual fact Freud himself, in 1922, mentions an unrepressed unconscious, deriving from the Id (for example, a part of the Ego and the Super-Ego) but his concept is different from our idea of the unconscious today, which is not the result of repression and is linked to the first significant experiences of early childhood. This unconscious is more passive than Freud's "dynamic" unconscious which is actively produced by repression.

In the 1930s psychoanalysis enjoyed an exceptional moment in its history, when Melanie Klein entered the international scene. She came from Hungary, where she had been analyzed by Sándor Ferenczi and subsequently by Karl Abraham, and she launched a whole new perspective on the theory of the mind. Her arrival led to the Oedipus complex losing ground as analysts gradually lost interest in a concept that no longer seemed central to the theory of the mind, its place taken by the importance of the pre-Oedipal phases in the development of the infant's mind.

Deleuze and Guattari (1972) accuse the Oedipus complex of being a "mousetrap" that generates double bonds. They were in fact ahead of various contemporary analysts who suggest "dis-Oedipizing" the unconscious so as to tackle the real problems, which are pre-Oedipal, rooted in the mother–child relationship, in which the father figure, though important, is more symbolic than real, as an internal representation of the mother.

The Oedipus complex did not in fact disappear with Klein, but moved forward to the child's first months when, in its primary relationship, it passes through what Klein calls the paranoid-schizoid position (Klein, 1928). This involves splitting and projective identification, and the child then projects his or her sadistic and destructive parts onto the mother figure, which is expected to metabolize them and return them to the child, "cleaned up" as it were, for introjection (Bion, 1962).

In place of the *instinct model* Klein (1928) proposes a *relational model* of the mind, but even so she does not manage to distance herself completely from the dominant psychoanalytical thinking of her time. The paradox is that Klein proposes a relational concept of the mind while still remaining anchored to the idea of the death instinct, which she further develops by linking it to clinical practice. This gives rise to the "Kleinian school", which considers the mother–child relationship isomorphic with the patient–analyst relationship and enables the analyst to grasp these relations in the transference, with their resemblances to the growing child's early relational experiences.

Klein realized the decisive importance of primary relations, particularly with the mother and the child's surroundings as he or she grows up. Logically, therefore, Klein considered the unconscious not merely a product of repression, but the actual expression of the child's splitting off his or her sadistic and destructive parts that the child found hard to put up with, and projecting them onto the mother. This specific – and fundamental – modality appears to dominate Klein's relational model.

The shift from an instinctual model to the relational model of the mind was already implicit in Klein's refusal of primary narcissism, justified by her conviction that the newborn infant is already able, at a tender age, to relate to the mother; this was in fact amply and substantially confirmed by subsequent research about growing children (Stern, 1985; Ammaniti and Stern, 1992; Fonagy and Target, 1997). However, Klein believed that the death instinct persisted in the newborn in the form of sadistic fantasies and primary anxiety.

One may ask why Klein never stepped back more clearly and less ambiguously from the Freudian model and why she remained anchored to the Oedipus concept, while simply shifting it to the child's first months (an "early Oedipus"), even though this seems to have little in common with Freud's Oedipus complex. And one wonders why she linked her theory so firmly and causally to the death instinct, raising it to the status of *deus ex machina* for so many mental disorders.

It is no simple matter to guess why Klein took this route. She might have felt that the psychoanalytical community was not ready just then to accept such a marked change as that implicit in the model of the development of the mind she offered in contrast to Freud's. She may therefore have decided to opt for a "half-revolution" that would succeed rather than a complete one that could well fail. The fact remains that her attempts to save some of the theoretical bases laid by the father of psychoanalysis – the Oedipus complex and the death instinct – definitely slowed the shift in scientific paradigm that eventually marked the second half of the twentieth century. The importance she attached to the death instinct, and its application in clinical work, had significant theoretical and clinical consequences, especially in the treatment of psychosis. However, this delayed the acceptance of more advanced concepts of this disease based on early trauma and defenses set up during early childhood.

Melanie Klein made several fundamental contributions to current psychoanalysis, one of them being *projective identification* (Klein, 1946). This figure serves numerous purposes (see Rosenfeld, 1965, 1987). The concept has been excessively extended and possibly also occasionally abused, but it is nevertheless still the most important discovery in contemporary psychoanalysis, comparable to Freud's announcement of the unconscious far back in 1897. It is impossible to even think of working through and adequately interpreting the many events arising in analysis without this basic concept. Even authors who do not normally employ it describe their clinical findings in a form that still follows Klein's concept closely. One typical example is Giancarlo Zapparoli's fine book *La paura e la noia* (*Fear and Boredom*) (1979).

Another of Klein's brilliant intuitions involved the similarities between the language of play and the language of dreams, both being representations of affective dynamics between internal objects and the fantasies and defenses organized in the unconscious. This enabled her to try analyzing very small children – this had not been done before – and, using games, she found she could formulate interpretations of the affects and emotions surrounding their primary representations, their fantasies and defenses. This approach on play was similar to work on dreams.

Klein's intuition caused much wider ripples in that it led to a new, more detailed way of working on dreams compared to Freud's method which was inevitably reductive as it was so closely bound to the wish and its fulfillment. Klein turned the dream into an experience that could reveal the "state of the relation" between the analyst and patient in the here and now of the session, giving an overall picture of the whole transference. No longer was the psyche fueled solely by wishes, but a dynamic relation was established between internal objects (the intrapsychic dimension of the dream), which were related to the self and with the object in the transference (the intersubjective dimension of the dream).

The importance of Melanie Klein's work is clear from the solid group of analysts, of various nationalities – particularly South American and European – that has grown up around her figure. From the close circle of the master's followers, Hanna Segal and Herbert Rosenfeld dealt successfully with psychosis. They were among the first to use psychoanalytical methods to tackle the psychotic transference and offered their patients interpretations that did in fact significantly influence their personalities. Rosenfeld (1965, 1987) made a particularly substantial contribution, reflected in his wide range of articles, and the enlightening idea of the narcissistic object relation, with its arrogance, omnipotence, omniscience, and massive use of splitting and projective identification, denial and idealization. Rosenfeld takes credit for comparing the narcissistic personality with an organization like an internal "mafia" or a form of Nazism where perverted followers cover their own backs with the aim of attacking and subjugating the healthy part of the personality.

The countertransference, originally viewed as a disturbing element in the relation, was strongly valued by the Kleinian school, and Paula Heimann in particular (1950) turned it into a *compass* to orient the analyst on the patient's transference. This drew attention to the analyst's role and to his or her sensitivity in building up a culture of the couple. This was upheld by Willy and Madeleine Baranger (1961–1962), who were the first to mention a "bipersonal" field, a term picked up widely by various authors in Italy (Manfredi Turillazzi and Ferro, 1990), to cover the interpretation and working through of affects and emotions occupying the analytical "space".

Donald Meltzer (1978, 1980, 1988), an acknowledged expert in infant analysis and an expounder of Klein and Bion's opinions, never failed to point out how in adults in analysis infantile parts of the personality still operated. Betty Joseph (1989) was another analyst who was particularly sensitive and attentive to the here and now of the session and extended the idea, so as to perceive in items arising in the transference and countertransference any perverse aspects of the relation and of the patient's sexuality.

Roger Money-Kyrle and Wilfred Bion were the pillars of theory around which a new, modern epistemology of the mind was to develop. Money-Kyrle was an anthropologist and philosopher, besides being a psychoanalyst, and had been a pupil of Moritz Schlict in Vienna, where he had gained a profound experience in philosophy that stood him in good stead in his psychoanalytical work. It might have been this basic training that facilitated his reflections on "innate preconception" (which he shared with Bion), had close analogies with Kant's a priori principles, such as an attitude to meet the objects of reality (Longhin and Mancia, 1998) and on the development of thought (Money-Kyrle, 1978). Money-Kyrle was able to apply psychoanalysis to anthropology (1930, 1938), to politics (1951) and to social work (1961), promoting psychoanalytical thinking applied to society and work that was to be taken to its peak by Elliott Jaques (1970).[1]

Money-Kyrle's central theme was that humans are their representation of the world and that is where their cognitive dimension lies. Children's creativity leads them to build up their own model of the world, combining sensory recollections from their memory into one and binding the various images together in a world that makes up the essence of their thought. Today we know that this construction is achieved very early and is stored in the child's implicit memory, where it constitutes the unrepressed unconscious nucleus of the self that will influence the person's relations with the world even as an adult.

Money-Kyrle allows humans full responsibility for understanding themselves, which he says is essential if humans are ever to achieve their dream of a safer and more harmonious society; humans need a more reliable and greater capacity for managing their "negative" parts, which are an obstacle to achieving a better, more mature society. Here Money-Kyrle sees one of psychoanalysis's tasks, as total psychology: understanding and if necessary correcting our ethical, political and esthetic valuations, which are based on our models of the world.

Understanding the real situations outside us, including social and political reality, starts with an understanding of our internal world and the representations populating it, which largely reflect the experiences of our early infancy. This brings us to another of the tasks of psychoanalysis: to bring back to life and rework in the transference each individual's childhood experiences, so as to "correct" the errors and straighten up the "misunderstandings" implicit in the model of the world each person has built up. In this framework, psychoanalysis offers itself as a method for changing man and his view of the world.

It was inevitable that Money-Kyrle showed interest in an anthropological and psychoanalytical definition of "normal". After several phases of elaboration and thought Money-Kyrle defines a normal person as one who is free of inhibitions, though he also considers people normal if they do not defensively use primary mechanisms such as splitting and projective identification. Equating normality with rationality is a pivotal point in Money-Kyrle's work, but he specifies that though normality implies freedom from delusion it does not imply freedom from conflicts and ambivalence. Normality does, however, require a person to be relatively free of persecutory and depressive anxieties.

Money-Kyrle traces morality back to the unconscious guilt feeling, referring to a child's aggressive feelings aimed at the maternal object. The moral attitude becomes a drive to do or not do certain things, bringing us back to the introjected parental figures, meaning the Super-Ego, guardian of morality and also a severe judge who can condemn mental illness. It is interesting to see how envy is viewed by different societies, too. For instance, in a capitalist society envy pushes people to use their projection competitively, whereas in old communist societies it was expected to repress and deny this urge. But envy always showed its face in some other form.

Another of Money-Kyrle's major contributions regards cognitive development. He maintains that the child's basic concepts emerge from the "innate preconceptions" which, when they meet up with the object (the breast), formulate a concept. This has then to be slotted into a spatial-temporal system. This model of the world forms before language develops, when the child is still not capable of putting things into words, or even symbols. Various affects, including envy, can disrupt this process and set up a "misunderstanding" that can disturb thought.

Today we can see clearly how important are these intuitions. A child's early cognitive experiences, preverbal and presymbolic, can be stored only in the child's implicit memory, where they form a structural part of the unrepressed unconscious that will carry on working even in the adult, and which will surface in our patients' transference – and dreams.

Wilfred Bion (1962, 1965, 1967, 1970, 1975) provided the psycho-analytical community with a new way of tackling the questions arising within the analytical relationship.[2] First of all, though he never actually declared himself, Bion kept his distance from the death instinct theory and put into play his interest in relationships. Here the concept of *rêverie* is very important: this light, dreamy mood of the mother (or the analyst) is essential to grasp, work through and transform the suffering and persecutory parts of the child's – and the patient's – self, split and projectively identified in her (and in the analyst).

Bion tried (but failed) to render psychoanalysis in mathematical terms and then introduced a series of reflections on how the mind works which enabled theoretical-clinical psychoanalysis to extend itself and offer new scientific paradigms. This started with the systems whose basic workings Bion guessed at, and moved on to studies of the psychotic personality, defined by mental workings manifesting themselves through certain communication pathways, and the effects these had on the listener.

It was Bion who conceived of a mental space open to infinity and of the multidimensional nature of things mental. At the center of psychoanalysis he placed an "apparatus for thinking thoughts", causally connected to pain due to the absence of the object, and analyzed like an operation designed to set up links (with a play on the rhyming words *to think* and *to link*). This was an extraordinary intuition, and applied to the analytical relationship it focused and identified the patient's ability to think and the analyst's ability to establish links: between past and present, internal and external reality, material and metaphorical reality, and between metaphorical reality and the transference.

Underlying thought formation, Bion – like Money-Kyrle – sees "pre-conceptions". If these cannot be fulfilled (for instance because there is no breast) the child becomes frustrated. If he can put up with this, thanks to innate factors among other things, the child creates a thought and develops the "apparatus for thinking" (alpha function). Intolerance will impair this process and facilitate the organization of defenses, such as splitting, projective identification, denial and idealization. The child's own internal "equipment", which is genetically determined, has a major role in this process, and maternal *rêverie* becomes a decisive factor in the development of emotions, affects and thought.

Bion says that every patient has "an ancient civilization" buried within him or her, and this spotlights a central feature of contemporary psychoanalysis: the role of the oldest unconscious made up of childhood experiences, fantasies and defenses deposited in the patient's memory. Bion could not know then that these primary experiences, dating from the child's preverbal and presymbolic days, were filed in the child's implicit memory, where they make up the unrepressed unconscious (Mancia, 2003a, 2003b).

Along this same line we can assess the importance Bion attributed to the emotions and their inextricable interweaving with language, carrying meaning. Once again, Bion was ahead of his time, focusing the listener's attention on the word as bearer of significance, and on its "musicality", through which the speaker can present deeper meanings. Many analysts today consider this aspect of communication of prime interest (Ogden, 1999, 2001; Di Benedetto, 2000, 2003; Mancia, 2003a, 2003b).

As we said, Bion centers his interest on the emotions. Humans need to dream, by night or by day! And one of Bion's main contributions to knowledge lies in his vision of the dream: it becomes a "barrier" preventing contact between the unconscious and the conscious mind, the unconscious exploiting the selective "semipermeability" of this barrier.

Closely linked to the dream is Bion's *alpha function*, a metaphor symbol-izing the mind's work as it "metabolizes" sensory and emotive experience, using it in dreaming. Upstream of the alpha elements are the *beta elements*, which are undigested sensory impressions of emotive experience. They are destined to be evacuated through projective identification if the alpha function does not convert them to alpha elements. Beta elements tend to dominate in psychotics, where their projection to the external world creates persecutory "bizarre objects".

Bion also added important information to the concept of projective identification. Besides the patently psychopathological aspect, this process also has a "physiological" function as the natural way for a child to relate to the mother and try to get to know her. We would say today that projective identification and the mother's response to it enable the child to organize his or her "theory of the mind", meaning the ability to recognize the mother's feelings and relate them to the child's own (Fonagy and Target, 1997).

Yet another outstandingly original concept produced by this exceptional – and prolific – author involves the vertex and the transformations (rigid, projective and in hallucinosis) always linked to a change at the vertex. To grasp these transformations in a patient, the analyst's mind must be free of memory and desire. Bion meant this valuable advice as a suggestion to analysts to keep their mind unencumbered with excessive recollections, or an obstinate desire to "cure", so as to grasp the unconscious shifts perceptible in the patient's way of communicating, and in his or her narrations.

Bion provided extraordinary insights into psychoanalytical practice, the inevitable pain accompanying any analysis, but the fact that the patient must, all the same, put up with the painful moment, as they foster mental growth. Both parties must tolerate the uncertainty, non-knowledge (–K) and incomprehension. Many of Bion's ideas have thus literally revolutionized some of our ways of thinking and have enormously enriched psychoanalytical epistemology.

The risk implicit in Bion's various elaborations – as for any figure of his standing – is that some of his formulations and working hypotheses may end up being used as "formulas" for use in any clinical situation. The result is that with time they lose significance and impede, rather than facilitate, our understanding of the affects and emotions that really fill the patient's and the analyst's minds during analysis.

★ ★ ★

Interwoven with the contributions of Klein's school to psychoanalysis today we find Ronald Fairbairn and the mastery of Donald Winnicott. Fairbairn (1952) was one of the group of analysts not satisfied with Freud's instincts model, who proposed a relational model of development, considered central to the organization of the personality. One of Winnicott's reflections back in 1958 that might summarize his ideas was that one of the difficulties of our analytical technique is knowing at any time the patient's age in the transference. The idea of regression to early stages of development is a vivid and original central point in his thinking.

Winnicott was one of the first to mention explicitly the mental life of the fetus, whose relationship with the outside environment becomes closer and more intense as birth comes nearer. One of Winnicott's statements was that in the natural way of things, the experience of birth is a large-scale sample of something the child is already familiar with. The question of the importance of prenatal life in relation to mental development was subsequently tackled by Rascovsky (1977) and in Italy by myself (Mancia, 1980b, 1981) and by Imbasciati (1998).

Winnicott sustained that if we are to understand the psychology of the newborn child, including the trauma of birth, we have in psychoanalysis to grasp the moment of "regression". There is a relation between the trauma of birth and psychosomatic and hypochondriac disorders (Winnicott, 1965). This is because from conception onwards the body and mind develop together, gradually taking separate paths as the child grows. The self develops early in this process, from the union of body and mind. It seems appropriate here to note the importance of Eugenio Gaddini's (1981) proposals on the relations between mind and body and the bodily expression of mental suffering in a growing child.

Winnicott (1965), however, was the first to highlight the notion of separation, especially the experience of a baby and small infant alone with the mother, as a paradoxical moment, as it involves being alone but in the presence of another person. On this experience the child's emotional maturity is based.

Winnicott highlighted the relational model of development built around the presence of a mother who had to be good enough to adapt to the child's needs and wants, and the development of the child's own capacity to "worry" and take responsibility. It was Winnicott (1971) who proposed the idea of transitional objects and phenomena, creating a mid-way stage during which the child's ability to recognize and accept reality develops. The transitional object is symbolic, standing for the breast or for the object of the child's very first relation; it therefore belongs in the area of *illusion* a mother who can adapt to her child's needs sets up. The illusion enables the child to think there is an outside reality consisting of the objects he or she needs and that the child creates with his or her imagination.

Winnicott's idea is obviously very important, linking the transitional zone to the play of artistic and scientific creativity as well (and, for that author, also to religion). Winnicott even sees cultural experience as an extension of the transitional phenomenon of play, which itself is what enables the child to make fundamental transformations, from the system of representation to that of signification, starting with language.

At least to begin with, Winnicott was much influenced by Klein's theories, especially on the role of transitional objects and the importance she attached to the mother setting up that illusory space so important for the development of the child's creativity. I think the most striking break from Klein was Winnicott's (1971) refusal of the death instinct, although, paradoxically, when talking about the origin of aggression, he stated that there was always the assumption, in orthodox theory, that aggression was related to the encounter with reality, while here it was the destructive instinct that decided the quality of external reality. This was the main pillar of his reasoning (Winnicott, 1971). But what instinct is he talking about? Why does he mention the primary use of an instinct when his whole theory is rooted in the child's *relation* with the mother and the surroundings where the child grows up?

The neurosciences' contribution to psychoanalysis

Background

Advances in knowledge in the field of neurosciences and the launch of a new generation of psychoanalysts who are much more open than their predecessors to comparisons and exchange with other disciplines have made it easier to meet up and overcome diffidence. On the resulting shared base a language has been established that fosters research into the mind's functions – a topic close to psychoanalysts' hearts, but that is also attracting the neuroscientists' attention.

There are many fields in which the separate disciplines can open up vistas and share them (see Solms and Turnbull, 2002; Mancia, 2004c, 2006c; Cooper, 2005; Scalzone, 2005). The main route to fruitful interaction lies in respecting each one's methodological limits, so as to avoid dangerous, and sterile, epistemologic confusion.

There is no question that normal and pathological mental activity depends on the brain, and its complex circuits and connections that respond to the plasticity typical of the brain's multiple functions. We know of only a few of the links in the chain that connects synaptic activity in certain brain circuits to the mind and its functions, but we can nevertheless still try and tackle these complex processes while remaining faithful to ontological monism. Psychoanalysis is based on intersubjectivity, while the neurosciences are based on a relationship in which the subject studies the object of interest. We also know that different "logics" lie behind the two disciplines: the neurosciences work from a "*logic of explanation*", while psychoanalysis uses a "*logic of understanding*".

There are still, however, numerous areas of common interest where significant interdisciplinary contributions are possible:

- emotions and their role in mental development, the organization of memory and human behavior
- the different types of memory and their relations with the unconscious
- the dream in relation to the different phases of sleep (REM and non-REM)
- empathy, intentionality, imitation, embodied simulation and shared affective states, investigated using bioimaging and electrophysiology of mirror neurons
- consciousness and the unconscious
- prenatal and perinatal life as it relates to early communications between the mother and child
- the development of language.

The final aim of interdisciplinary research would be to convert metapsychology, the "witch" which Freud discovered, to psychology open to experimentation and scientific observation to facilitate the gradual integration of psychoanalysis with the neurosciences.

Emotions and memory

Darwin's *The Expression of the Emotions in Man and Animals* in 1872 made a scientific contribution to the question of emotions but it was LeDoux (1996) who studies the neurophysiological processes underlying them and how they influenced the workings of the explicit and implicit memory. LeDoux noted the role of the amygdala and the hippocampus in the organization of both memory systems, and that the amygdala matures before the hippocampus. This suggests that the implicit memory becomes active before the explicit one, helping differentiate the two systems as regards learning and the unconscious. LeDoux also provided information on how early trauma could affect the amygdala and the systems of memory and emotion. Trauma of various types can bring out apparently extinct conditioned responses even after long intervals.

This experimental finding was extremely interesting for psychoanalysts as it meant we were justified in believing that certain traumatic experiences, even from long ago and apparently extinct in the sense that they could not be remembered, could nevertheless surface in the transference within the dreams when they were dug out from the implicit memory. The apparent extinction did not cancel out the experience, which carried on influencing the person's emotional affective and cognitive life.

LeDoux (1996) suggested this was due to the "plasticity" of the amygdala's neurons which enable emotions to be recorded in the implicit memory where, though they are not recollectable, they cannot be erased. Important in this process is the relation between the amygdala and cortical areas, especially in the right hemisphere, which is essential for cortico-amygdaloid self-regulation of emotions.

Damasio (2003) suggested that emotional stimuli lead to the organization of neural "engrams" or "configurations" referring to different maps of the body. He compares the somatosensory cortical areas to "control boxes" that transmit emotional signals to the amygdala, the cingulate cortex and the insula. These contain the body maps and distribute the emotions and feelings involving other areas of the brain. Adolphs et al. (2000) made an interesting observation on this point, stressing the role of the somatosensory cortex – especially in the right hemisphere – in recognizing emotions expressed on the face. Microphysiological research has since confirmed that the amygdaloid neurons are particularly sensitive to facial expressions (Sergerie and Armony, 2006). Bioimaging has shown that a person's emotions, revealed in their face, activate the observer's left frontal operculum and the right parietal cortex (Iacoboni et al., 1999). Therefore the cortical areas, with the amygdala, work as two parts of a neurophysiological system that enables us to understand a person's facial expressions.

Panksepp (2001) suggested that early emotions influence the brain's development, particularly its neuronal plasticity. This explains Edelmann's references to "neural Darwinism". Early trauma, abandon, or severe stress all cause the release of oxytocin and corticotropin releasing factor (CRF) which in mammals is affected by the emotional stress of the newborn's separation from the mother. These hormones also influence brain development and neuronal plasticity.

That early environmental influences affect neuronal plasticity was shown by Joseph (1996), who found the brainstem was the structure that matured early enough to control the organization of motor activity and vital auto-nomic functions. The limbic system also matures early, controlling not only hunger and thirst but also the expression of emotions like anger, fear, pleasure and desire for social contact. Early environmental experiences can influence the organization of these neural networks, with subsequent effects on the social, emotional and intellectual aspects of development.

This all provides some explanation of why newborn babies have such need of emotional stimuli in their first months, and seek social contact. The stimuli act on the amygdala which promotes synaptic plasticity, facilitating interactions between the non-cortical areas involved in laying down information, and the temporal cortical structures which more directly consolidate the memory (Paré et al., 2002).

There are significant differences between the right and left amygdalas as regards memorizing. The left amygdala seems involved in memory organization in women, while the right-hand one seems more active in this task in men. Bioimaging findings suggest the implicit and explicit memories influence each other – as the amygdala and hippocampus can do so – in relation to how essentially emotional events are "coded" (Phelps, 2004). The amygdala influences the deposition of emotional memories in various parts of the brain (hippocampus, striatum, cortex) but only the hippocampus is needed to remember them (McGaugh, 2002). This is important for psychoanalysis, as it indicates that emotional experiences can be recalled only if they involve the hippocampus, hence the explicit memory, while if they remain in the implicit memory they cannot emerge to the surface.

The interaction between the amygdala and hippocampus in limbic regulation of memorization is important in relation to how early trauma and stress affect the organization of the memory. Stress raises the levels of corticosteroids, causing atrophy of the hippocampal dendrites and pyramidal cells, inhibiting neurogenesis of the dentate gyrus and impeding learning and memorization of experiences stored in the hippocampus-dependent explicit memory (McEwen and Sapolsky, 1995; Phelps, 2004). In small mammals, deprivation stress and separation from the mother reduces hippocampal neurogenesis, thus again impeding learning and hippocampus-dependent memorization (Karten et al., 2005).

These are very important findings for the psychology of development and for psychoanalysis, which can thus trace many aspects of mental diseases to distortions or trauma affecting the child in its earliest development.

The amygdaloid neurons selectively respond to faces and influence the processes of attention through their projections to numerous other brain areas, particularly the orbito-frontal cortex which is considered an "interface" linking the early warning system for threats – the amygdala – with the attention system in the fronto-parietal cortex (Sergerie and Armony, 2006). The amygdala is, from all viewpoints, essential to emotional memory, the left amygdala also helping reinforce the emotional dimension of declarative memory for verbal and non-verbal stimuli. It does not appear to have a part in remembering emotional experiences, which is where the hippocampus comes in.

This is another interesting point for psychoanalysis as it lays a neurophysiological basis for the distinction between the implicit memory – managed by the amygdala – and the explicit memory controlled by the hippocampus. Thus only events stored in the latter can be remembered, not those in implicit memory. This is obviously vital in repression, and in the transference. Emotions and memories are all parts of an adaptational process asymmetrically involving mental functions: the right hemisphere is needed for various types of non-conscious emotional memory, and plays a part in the organization of the implicit memory (Gainotti, 2006), hence of the unrepressed unconscious (Mancia, 2003a; 2006a). The left hemisphere is dominant in intellective and rational functions, and naturally for language (Sperry, 1974).

Memory and the unconscious

Vast new horizons have been opened to psychoanalytical theory and clinical practice by the discovery of the dual memory system: explicit or declarative memory is conscious, verbalizable and recollectable, and is essential for our identity and life story; implicit memory on the other hand is neither verbalizable nor recollectable. Only implicit memory develops early in life – it is present and active in the last weeks of pregnancy and is the only memory available to children in their first two years. Its *procedural and emotive-affective* dimension means that children can file away their earliest experiences relating to the mother's voice and language and the child's surroundings. It stores the mother's relations with the child's body, how she speaks to him or her, watches and touches the child, in other words her *rêverie* with all its affects and emotions.

If we now return to Freud (1912) who considered every event stored in memory as part of the structure of the individual's unconscious, we see a potential connection between implicit memory and the unconscious functions of the newborn mind. This early unconscious is surely not the result of repression, because the structures – especially the hippocampus – needed for explicit memory, which is the one used for repression do not mature until a child is at least 2 years old (Joseph, 1996; Siegel, 1999). Therefore presymbolic, preverbal experiences filed away in implicit memory are not lost, even though the person cannot consciously recall them. They do in fact form the structure of *an early unrepressed unconscious* that will govern a person's affective, emotional and cognitive life right through adulthood (Mancia, 2003a, 2004c, 2006a, 2006b).

Another link can be drawn between the unrepressed unconscious and clinical practice, and we shall look at it in this book. At this stage it is enough to mention the musical dimension of the transference, related to the patient's voice and language, that helps recollections emerge from implicit memory. This dimension is like a metaphorical bridge linking the patient's emotions in the transference to those of early infancy, re-evoking the mother's tone of voice and the structure of her language. This infra-verbal musical dimension can communicate affects that do not come to light in a narration. Obviously, this new view of the unconscious involves an expansion of the concept of *Nachträglichkeit*, which Freud restricted to the repressed unconscious, but which we can now extend to the unrepressed unconscious too. It is a means of "writing the story" of the patient's whole unconscious starting from his or her very first experiences.

As part of the interdisciplinary approach I am trying to lay out here, it is interesting to apply to implicit memory the reflection already made for the explicit one: memory can no longer be considered a static "filing system" but becomes a dynamic function in which things are continually being re-categorized, according to Edelmann's model (Leuzinger-Bohleber and Pfeifer, 2006). This process can be used as the neurophysiological basis for the changes in a patient's memory resulting from the interpretation, construction and reconstruction that mark the analytical encounter.

The dream

The dream is an ideal tool for recuperating recollections from the patient's repressed and unrepressed unconscious. It can be used in the here and now of the session, where the dream serves as a sort of window open onto the transference, or in a reconstructive diachronic process, which is made easier by the dream's capacity for creating symbols to represent presymbolic and preverbal experiences that thus become thinkable and verbalizable.

This book takes an interdisciplinary view of the dream, keeping an eye open to the knowledge added by neurophysiology, psychophysiology and neuropsychology. *Neurophysiology* provides the basis for understanding which brain structures are involved in sleep and the phases where the dream is organized. *Psychophysiology* studies the mental functions that develop in the different phases of sleep – REM and non-REM. *Neuropsychology* calls on bioimaging to tell us which structures and circuits are indispensable for dream formation and its narration.

Much of the neuroscientific data provided by research into the brain's workings while dreaming also contribute to various psychoanalytical hypotheses. For instance, Bion (1962) and Meltzer (1984) both suggested that unconscious fantasies were similar to those of dreaming in sleep. In other words, there is no break in mental activity as we pass from waking to sleeping except, clearly, the neurophysiological changes related to this change in consciousness.

The neurosciences tell us that the brain does not process information in a uniform manner, but according to its functional state at any specific moment. It controls the emotional and cognitive contents and brings them up from the different types of memory in response to changes in cortical and subcortical function during the different phases of sleep and dreaming (Lehmann and Koukkou, 2006). Research (Massimini et al., 2005) has shown that stimuli applied to a cortical area can spread through the same and the opposite hemisphere while we are awake, but remain in the area of application during synchronous sleep.

These findings show that as we pass from waking to sleep the functional processes of the neocortex change, so there may possibly also be differences in our emotional and cognitive processes in the various states of consciousness.

Empathy, simulation and shared affects

Neurophysiological and neuropsychological findings from bioimaging investigations have provided important recent information on empathy, embodied simulation, imitation, intentionality, and shared affective and emotional states. Bolognini (2002) looked into the history of empathy and described its specific characteristics in the analytical relationship, distinguishing it from shared affects, merging, and other unconscious relational methods. It is not clear from his writing exactly how empathy is related to projective identification, but this would be important in interpreting neuroscientific findings on shared emotional and affective states and embodied simulation.

Bioimaging investigations show that human pain response areas – the anterior cingulum and insula – are activated not only in the brain of someone receiving painful physical stimuli but also in anyone with an affective bond watching the subject undergoing the stimulus in a mirror (Singer et al., 2004). The same pain-affective areas are activated in response to verbal stimuli mimicking a painful experience (Osaka et al., 2004; Osaka, 2006). Activation of the same two brain areas (cingulum and insula) in the person directly suffering pain and in someone watching was confirmed recently and described as a form of empathy (Avenanti and Aglioti, 2006).

The discovery of mirror neurons (Rizzolatti et al., 2001; see also Gallese, 2001) showed that intentional syntonization between people can be achieved through embodied simulation. The mirror neurons are the neuronal correlate of this mechanism which permits empathy, a shared modality of intersubjectivity and intentionality (Fogassi et al., 2005). Dapretto et al. (2005) reported the interesting finding that mirror neurons are not activated in autistic children. However, in this case it is hard to establish whether the mirror neurons are lacking from birth, for genetic reasons, or have not developed on account of some traumatic environmental situation that has prevented the gene expression needed for them to function early in life and during the child's mental development.

These neuroscientific findings provide interesting material for theoretical and clinical psychoanalytical speculation. Shared emotional and affective states are obviously a basic element in the analytical relationship where each party's unconscious communicates with the other through many verbal, infra-verbal and extra-verbal channels. Therefore, for psychoanalysis, the neurophysiological findings to date can lay the functional grounds for the unconscious process defined as *projective identification* (Klein, 1946).

Consciousness and the unconscious

An interdisciplinary dialogue between psychoanalysis and neurosciences cannot ignore consciousness and its different functional levels. Freud dealt with consciousness in relation to the unconscious in 1922 in *The Ego and the Id*. The opening words of the work are:

> The division of the psychical into what is conscious and what is unconscious is the fundamental premiss of psycho-analysis; . . . psychoanalysis cannot situate the essence of the psychical in consciousness but is obliged to regard consciousness as a quality of the psychical, which may be present in addition to other qualities or may be absent.
>
> (Freud, 1922: 13)

Nevertheless, according to Freud there is an intermediate area between the unconscious and consciousness, a psychic limbo that he called the pre-conscious. This corresponds to psychic material that is latent, but very close to the conscious: "We restrict the term *unconscious*," – clarified Freud – "to the dynamically unconscious repressed" (1922: 15).

In his metapsychological work, Freud (1915a, 1915b) specified that the unconscious was the dynamic result of a repression starting at the beginning of life (*original repression*) and continuing as *repression proper*. It can affect the conscious. As word representation, language serves to bring the unconscious thing representations to the level of consciousness.

The Ego is part conscious and part unconscious, deriving from the Id. This complex structure has some psychological processes linked to the conscious and others to the unconscious (repressed and not). This dual nature of the Ego casts light on the ontogenesis of the human mind, where the formation of the conscious and the unconscious runs parallel. The conscious thus becomes a complex function, but is never autonomous, as it is influenced by experience, and unconscious fantasies and defenses that influence symbolization and the whole process of transformation, from affective representations to signification systems, starting with language. Clearly, therefore, for psychoanalysy the conscious is closely dependent on unconscious representations. It is a sort of sensory organ of psychic qualities, linked to language, a function that enables a subject to relate to his or her own unconscious reality (Semi, 2003).

★ ★ ★

The neuroscientific approach to consciousness is different. It looks at two forms: *basic consciousness* (or primary consciousness, according to Edelmann) and *differentiated consciousness* (Edelmann's higher-order consciousness). The first is the equivalent of alertness, and its roots are in the brainstem, particularly the ascending reticular system that reaches the thalamus, and controls the whole neocortical mantle. It was in this ascending reticular system, discovered by Moruzzi and Magoun in 1949, that Alfred Fessard (1954) suggested the presence of a state of consciousness or alertness expressing what he called *experienced integration*. The reticular formation does in fact integrate various sensory afferents, and sets up a feedback loop to keep its activity at the optimal operative level to maintain various states of consciousness, from waking to sleep. It is sensitive to circulating hormones; it changes its neuronal activity from continuous to oscillating, as the electrophysiological equivalents of waking and sleep, respectively (Moruzzi, 1972; Mancia, 1982).

The differentiated, or higher-order consciousness, can analyze experiences and integrate them in a coordinated spatial-temporal system. Jasper (1964) specified four fundamental features of this consciousness: its own identity, its own uniqueness, its own activity, and its state of antithesis to the outside world and others. It is the series of processes that enable individuals to be aware of themselves and their surroundings, and of their own psychological life, to be able to integrate past and present, to use external and internal perceptions, and to be capable of intentionality (Mancia, 1989).

There are various psychophysiological processes underlying consciousness: perception, attention, memory, ideation, criticism, judgment, will, affects, emotions, and thoughts. All are essential for the complex parts of the conscious to integrate and manifest itself. One possible link between these neuroscientific and psychological concepts is suggested by various authors who have dealt with the topic. Edelmann (1992) maintained the cerebral cortex was responsible for elaborating information, selecting and transferring it to the other cortical areas. His theory was that groups of cortical neurons selected schemes for responses to specific stimuli, forming cerebral maps. These then interacted, permitting re-entry to facilitate the organization of complex cortical functions such as the memory, symbolization and thought.

Dennet (1991) saw the conscious as linked to the brain's plasticity which, since the times of *Homo habilis*, has organized the software running on the brain's hardware, transferring these changes in the genome (this is the *Baldwin effect*). Damasio (1994) identified the mind with representations or "neural configurations" involving the prefrontal cortical areas; these underlie higher-order consciousness. This is the result of integration of processes involving associative and sensory areas, that enable us to classify perceptions and organize them in concepts.

Edelmann and Tononi (2000) subsequently suggested that consciousness is the outcome of a re-entry process that ensures the integration of information in the thalamo-cortical system. They suggested the idea of *qualia*, as specific qualities of subjective experience resulting from the activity of groups of neurons through a process of re-entry. To start with these neuronal groups involve the brainstem – the oldest part of the brain, that matures early (Joseph, 1996). Its structures and circuits regulate the autonomic nervous system, governing motor activity and respiratory work, and sleep, in its cycles of rest and activity (Mancia, 1981; Piontelli, 2006). This suggests that the *qualia*, as proto-mental subjective experiences, emerge from these re-entry processes involving the brainstem. This brings us back to Fessard (1954) and confirms the brainstem's essential role in early integration of the fetus's sensory afferences that give rise to the earliest consciousness.

Prenatal and neonatal life

Starting with Rascovsky's pioneering work in 1977, interest has grown enormously in fetal life, its motor, sensory and integrative components, and particularly sleep and its phases (Mancia, 1981). Observations on fetuses between the tenth and twentieth weeks of gestation indicate that generalized and partial movements tend to alternate with respiratory movements (Piontelli, 2006). This suggests that the brainstem, which, as we said, matures sooner than other brain areas (Joseph, 1996), has a complex organization in which inhibitory interneurons become active early, to govern these alternating functions. Active sleep too is organized early in this brain structure, similar in some ways to REM sleep for the mature brain (Mancia, 1985).

From about the fifth month of gestation the fetus perceives the mother's heartbeat and respiration, as well as her voice. The voice is an important stimulus, containing the fetus psychologically and conveying emotional and affective aspects of the mother's personality. The fetus stores these experiences in its memory (De Casper and Fifer, 1980; see also Kolata, 1984). Its sensitivity to the mother's language and the surroundings in which it grows enable it to grasp her tone and stresses very early. From the sixth month of life, babies can represent in their own mind the sequences of vowels and consonants they hear in speech.

Besides the voice and language, the infant's visual contact with the mother is also a very important way of communicating affective states (Farroni et al., 2002). Her body is a pivotal element in the primary relation: how the mother contains her newborn infant, talks to and looks at him or her, and her level of *rêverie*, are all prime bearers of affects and emotions the child will store in his or her implicit memory. These will affect the development of the young mind and the child's emotional and cognitive life even as an adult.

The infant's interaction with the mother reaches a peak during breast-feeding, when the suckling child is in intimate contact with the mother's skin. From this interaction the child's body Ego develops, on the lines of a primordial *matrix-like structure*. This confirms Gaddini's (1969) intuitions based on clinical evidence. During breast-feeding the amplitude of EEG waves changes in the posterior cortical areas of the child's right hemisphere. At 6 months theta activity is detectable during suckling, as the connections between cortical and subcortical areas mature (Lehtonen, 2006). Theta activity is also seen in an infant shown pleasant pictures, and has therefore been called hedonistic theta (Maulsby, 1971).

Psychoanalytic interest in this prenatal and perinatal life is clearly related to the fact that this is when the early bases of an unrepressed unconscious are first laid down, to appear later in the transference and represented symbolically in dreams, as we shall see in this book.

The development of language

There are reports (Sakai, 2005) that a newborn infant can perceive language and start developing its elementary grammar in the first month of life. The linguistic factors that are organized so early are auditory-phonological then, later, lexical-semantic. The former involve the posterior superior temporal gyrus (Brodman's area 22), and the latter the temporo-parietal regions (angular and supramarginal gyrus: Brodman's areas 39 and 40) in the left hemisphere.

Grammar and syntax are vital for selective integration of lexico-semantic information and operate in the inferior frontal gyrus of the left hemisphere, comprising the opercular and triangular areas (44 and 45), and the left premotor lateral frontal area (6, 8 and 9). These areas constitute the grammatical center of language. It is activated by any language the child hears, confirming Chomsky's (2002) universal nature of grammatical processes. However, the child responds with generalized motor activity to the adult's language (heterosynchronic activity) and the child's first attempt at speech (autosynchronic activity) (Condon and Sander, 1974). This implies that all the sensorimotor areas of the two hemispheres are involved in the initial stages of development of language and only later are the various centers of grammar, syntax and semantics organized. This is when the linguistic functions concentrate in the specific areas of the left hemisphere.

★ ★ ★

The book is in three parts, reflecting the fact that it deals with different mental functions pivotal to psychoanalysis, relating to the different brain functions studied by the neurosciences:

- memory and its relation with the unconscious
- the dream as regards its organizational aspects and its complex role in the analytical relation
- clinical work as a "laboratory" where affects and emotions can provide evidence for or against the various theories put forward in the rest of the book.

27

PART ONE

Memory and the unconscious

This part deals with the two dimensions of memory: implicit and explicit. We look at the neuroscientific literature on this function, focusing on the time the amygdala and hippocampus take to mature. The amygdala is responsible for the emotions and for the implicit memory circuit, while the hippocampus selects and codifies information for the explicit memory. The fact that the amygdala matures sooner than the hippocampus explains why implicit memory is available before explicit memory.

This dual memory system leads to the idea that the unconscious too may be organized as a double function: unrepressed, regarding implicit memory, the storehouse of affective and emotional experiences dating from very early in life – possibly even the last weeks of gestation too – and repressed, connected to explicit memory, which matures once the child has reached the age of 2.

The unrepressed early unconscious can come to light in the transference and in dreams. It reveals itself in the transference through the "musical dimension" based on the child's earliest affective and emotional experiences, conveyed through the mother's tone of voice and the prosody – the stresses and tempo – of her language. The dream achieves the symbolization of presymbolic, preverbal experiences, so they become verbalizable and "thinkable". The dream also provides a means of figuratively filling the gap of non-representation, serving as a means of reconstructing the person's unconscious affective and emotional life story.

This part also looks closely at the part played by the unrepressed early unconscious in artistic output – poetry, music, art – according to Jakobson's principle for grasping the analogies between the languages of the transference and of poetry and music.

1

Memory between neuroscience and psychoanalysis

Memory has fascinated psychoanalysts ever since Freud. It is essential for an individual's identity and for the organization of the person's conscious and unconscious.[1] Since the late 1990s interdisciplinary studies of the memory have aroused much interest, and the ground is increasingly shared by psychoanalysts and neuroscientists. In 2000 an issue of *Psiche* in Italy bore witness to this: dedicated to "Memory and memories", it offered articles by F. Scalzone, A. Palmisano, C. Semenza and others, plus one of mine, all on this one topic. Other important papers have appeared on the subject (Fonagy, 1999; Pally, 1999; Davis, 2001), which was also dealt with at a neuropsychoanalysis conference in 2001 in New York, where M. Solms, C. Semenza and H. Shevrin presented reports. These contributions suggest that memory is a complex function of the brain structures and mind, of interest to many fields of research, from neuropsychology and molecular biology, to experimental psychology and psychoanalysis.

Memory comes in various shapes: there is *motor memory*, essential for everyday movements and exercises learned; *sensory memory*, where the experiences of the five senses are stored; *cognitive memory*, for learning in general; even *musical memory*, which seems complicated as it involves the motor and positional memory as well as the visual and auditory mechanisms; *genetic memory* helps in adaptation to the environment, and *historical memory* can be shared by a whole nation.

All these memories come in short- and long-term versions. In this chapter I shall look particularly at the anatomo–functional correlates of the long-term memory, and its importance in analysis. *Short-term memory*, sometimes called *operative memory*, stores information only for a few minutes; *long-term memory* is where things are filed away for a whole lifetime. The two types of memory are, however, related. According to Atkinson and Shiffrin

31

(1971), information stored in long-term memory has first to pass through short-term – operative – memory where it is screened and selected before being moved forward for long-term storage. This is a sort of cascade. However, in other "parallel" models information is sent directly to long-term memory, without necessarily going through the operative system (Vallard, 1983).

Long-term memory comprises explicit, or declarative, memory, and implicit, non-declarative memory (Squire, 1994; Schacter, 1996). Recollections from explicit memory can be consciously brought to the surface and expressed in words. This memory can be selective, episodic – meaning only certain specific events in the person's life are stored there – or it may be semantic, regarding facts, knowledge and the ability to make sense of very old recollections. Explicit memory therefore enables a person to "reconstruct" their own life story.

Implicit memory, on the other hand, stores experiences that are not conscious and cannot be described verbally. Here various forms of learning are filed, such as *priming* (meaning a person's ability to identify an object visually or auditively as a result of having already been exposed to it, possibly not consciously but only subliminally) *procedural memory*, which keeps track of motor and cognitive skills such as the movements needed for certain sports, or to play musical instruments, and the memory of numerous everyday things we do automatically without even being conscious of how; *emotional and affective memory*, where the brain stores its recollections of emotions arousing from affective experiences of the child's earliest relations with the environment, and particularly with the mother. This type of implicit memory may also operate in the late stages of pregnancy, when the fetus lives in close *rapport* with the mother, feeling her heartbeat and breathing rhythms, and particularly her voice. These build up a model of constancy, rhythm and musicality around which the infant will organize his or her first representations at birth (Mancia, 1981, 1989; Imbasciati, 1998; Cheour et al., 2002). This implicit memory may also store sensory experiences from the outside world that the newborn perceives and memorizes (De Casper and Fifer, 1980).

Psycholinguists consider the mother's voice, memorized by the fetus, very important; the memory is reactivated during breast-feeding, as indicated by the changes in heart rate and the infant's rate of suckling when it hears its mother's voice, rather than others (Mehler et al., 1978; Michnick Golinkoff and Hirsh-Pasek, 1999).

At birth and in the first two years or so, while the child's systems of symbolization and language are developing, the affective experiences in the child's primary relation with the mother are extremely significant, and are quite likely put away in the memory. While many of these will be positive, and essential for the child's mental and physical growth, some may be traumatic – the parents may be neglectful and inadequate; they may have mental illnesses; frustrations, violence and abuse from the family and environment can all cause harm to the child and will form the core of the child's implicit memory. To the extent that these emotion- and affect-laden experiences, with the fantasies and defenses they set up, are memorized in this preverbal and presymbolic stage of life, they will form part of an early unconscious nucleus of the child's personality, coloring his or her affects, behavior and personality right into adulthood. This nucleus will create an implicit way of establishing relations with others (Stern et al., 1998).

This is not the unconscious related to repression (Freud, 1915a, 1915b) as in early childhood the structures needed for the complex process of repression (the hippocampus, temporal and orbito-frontal cortex) are not yet mature (Perner and Ruffman, 1995; Siegel, 1999). These are more like memories "filed" in the temporo-parieto-occipital posterior cortical areas, particularly in the right hemisphere, from the child's preverbal and presymbolic stages; they are therefore beyond the reach of consciousness and never surface to the level of verbal expression. This implies that experiences, fantasies and defenses stored in the implicit memory are fundamental to the psychoanalytical theory of the mind, and in particular to the theory of dreams.

In the sections below I take an interdisciplinary look at memory, discussing the latest neuropsychological and molecular biology findings and relating them to memory's part in psychoanalytical theory and clinical practice. Finally, I shall focus on the potential for interaction and integration between neuroscientific findings and psychoanalysis as they relate to this mental function.

Neuroscience and memory

The contribution of neuropsychology

Clinical experience in the past hundred years has offered numerous examples of short- and long-term memory disorders. Much of today's information on memory was obtained in human beings with brain lesions. Short-term, operative, memory involves neurons in the prefrontal cortex (Fuster, 1997) and the inferior temporal cortex (Miller et al., 1993). This system comprises the hippocampus, which selects information, and the amygdala, which has an indirect part through the emotions; this is where information is "processed" for permanent storage, as long-term memories, in various parts of the associative cortex.

Alzheimer's disease is a classic illustration of a memory disorder, resulting from loss of the ability to store new information and persistent retrieval of experience dating from before the onset of the disease. These patients also have an abnormality of semantic memory, which draws on recollections of past events to give meaning to new experiences. Bioimaging investigations in these patients have shown a reduction in the function of hippocampal neurons bilaterally, of the cingulate cortex and the fronto-basal areas. Therefore structures of the medial temporal lobe (MTL) – particularly the hippocampus – and frontal areas are necessary for the selection of information and its storage in long-term memory.

Another cause of amnesia in humans is Korsakoff's syndrome, where patients can recall events from before the onset of the dysmnesia, but are no longer able to select, process and transfer recent events to long-term memory. Here again, bioimaging shows alterations to the hippocampus and dorsal medial nucleus of the thalamus, through which information reaches the prefrontal cortex.

A useful confirmation of these clinical observations is provided by patient HM, who had undergone bilateral removal of the hippocampus and temporal lobe cortex for therapeutic purposes. His subsequent memory disorder meant he could no longer memorize new experiences, but had no problems with older recollections.

Alexander Luria (1973) tells the fascinating account of Lieutenant Zasetskij, who had suffered a lesion to the parieto-occipital region of the left hemisphere, in the areas of the angular and supramarginal gyri (Brodmann's 39 and 40). Zasetskij lived in a state of "mental aphasia" which made it hard for him to read because he immediately forgot the first letter of a word, then if he finally grasped a string of words he forgot the one he had just read. He could never get the meaning of a whole sentence (semantic amnesia).

These clinical examples show that the brain structures needed for the long-term memory are in the MTL, which comprises the rhinal, perirhinal and parahippocampal cortex, and the hippocampus. The amygdala is needed for the emotional component of the process. Information is "archived" in various parts of the associative cortex, depending on the nature of the sensory experiences involved. All the cortical associative areas can potentially store information.

This was the background to early experiments in rats which showed that memory persisted even after extensive cortical lesions (Lashley, 1950; Pribram, 1969). This is why memory is considered a holistic phenomenon as it concerns the whole of the neocortical associative mantle in both hemispheres. The more specific process of selection, modification and processing of information for storage in the memory requires the MTL, particularly the hippocampus. The amygdala participates by controlling the emotions (Mishkin, 1978).

★ ★ ★

Recent electrophysiological and neuropsychological investigations confirm that the hippocampus and MTL are essential for memory. Operative memory essentially needs the prefrontal cortex, where specific neurons organize "memory fields". These illustrate how the process of memorization is divided up into compartments, as each neuron is selectively activated for specific information – such as a face, or a peculiarly shaped object – and is functionally connected to other associative areas, particularly the posterior parietal cortex (Goldman-Rakic et al., 2000).

The cognitive neurosciences have focused closely on the distinction between explicit, declarative memory and implicit, non-declarative memory (Schacter, 1995; see also Siegel, 1999). Explicit memory needs an intact MTL (rhinal and parahippocampal cortex), hippocampus and diencephalic nuclei of the median line. The amygdala, though indispensable for remembering emotions, does not seem essential to declarative memory (Squire and Knowlton, 2000). Implicit memory, in contrast, does not depend on the MTL and diencephalic structures (Squire et al., 1993) which are vital to declarative memory.

Implicit memory was in fact "discovered" in patients with amnesia due to lesions to these structures, through *priming* (Warrington and Weiskrantz, 1974) and others in relation to procedural memory (Schacter, 1996). Implicit memory seems to involve the posterior associative cortical areas and, for motor activity – procedural memory – other parts like the basal nuclei and cerebellum (Markowitsch, 2000).

The MTL is explicit memory's mainstay, as information is stored in the rhinal cortex (comprising the inter-rhinal and perirhinal parts), which is believed to be responsible for recognizing objects from their shape and remembering them. The hippocampus helps locate the object in space and the amygdala instigates the emotional responses to that object (Murray, 2000).

Patients with lesions to the right occipital lobe have an intact explicit memory but their implicit memory for words is damaged. This confirms these two memories probably use separate "processing" systems and the system in the right occipital cortex governs the visual implicit memory for words (Gabrieli et al., 1995).

Bilateral lesions to the hippocampus make it impossible to code information and recuperate new information, besides that acquired before the onset of amnesia (Cipolotti et al., 2001). These authors describe a patient with hippocampal lesions who could not recall autobiographic episodes from any time in his life. It is episodic explicit memory that is particularly damaged, while semantic memory's role is less clear, as if these two forms of explicit memory involved the hippocampus differently. In the light of this case, Nadel and Moscovitch (2001) suggested that all the structures of the MTL were required for retention and recovery of autobiographic memory.

The question of how explicit and implicit memories are organized and how we retrieve their information is still very much open, as shown by Stickgold et al. (2000). Subjects with bilateral lesions to the MTL and hippocampus were asked to learn a simple computer game requiring spatial organization, in order to test their memory. People with no lesions had no problem, after a few test runs, in remembering the game. The hippocampal lesion patients, on the other hand, could not remember the rules at all, but they reported having dreamt of them, at sleep onset.

This finding is interesting because it shows that something learnt can still be remembered outside the hippocampus through circuits that file information directly in the neocortex. In Stickgold's patients, declarative memory had been eliminated by the hippocampal lesions, but an "unconscious", non-declarative memory remained which surfaced in a dream in early sleep – a sort of implicit memory. The authors do not guess at what specific cortical areas might be involved.

Sperry (1974) reported that commissurotomized patients worked with their left hand obeying visual commands received from the right hemisphere, but not consciously, and without verbalizing the fact. On the basis of this finding and subsequent observations in primates (Schacter and Curran, 2000) we are led to suggest that information that does not reach the level of consciousness may be stored through the posterior cortical areas (parieto-temporo-occipital), particularly in the right hemisphere.

The contribution of molecular biology

Current biological research has made substantial contributions to our knowledge of the molecular mechanisms involved in "archiving" information. Molecular biology works on the assumption that memory involves biochemical-molecular and structural events at the junctions where neurons meet, which Charles Sherrington in 1906 called *synapses*.

Early electrophysiological investigations of learning showed, for example, that if the dorsal root of the spinal cord (which conducts sensitivity) is stimulated with high-frequency electrical impulses (tetanization) and the reflex response is recorded in the ventral root (conducting motor impulses), which is connected to the dorsal root through only one synapse, the stimulation potentiates the normal response, and the potentiation is lasting (post-tetanic potentiation). This simple procedure suggested that this synaptic junction in the spinal cord underwent stable "plastic" structural changes to its membrane, which explained why the potentiation lasted (Bliss and Lömo, 1973).

Similar conclusions had already been reached by Di Giorgio (1929) from observations of the persistence in spinal animals of postural and motor asymmetries induced by the cerebellar ablation preceding the spinal cut.

Long-term potentiation (LTP) experiments have provided interesting information on biological memory. These involve repeated stimulation of central structures (the hippocampus has been particularly widely studied) that potentiates their responses for a long time, as if they "remembered" the stimulus (Kornhuber, 1973). The synapses, therefore can undergo permanent plastic and structural modifications in response to stimulation: hypertrophy and the creation of new synapses after repeated stimulation, atrophy and a reduction in the number of synapses when stimulation is lacking.

A major step in our understanding of the biological events underlying the memory was achieved through neurochemical research by Stephen Rose (1992). Working in chicks he showed they had a genetic memory based on chromosomal DNA which explained their specific, innate behavior in response to certain stimuli – such as a moving figure, like in Konrad Lorenz's classic example of the duckling. The learning from these stimuli lasts throughout life and is fundamental to the survival of the species. Rose also showed that while the chick was learning, biochemical changes took place in the brain in the ribonucleic acid (RNA) required for protein synthesis. This is obviously essential for the formation of new proteins, hence also new synapses, which lay the foundations for new neural networks and circuits for long-term consolidation of information.

We now have ample proof that long-term memory even of a motor behavior, such as sport or playing instruments, increases RNA levels in the synapses of the neurons involved, with a consequent increase in their protein synthesis that facilitates synaptic hypertrophy, the organization of new synapses and therefore new nerve circuits.

Kandel et al. (1994) investigated learning and memory in a marine gastropod, *Aplysia californica*, in which repeated stimulation of the siphon mechanoceptors caused retraction of the gills. This elementary reflex, basically involving only two or three neurons, that are easily recorded, may become *habit*. Habit is an elementary form of learning that lasts a long time, and with repeated stimulation the response gradually becomes weaker, eventually disappearing altogether. Recording the neurons involved in the reflex Kandel et al. (1994) found that with repeated stimulation the post-synaptic excitatory potentials of the neurons that moved the gills became progressively weaker, and finally disappeared. This was caused by inactivation of the Ca++ channels of the presynaptic terminations, which caused less neurotransmitter release, leading to a weaker post-synaptic response.

This chain of events is linked to modifications in the ion channels following a change in gene expression, which in turn has a lasting effect on presynaptic membrane protein synthesis.

Unlike habit, sensitization of a reflex – meaning its increase, which is another form of learning that can be remembered – is based on presynaptic facilitation by the axo-axonal synapses that use serotonin as their transmitter. This facilitation, which is lasting, is due to an increase in the entry of Ca++ ions resulting from a change in presynaptic membrane protein synthesis, with an increase in the number of synaptic contacts and more power to the synapses themselves.

Kandel (2001) later reported that in mammals, *dopamine*, whose production increases with attention, facilitates the fixation of proteins expressed by the genes on specific synapses, responsible for long-term memory of certain experiences. This suggests that in humans too – which after all are mammals – dopamine, which we know controls the pleasure and sexuality pathways, may also be needed for the attention processes underlying the persistence of information, through the plasticity of the synapses involved in memory.

These findings confirm Kandel's (1999) earlier suggestion that environmental stimuli such as speech, attention, and the emotions and affects they convey, may cause stable modifications in the protein expression of genes and their fixation on the synapses; the resulting condition of neuronal and synaptic plasticity might be the organic basis for memorizing an experience. This will be discussed in greater detail in the third main section of this chapter.

Psychoanalysis and memory

The idea of memory runs through all Freud's work, starting with his *Project for a Scientific Psychology* in 1895. Here he outlines a model of the brain–mind relation and, using what sounds like neurophysiological language, but in fact is metaphorical, sets out the basic lines of the new psychology he was opening up (Mancia, 1987, 1998b).

Freud starts with the idea that the memory is a fundamental feature of the nervous system, the *faculty of undergoing permanent change after an event*. He suggests that the neurons retain traces of the energy that has flowed through them, while at the same time keeping their original receptivity unchanged, thus always taking a fresh approach to reality. He solved the complexity of the problem by suggesting there were two types of neurons: φ permeable neurons whose function was perception, and ψ impermeable ones responsible for memory.

Freud's "hydrodynamic" concept thus sees nervous energy as a fluid which, as it runs, digs its track through a medium that puts up some resistance, so that the next time it goes that way the fluid tends to take the path it has already traced. Thus the neurons are permanently altered by the exciting fluid. His theory is that the memory involves facilitations between φ and ψ neurons, or that it is based on the different levels of facilitation between the neurons, as memory itself involves distinguishing and selecting one path of nervous conduction rather than another. The different extents to which neuronal permeability is altered forms the basis for this selection (Freud, 1895: 206).

The hydraulic metaphor of the *Project* suggests that just as a river bed becomes wider and deeper as more water flows through, flooding it more often, so the memory depends on a factor termed

> magnitude of the impression and the frequency with which the same impression is repeated: translated into theory, facilitation depends on the Qή which passes through the neurone in the excitatory process and on the number of repetitions of the process.
>
> (Freud, 1895: 300)

Later, in *Neurosis and Psychosis* (1923b), Freud came back to this point, speaking of a mnestic patrimony of earlier perceptions which, as part of the internal world, are a possession and constitutive element of the Ego itself.

In his *Interpretation of Dreams* he did not change the concept of memory much. Visualizing the psychic apparatus as an instrument made up of systems aligned in a constant spatial orientation, Freud (1900) writes:

> We shall suppose that a system in the very front of the apparatus receives the perceptual stimuli but retains the trace of them and thus has no

memory, while behind it there lies a second system which transforms the momentary excitations of the first system into permanent traces.

(Freud, 1900: 538)

The basic idea is still that of neurons in the two systems, φ and ψ. However, *The Interpretation of Dreams* offers a much more advanced theory of the memory, suggesting it is responsible for linking experiences and perceptions.

In the years when he was working on his theory of dreams, however, Freud was curious about how we forgot the facts and experiences of our early infancy, and stressed the pathogenic implications of these forgotten impressions which, though repressed, still left indelible traces in our mind (Freud, 1899). He writes: "No one calls in question the fact that the experiences of the earliest years of our childhood leave ineradicable traces in the depths of our minds" (p. 303). Freud seems to have guessed here at the idea of an implicit memory, but this brought up another topic: that of screen memories, resulting from repression of some events and their shift onto contiguous facts (in the spatial-temporal sense).

Our early childhood memories will always be subject of special interest, because the problem mentioned at the beginning of this phrase (how it comes about that the impression which are of most significance for our whole future leave no mnemic images behind) leads us to reflect upon the origin of conscious memories in general.

(Freud, 1899: 321)

Freud seems to be referring here to what we now call the implicit memory, but he considers it confirms his hypothesis relative to the unconscious: that of *repression*. He sees screen memories as tendentious falsifications of the memory that serve to repress and replace perturbing or otherwise unpleasant experiences, a bit like the manifest content of a dream in relation to its latent content.

From *Screen Memories* we have the impression that at that time Freud (1899) did not sense the importance of the implicit memory for reconstruction in analysis as he was too tied up with the Oedipal phase of development in his theory of the mind, with its language and symbolic thought. As a consequence he underestimated the earliest profound Oedipal and dyadic pre-Oedipal experiences (Klein, 1928) referring to preverbal and presymbolic infancy, filed away in the implicit memory, where they cannot be repressed. This is why the references in *Remembering, Repeating and Working-Through* (Freud, 1914b) seemed aimed at explicit – autobiographic – memory that can be brought to the surface through free associations in analysis, even through Freud shows some intuition that links his ideas with a sort of implicit memory. He writes:

> There is one special class of experiences of the utmost *importance* for which no memory can as a rule be recovered. These are an experience which occurred in very early childhood and were not understood at the time but which were *subsequently* understood and interpreted. One gains a knowledge of them though dreams.
>
> (Freud, 1914b: 149)

We have started to clarify this only in recent years, and Freud could neither prove nor use it. He does not in fact go any further into this possibility, and considers this sort of memory as the expression of (original) repression.

In talking of screen memories as a means of masking experiences memorized in infancy and repressed, Freud seems to suggest an analogy between this memory and false memory. Screen memories do in fact have some resemblance to false memories as they reflect things that never happened and were therefore never actually lived, but which have "illegally" worked their way in among our recollections of early infancy. Neuro-cognitive research raises an interesting point here, attributing implicit memory and false memory to the same parieto–occipital cortical structures (Schacter and Curran, 2000). It is interesting to report that lesions to these posterior cortical associative areas make a person unable to dream (Solms, 1995). The third main section of this chapter will look at this more closely.

Freud comes back to the question of memory in analysis in *A Note upon the "Mystic Writing-Pad"* (1924c), where he picks up once more the ideas of his *Project for a Scientific Psychology* from 1895. The "mystic writing-pad" was a resin or wax block covered with two sheets of transparent paper on which new messages could always be written, while traces of previous ones remained underneath. Freud notes the similarities between this writing-pad and our memory, since our mental apparatus can offer both the services of the pad, by dividing things between the two connected φ and ψ systems.

A Note upon the "Mystic Writing-Pad" is particularly interesting because it is through the work of construction and reconstruction in analysis that the two systems come into contact. The events deposited and the emotions felt in the past and filed in the memory are brought to the surface, relived in the transference, and represented in dreams. Freud sustains that we are that doubly mystic writing-pad, because in the right conditions we manage to bring to light what repression "wrote" in our minds. The right conditions arise in analysis, which encourages the patient to re-establish memories of certain episodes, and the emotional responses they produced, which the patient may at the time think he or she has forgotten. Freud (1937b) concludes that the patient's current symptoms and inhibitions are the consequence of this repression.

Freud uses a historical or archaeological metaphor in *Civilization and its Discontents* (1930) to show that what has happened can anyway not be erased:

> Perhaps we ought to content ourselves with asserting that what is past in mental life *may* be preserved and is not *necessarily* destroyed. It is always possible that even in the mind some of what is old is effaced or absorbed . . . to such an extent that it cannot be restored or revivified by any means; or that preservation in general is dependent on certain favourable conditions. . . . We can only hold fast to the fact that it is rather the rule than the exception for the past to be preserved in mental life.
>
> (Freud, 1930: 71–72)

Analysis therefore works on the past surviving in the present, through the transference, which fosters the retrieval of affective relations that were significant for the patient. In *Constructions in Analysis* (1937b), Freud tackles the question of memory and recollection face on as the foundations of construction, and reconstruction, in analysis:

> The analyst has neither experienced nor repressed any of the material under consideration; his task cannot be to remember anything. What then *is* his task? His task is to make out what has been forgotten from the traces which it has left behind or, more correctly, to *construct* it.
>
> (Freud, 1937b: 258–259)

In the same work, Freud goes on to offer another, more precise, archaeological metaphor: "His work of construction, or, if it is preferred, of reconstruction, resembles to a great extent an archaeologist's excavation of some dwelling-place that has been destroyed and buried or of some ancient edifice" (p. 259). Freud seems to use the terms construction and reconstruction interchangeably but the "if it is preferred" looks highly ambiguous to our eyes (Mancia, 1990). Both the archaeologist and the analyst have to patch up and recompose the material they find. But the analyst has an advantage over the archaeologist because the former enjoys more favorable conditions: the transference serves as the search engine and gives some guarantee that patients' reactions are repetitions of their past, and actually date from their very early life.

In the transference, therefore, history emerges in the present; everything essential is there, and some things that seemed forgotten are nevertheless present too, in some way and in some part. The analyst has therefore to work as a historian and an archaeologist. We can define the analyst's work as "anastylosis" – uncovering and reassembling the dirt-encrusted fragments of an ancient column from a temple, for instance, giving them a new meaning. But the analyst is required more specifically to "transform memory", working on traumatic experiences that either have been repressed or were "filed" when the infant was still preverbal, and are therefore not repressed. This work transforms the persecutory ghost created by the trauma and a source of suffering into fantasy and thought (Giaconia and Racalbuto, 1997).

But what exactly is our forgotten history? I think it is the preverbal and presymbolic history of our first relationships, regarding the part of our life that is tucked away in implicit memory, serving as the foundation for our personality and character. Studies of the infant's mental development starting before birth confirm that memory is important in organizing his or her first representations. The fetus's sensory experiences in the mother's womb, particularly the sensory-motor and auditory impressions of the constant rhythms of the maternal container, and from the outside environment, all lay the foundations of the implicit memory that assists babies at birth and will help them achieve psychic continuity on their way from the inside to the outside world – a shift that apart from anything else is physiologically traumatic anyway (Mancia, 1981).

At birth the infant's experiences – and consequently his or her memory – are purely sensory (*aesthesis*): the mother's odor, her words, how the baby feels contained and watched, all convey affective messages essential to the organization of these very first representations. These preverbal experiences are filed in the implicit memory. But the baby may also have occasion to file gross or microscopic trauma there too: loss of the parents, abandon, neglect, serious frustrations, humiliation, incomprehension, physical, mental and even sexual violence or abuse. These trauma may undermine the baby's attachment system (Bowlby, 1969; Fonagy and Target, 1997) and endanger the organization of his or her self (Stern, 1985).

These processes filed in implicit memory form part of the infantile amnesia partly reflecting the incomplete maturation of the sense of self, besides the newborn's verbal and semantic incapacity (Rovee-Collier, 1993; Newcombe and Fox, 1994; Meltzoff, 1995; Siegel, 1999). On the neuropsychological level, this amnesia can be explained by neuronal immaturity of the infantile hippocampus, which implies the system used to file these happenings is different from the explicit memory (Perner and Ruffman, 1995). Implicit memory is therefore the storehouse for these important, early experiences, including the fantasies and defenses, such as splitting, projective identification and denial, that the newborn sets up to limit the anxiety caused by the most serious traumata.

This is a new view of the unconscious, different from Freud's (1915a, 1915b), a series of traumatic events of differing severity that were never repressed but were stored in implicit memory; as preverbal, presymbolic representations they never reached the level of consciousness but their effects are nevertheless felt throughout adult life. They surface in the transference, and particularly in dreams, which are memory's very own theater.

The dream is a special place where memory encounters no resistance, and can bring forth not only the wish that was repressed and filed but also all the unrepressed trauma I have listed, with the fantasies and defenses typical of the dreamer's own personality, which might be denial, splitting and projective identification – all independent of language. Projective identification works massively in dreams, enabling parts of the self and their unconscious conflicts to manifest themselves. Memory, particularly implicit memory, comes actively into analysis – more today than in Freud's time – and in dreams, from which it can be recuperated so present and past experiences can be compared. It serves as a *pontifex*, linking current reality with the events of the past, and combining in one the child's and the adult's object worlds, the former built up in the preverbal and presymbolic stage.

★ ★ ★

Memory is therefore an important actor of the transference, becoming an integral part and ontological structure. Memory today means not so much a reactivation of historically definable experiences, as a means of easing the comparison and integration of current life with things from the past, emerging in the transference. Memory is therefore a pivotal part of reconstruction in analysis, not only in historical terms but also for re-evoking the emotions and affects of past events – especially traumatic ones – filed in the implicit memory, and integrating them with current experience in the transference. It is an obligatory step to link the emotions and defensive modalities in the transference with the patient's experience with the most significant figures of infancy, especially in his or her preverbal, presymbolic life, since these – as we have said – are filed in implicit memory.

Retrieving things from this specific memory, which cannot be recollected, in analysis, and particularly in dreams, forms the basis for the emotional reconstruction that Freud called *Nachträglichkeit* (although he obviously had in mind only explicit memory); this refers to the mind's ability to relive its oldest experiences in the transference and to assign them fresh significance by retranscribing the memory, so they can be rendered verbally, thanks to the work of analysis. This "plasticity" of the mind is therefore the basis of therapeutic work by the analytical couple (Fonagy, 1999; Mancia, 2003a).

Explicit and implicit memory pull together as a team in the analytical relationship to achieve reconstruction. The first works as part of auto-biographic memory, the second supplies the unconscious preverbal and presymbolic experience that can be brought to the surface and represented in dreams and relational experience, dominated by projective identification, recognizable from the countertransferential affects it arouses in the analyst (Heimann, 1950; Joseph, 1985; Rosenfeld, 1987; Mancia, 1995; Fonagy, 1999). Memories deposited in this system cannot be "remembered" as such, in contrast to those stored in explicit, declarative memory. As they are not conscious, they obviously cannot be rendered in words, and can be repre-sented only in dreams or lived in the analytical relation or in the patient's relations with his or her body, through preverbal modalities, primarily projective identification (Klein, 1946).

Even without any specific reference to implicit memory, Francesco Siracusano (1982), in his paper to the Palermo meeting, points out that remembering has features of autobiographic memory that can be recalled, while forgetting has qualities that bring it closer to implicit memory – a modality of storing a recollection, an aspect of memory not linked to repression.

Transcription from memory, starting from implicit memory, is a means of writing the history of the unconscious and provides a continuous "record" of the discontinuous experiences spread diachronically over time. Resistance and defenses may operate in dreams and in analysis, impeding activation of memory and the mind's plastic functions, and preventing the formation of elaborative and symbolic thought. Therefore an attack on memory becomes an attack on analysis and the reconstructions – often painful – that analysis involves.

To recapitulate, therefore, retrieval from implicit and explicit memories is part of reconstruction in analysis. From implicit memory we can recu-perate preverbal – possibly even prenatal – experiences that laid the foundations of the child's inner world; from explicit memory we can obtain an autobiography but it also facilitates the emergence of recollections from implicit memory for use in reconstruction (Holmes, 2000). Explicit and implicit memories can also interact, influencing relational behavior (Davis, 2001), although in many patients, attempts at retrieval from auto-biographic memory may be a form of defense as analysis proceeds and access to implicit memory comes into sight.

As a whole, therefore, in analysis the memory:

- links the experience of the different sessions, giving continuity to what is actually a discontinuous analytical relation
- fosters the recollection of past events by recovery from explicit memory
- stimulates affects and emotions, even if they cannot actually be recalled, connected to preverbal and presymbolic experiences stored in implicit memory, facilitating their verbalization and symbolization (this is essential to reconstruction)
- eases the recollection of dreams and, through them, the symbolization of presymbolic experiences that cannot be rendered verbally
- helps work through what has been said and done in the session once the patient is outside
- upholds the internal representation of the analyst, during separations, as a stage of working through and as a containing object that helps stabilize the patient's inner world
- has a vital role in conserving the analytical experience (which may also be implicit) once analysis has ended.

The neurosciences and psychoanalysis face to face

From this analysis of the different types of memory, their anatomo-functional positions and their roles in analysis, various intriguing questions come to mind.

- How relevant to psychoanalysis is neuropsychological research into explicit and implicit memory?
- Where do the two disciplines meet as regards studies of memory, particularly implicit memory?
- Can current research on memory extend and deepen Freud's classic concept of the unconscious?
- How is the neuroscientific idea of non-conscious and unaware related to the unconscious of psychoanalysis?

To take the first question first, neuropsychology helps locate the structures and "neuronal fields" needed for organization of short-term, operative memory and for storing experiences in long-term memory. The latter needs an intact MTL and hippocampus. The amygdala has a part in emotional processing of the information to be consigned to memory. Implicit memory can do without the hippocampus and seems to be located in the posterior

46

temporo-parieto-occipital cortex of the right hemisphere (Schacter, 1996; Siegel, 1999).

The importance of implicit memory in the development of the child's mind and personality has attracted psychoanalysts' attention as the expression of classic conditioning (Davis, 2001). At the same time it is the storehouse of unconscious, non-verbalizable experiences that can be represented only in dreams or reached through the analytical relation. These experiences can also be expressed by the patient's relations with his or her body, through preverbal modalities, primarily projective identification, respectively intrapsychic (Heimann, 1952), intersubjective (Klein, 1946) and intrasomatic (Mancia, 1994).

★ ★ ★

The possibility of identifying explicit and implicit memories with respectively the repressed and unrepressed unconscious offers exciting prospects for integration between the neurosciences and psychoanalysis, and possibly establishing some anatomo-functional correlations. This implies one assumption: that the experiences, life events, emotions, fantasies and defenses around which the person's unconscious psychic reality has been organized, from birth and throughout life, are in fact stored in the nervous structures used by implicit and explicit memory. This hypothesis simply follows Freud (1912: 260) when he says: "As for latent conceptions, if we have any reason to suppose that they exist in the mind – as we had in the case of memory – let them be denoted by the term 'unconscious'".

We can speculate that the *repressed unconscious* is located in the structures of the explicit, autobiographic memory. This is to some extent upheld by Anderson et al. (2004) who showed that purposely forgetting mental experiences, which they compare to *Freudian repression*, is accompanied by increased activity in the prefrontal areas and a parallel reduction in hippocampal activity. This is the opposite of the *de-repression* in dreams (during REM sleep), when hippocampal activity increases and there is deactivation of the dorsolateral prefrontal cortex (Braun et al., 1998).

The organization of the *unrepressed unconscious*, however, with implicit memory, appears to be sited in the posterior (temporo-parieto-occipital) associative cortical areas of the right hemisphere. There is experimental and clinical proof of this: these areas are more active during REM sleep (hence also during dreams) than the left hemisphere (Antrobus, 1983; Bertini and Violani, 1984) and in these areas information connected to speech is stored in implicit memory (Gabrieli et al., 1995). Indirect proof is provided by Solms (1995) who found that patients with lesions to the posterior associative areas did not dream and by Bischof and Bassetti (2004) who observed an absence of dreams in a patient with posterior cerebral lesions, more evident in the right hemisphere.

As it is formed in the earliest, preverbal and presymbolic stages of life, implicit memory can hold extremely significant information, that may form an unrepressed, unconscious nucleus of the self around which a person's whole personality is organized. This memory, being neither conscious nor verbalizable, can be represented only through the preverbal modalities arising in the analytical relation through forms of communication largely relying on the voice and language. Through this "formal" aspect of the transference, the patient can split and projectively identify part of the self into the analyst. Dreams have a major role, with their ability to generate symbols that serve as the basis for symbolic transformation of presymbolic experiences, which can then be put into words and made thinkable.

★ ★ ★

Molecular biology has provided important pointers to how an early rela-tionship, with its affects, emotions, fantasies and defenses, can be filed in memory and remain there for the rest of a person's life. Our imposing point of reference on this question is Eric Kandel's (1998) work on memory; he proposed a biological "framework" to hold psychological and psychotherapeutic processes that could be stably memorized. This can be outlined in five main points:

- All normal and pathological mental processes derive from work by the brain.
- Genes and the proteins they express decide how neurons are joined (synapses) so some mental functions, whether normal or pathological, have a genetic component.
- Relational and social factors act on the brain, stably modifying the function of genes, i.e. their protein expression as it affects the synapses and therefore whole neuronal circuits. Thus "culture" can express itself as "nature".
- Mental abnormalities may be induced by traumatic relations and social situations through changes in the genes' expression of proteins.
- Psychotherapy (and a fortiori psychoanalysis) may induce long-term changes in behavior and mental functions, acting on the genes' expression of proteins that modify the structure and potency of the synapses.

Kandel (2001) has published further observations that attention, pleasure and sexuality use the same neurotransmitter − *dopamine* − that serves to fix the proteins expressed by genes in specific synaptic sites in the nervous circuits responsible for memorizing experience.

These principles and findings are particularly pertinent to the interaction between psychoanalysis and the neurosciences. If gene expression is affected by relational experiences based on words, pleasure, sexuality, affects and emotions, besides more general social factors, then all these experiences are biologically incorporated in the patterns of synaptic fixation of specific proteins expressed by specific genes in specific nerve cells of specific brain regions. Therefore, if relational experiences influence the expression of genes, affecting how DNA transcription regulators bind with each other and with the gene-regulating regions, it is logical to suggest that personality disorders from neurosis to psychosis may well be due to reversible defects in this complex process.

Clearly these changes are not transmitted genetically, as it is not the gene structure that is affected but only its function. They are therefore the engine of cultural evolution that helps explain the enormous changes that have taken place in humans over thousands of years. As there is no learning, no interpersonal experience, or culture without changes in the expression of genes, we can assume – this was Kandel's (1998) idea – that every mental process is to some extent organic. Current technology, though sophisticated, does not yet give us a direct view of the cellular or synaptic changes underlying the mental process so there are still many missing links in the chain from the neuronal and synaptic event to the psychic moment.

We can take a similar approach to look back at and try to interpret the findings of a study on children and adolescents with epilepsy documented clinically and electroencephalographically (EEG) by Mariateresa Bonaccorsi (1980). These patients showed significant EEG changes, with parallel improvements in their clinical picture after psychotherapy.

Today we can opine that the psychotherapeutic relation may in these cases have affected the expression of certain proteins, changing the activity of synapses, neurons and whole circuits responsible for these children's pathology.

★ ★ ★

On the last question – the relationship between the concept of unconscious in psychoanalysis and the non-conscious, or unaware, used by the neurosciences – this is an important point that needs a clear definition if we are to avoid semantic and epistemological confusion.

Neuroscientific, particularly neuropsychological investigations, mainly focus on *unawareness* of events outside one's self. For instance, some brain lesions make a person unaware of extracorporeal space (neglect), or time, body parts (asomatognosia), familiar faces (prosopoagnosia), a personal illness (anosoagnosia), or the meaning of a perception or an experience (visual, auditory agnosia, etc.). These forms of unawareness have nothing to do with the self as such because they do not involve the person's affects and emotions, or the implicit or explicit memory. These aspects are, however, related to the concept of unconscious in psychoanalysis as Freud classically saw it – a dynamic unconscious linked to repression, and to the unrepressed form linked to affective and emotional experiences and essentially pre-verbal and presymbolic trauma from the child's earliest relations with its surroundings, filed in the implicit memory.

Some cognitivists (Kihlstrom, 1987), on the subject of emotions, speak of a "cognitive unconscious", stressing that emotions and unconscious are identical and suggesting this as a point where psychoanalysis and the neurosciences converge. De Masi (2000) picked up this suggestion, also referring to work by LeDoux (1996), distinguishing Freud's "dynamic unconscious" from the "emotional unconscious" as a function of the mind, proposed by Bion (1967). However, since the unconscious, whether dynamic (repressed) or unrepressed, is always rooted in the emotions and affects, I feel it is preferable to distinguish Freud's *repressed unconscious*, which is dynamic and based on repression as the expression of the instincts model, from the *unrepressed unconscious*,[2] which expresses a relational model and container for early preverbal experiences that helped organize the affective representations of the most significant figures of childhood, with the fantasies and defenses set up to deal with the disappointment, frustration and trauma a child meets as he encounters reality. High on the list of these defenses are splitting, projective identification, denial and idealization. These are the early relational experiences filed in implicit memory, where they form an emotional and affective history that may manifest itself in analysis even though their roots go back to preverbal infancy or even pre-natal life.

This might have been the line of thought that dictated Sandler and Sandler's (1987) distinction between present and past unconscious; however, manifestations in the transference and unconscious defenses in the here and now of the relation (present unconscious) are also rooted in the past, in the most significant experiences stored in implicit memory (past unconscious). This unconscious function of the mind, which summarizes a person's emotional and affective life, is exclusive and specific to psychoanalysis.

2

Implicit memory and unrepressed unconscious: their role in creativity, in the transference and in dreams

One of the possible definitions of *aesthetics* is related to the theory of "sensitive knowledge". This definition is used to underline the relationship between esthetics (*aestesis*) and sensitivity. The latter relates to the body and the sensory sphere which, in the infant's primary relations with the mother and the environment in which the child grows, convey emotions and affects. Through those esthetic experiences, children complete their very first creative task, forming their earliest representations (proto-representations), allocating them a position in time and space, and organizing the internal world around them.

As suggested in Chapter 1, all the earliest experiences take place at preverbal and presymbolic stages. These experiences, so important for the creative work, constitute the basis of an *unrepressed unconscious nucleus* of the self which governs a person's affective, emotional, cognitive and creative life through adulthood.

Human creativity, against this theoretical background, actually appears as a form of *re-creating* linked to implicit memory not available to recollection, but which can be represented and "acted" in creative work (poetic, musical, scientific and artistic activity in the widest sense). This creativity can be modeled only on the child's earliest relational experiences deposited in his or her unrepressed unconscious.

To explain the types of concept that children can form at birth when they encounter the objects of reality, several of the previous generation of psychoanalysts (Bion, 1962; Money-Kyrle, 1978) suggested the existence of innate *preconceptions* which may be transformed into concepts in the encounter with reality. The ideas they put forward have interesting analogies with Immanuel Kant's (1781) classical contribution on the origin of thought (see Longhin and Mancia, 2001).

Kant begins with the proto-mental concept that underlies the origin of the mind. He deals with the Ego's relationship with the object and its representation, a relationship dictated by a priori elements, i.e. ones that predate experience and are of a universal nature. The human way of knowing things can thus be investigated a priori, and is *transcendental* in the sense that it operates beyond the level of experience itself.

Kant, however, could not go beyond the idea of "I think" as the organizer of knowledge, nor could he include the concept of the unconscious. It was Bion (1962) who introduced the emotional and affective unconscious into Kant's proto-mental structure, completing its transcendental function. The idea of the child's "inner equipment", alpha and beta mental functions, and preconceptions and proto-representations all have analogies with Kant's a priori principles. These a priori ideas can be considered the natural, universal "presuppositions" for objective knowledge of reality in Kant. For psychoanalysis, this relational knowledge is also subjective and therefore affective and emotional as well as cognitive. Psychic events of this kind are preverbal and presymbolic and govern the way the Ego observes and interprets reality, just like the Kantian a priori principles that create objective knowledge, with all their similarities with the unconscious agencies we have just described.

I would like to suggest that we consider children's early emotional and affective experiences dating from their prenatal and post-natal relations with the mother and their environment as somehow being able to influence how the "presuppositions" actually meet up with reality and take an active part in the organization of an unconscious unrepressed nucleus of the self. This nucleus is composed of the affects and emotions, fantasies and defenses that may be triggered by this encounter.

Human creativity thus appears as one of the mental aspects that is organized according to an unconscious model formed early, as a result of the encounter between "presuppositions" (or innate preconceptions) and reality. The idea is that, during life, creative individuals repeat unconscious models laid down during their development and are conditioned by an *unconscious unrepressed* nucleus of the self that cannot be based wholly on the memory because the event is stored in the implicit memory. However, it can be indirectly represented in art (or in dreams).

★ ★ ★

There are multiple examples of the role this form of unconscious plays in human creativity. I would like to examine the *languages of poetry and music* and what one might refer to as the *language of the transference*, with the aim

52

of showing that they all belong to the same class, illustrating their analogies and capacities for representing the unrepressed unconscious affective and emotional structure of the individual.

In his *Writings* Jacques Lacan (1966), referring to the Hindu tradition, states that he believes the essential property of the word in analysis is to imply what is not said, meaning expressing and transmitting the message that speech hides. If this concept of the word in analysis indicates its function in repression, it can also refer to the unrepressed unconscious, but equally to poetry. In this case it would express and transmit whatever does not actually come out in words – and what is not said expresses a meaning that cannot be resolved in terms of significance (Agosti, 2002).

Following Jakobson's principle based on Ferdinand de Saussure's *Cours de linguistique générale* (1916), poetry can be said to involve the projection of the equivalences from the *axis of selection* (paradigmatic axis) onto the *axis of contiguity* (syntagmatic axis) (Agosti, 1996). A psychoanalytic approach to the poetic text, in line with the same principle, suggests that it involves the projection of the poet's affective and emotional unconscious structure (*paradigmatic axis*) onto the *syntagmatic axis* of the actual verses. This implies that poetic language is a set of metaphors (substitution axis) whose structure is isomorphic with the poet's affective and emotional unconscious structure. It is with this structure that the reader's unconscious identifies (see Figure 1).

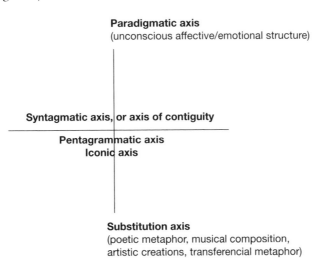

Paradigmatic axis
(unconscious affective/emotional structure)

Syntagmatic axis, or axis of contiguity

Pentagrammatic axis
Iconic axis

Substitution axis
(poetic metaphor, musical composition,
artistic creations, transferencial metaphor)

Figure 1 A psychoanalytic approach to poetic text, musical composition, artistic creations and transferencial metaphor. For explanation, see text.

Source: based on Saussure, F. De (1916). *Cours de linguistic générale* (amply modified)

Similarly, we can think of the *language of music* as a form of language *sui generis*, whose structure is isomorphic with that of our internal world (Langer, 1942). As with poetry, the language of music (*substitution axis*) can be considered a projection of the composer's emotional and affective unconscious structures (*paradigmatic axis*) on the actual notes (*pentagrammatic axis*). A fine example might be Robert Schumann's Fantasy in C major, Opus 17, composed in 1838, when the musician was in a state of tremendous affective suffering caused by his enforced separation from his beloved Clara Wieck. The three movements show regular, continuous swings between manic and depressive moods. The Fantasy ends with three descending low notes which Schumann feels represent a form of resignation to his state of depression. Does this signal the achievement of a more creative "depressive capacity"?[1] The same analysis holds for creative art in general, which as a "substitution axis" represents the artist's projection onto the work of art (*iconic axis*) of his unconscious affective-emotional state.

Finally, an analysis of *the language of the transference*, based on the same double semantics of language, shows the transferencial metaphor (substitution axis) as the expression of the projection of the patient's unconscious (*paradigmatic axis*) into the infraverbal component of the sintagmatic axis. From this viewpoint, words in the transference transmit in metaphors the message the patient is not saying – as we noted before, whatever does not actually come out in words.

From this it emerges that the languages of poetry, music and the transference all have their roots in the unconscious in that they all represent the projection and intertwining of a paradigmatic axis showing the subject's affective and emotional unconscious structure onto the axis of the specific languages (syntagmatic, pentagrammatic and associative).

In psychoanalytic practice, it ought thus to be possible to grasp the sense of the patient's communication not so much in the words themselves, but through the tone, timbre and volume of the voice, and the rhythm, stresses, syntax and timing of the language. The voice is attracting close attention as it harks back to the child's intra-uterine and post-natal experiences with the mother, stored in the implicit memory, as part of the unrepressed unconscious. In the analytical setting it is an experience of the self achieved through speaking, but also an expression of the self in relation to the other party. The voice of the couple in analysis arises out of a common area of unconscious experience in which the unconscious of both of them participates, although asymmetrically.

This is the shared area that Ogden (2001) calls the "analytical third party". This voice activates strong feelings – in the transference and countertransference. These are the "formal" aspects of communication that constitute the music in the session (Odgen, 1999), and which I have described else-where as the "musical dimension of the transference" (Mancia, 2003a), that creates a meaning that cannot be resolved simply in terms of significance.

★ ★ ★

I would now like to give a few examples of text analysis, starting from poetry and ending with a couple of clinical cases.

From the poetry collection by Annalisa Cima (1984), a contemporary Italian poet, entitled *Ipotesi d'Amore*, following Faggi (2001), I will analyze the first line of a poem dedicated to Mozart's *Cherubino*:

Amante amato amandoti

This lone line has its own musicality stemming from the stylistic image (grammatical and semantic) created by the repetition of the same syllables (from the root *amare*) which gives a rhythm and alliteration based on the same sounds – with the musical effect of a continuum of sound, a sort of *basso continuo* effect, for instance.

Another point in this analysis would be the order of the words with its near-*symmetry*, the word *amato* (loved) in the middle, the present participle *amante* (loving/lover) to the left and the gerund *amandoti* (loving you) to the right. The two side elements have an analogy in sound which stems from the double consonants (*nt* and *nd*) after the vowel *a*. The real musical appeal of this line, however, lies in the regular, insistent stress on the second vowel *a* in each word.

Perhaps to make the point by way of a pictorial analogy, one might visualize the symmetry of Parmigianino's 1529 painting of the *Madonna and Child with Saint Margaret and Other Saints*. Saint Margaret and the Holy Child, picked out in the same light, look lovingly at each other, their gestures creating symmetry. Saint Benedict and Saint Jerome are looking towards the center of the composition, reinforcing the symmetry. The Madonna is looking at Saint Benedict, and the Angel, watching the observer, seems to introduce an element of asymmetry (see Figure 2).

The symmetry (and asymmetry) underlying this analysis – or any other work of art – relates to the *symmetric (or asymmetric) logic of the unconscious* as described by Matte-Blanco (1975). This author himself, and the interpretation by Pietro Bria (1975), considers that humankind's being is marked by two thought processes: an *asymmetric* way of being which distinguishes and separates, and a *symmetric* way of being which homogenizes and makes no distinction between self and non-self, time or space. Matte-Blanco's

55

Figure 2 Parmigianino's 1529 painting, *Madonna and Child with Saint Margaret and Other Saints*, Bologna

unconscious presents a *bi-logic*: there is the asymmetric side (aristotelic) which respects the principle of non-contradiction, and the symmetric side which does not. The bi-logic structure therefore brings the unconscious closer to conscious thought through its asymmetric way of being, while the symmetric side moves it further away.

My idea is that the unconscious nucleus of the self, stored in the implicit memory, which is obviously outside the realm of consciousness, and pre-verbal, is dominated by the *symmetric*, homogenizing way of being and acquires a logic entirely outside time and space. This tends towards absolute symmetry. The unrepressed unconscious would therefore be marked by a single logic – *symmetric*.

The repressed unconscious, formed later once the explicit or declarative memory has developed fully, offers a double logic, both symmetric and asymmetric. The process of repression calls into play Freud's instincts model of the mind and, according to Matte-Blanco, respects the asymmetric relations, i.e. the way of being of conscious thought. The unrepressed, non-verbalizable unconscious, tucked into the implicit memory, is further from consciousness, so it should be totally dominated by symmetric relations.

This idea is upheld by the idea of "inexpressible", meaning not verbal-izable and not thinkable, which Matte-Blanco believes translates into the homogeneous, indivisible and symmetric parts of our being. This "inexpressibility" is therefore a feature of the symmetric unconscious. And what unconscious is more inexpressible, symmetric, homogeneous, indivisible, non-recollectable or thinkable, than the form organized in the earliest part of our lives, buried in the implicit memory?

Following this line of thought, poetry and art – like the work of dreams – would have the task of symbolically expressing the symmetric logic of the poet or artist's unrepressed unconscious (or the patient's). This is also the unrepressed unconscious of the reader, the listener to music, or the appreciator of art – or the analyst.

★ ★ ★

Another interesting example of representation of the unrepressed un-conscious in its verbal and musical dimension can be found in several compositions by Alberto Savinio, the younger brother of De Chirico. This painter, writer and musician was one of the leading Italian surrealists. Although we know that Freud did not show particular interest in the Surrealist theoretician André Breton, I believe Surrealism can provide psy-choanalysis with numerous points for creative reflection. In *Chants étrangers*, Savinio weaves music and speech-like sounds to create a composition that is simultaneously poetic and musical language. He himself described it as the representation of his unconscious. We also know that when he was writing music, Savinio intentionally left in wrong notes because he valued such "slips" as a creative expression of his unconscious.

Other contemporary authors, such as Paolo Castaldi, have created compositions that include meaningless words, but are used as *musical signifiers*, sung by two persons, one singing in the treble clef, the other in the bass clef. This exchange of vocal sounds forms a very moving duet, suggesting a metaphor of the encounter between two unconsciouses in analysis.

★ ★ ★

Turning now to associative language, there is no question that alongside the "dynamic" unconscious Freud described (1915a, 1915b), produced by repression and therefore stored in the explicit, autobiographic memory, there is also an unrepressed unconscious based on sometimes traumatic experiences of the child's very first relations, though also the late prenatal period (Stern, 1985; Mancia, 1994, 2003a). These experiences, with the resulting fantasies and defenses, are stored in the infant's implicit memory since they are preverbal and presymbolic, and the brain structures required for the explicit memory (hippocampus and temporal and baso-frontal cortical areas) are not yet mature (Joseph, 1996; Siegel, 1999).

This leads us to visualize the unconscious as a complex mental function with repressed and unrepressed components. The relations between the analyst and patient will therefore be colored by this unconscious structure, which has inevitably to involve both parties. It may manifest itself in the transference and in the countertransference.

In the transference, the "dynamic" unconscious resulting from repression will surface in the recollections brought to light by analysis, in the content of the patient's narrations and free associations, in the occasional slip of the tongue and in some dreams. The unrepressed unconscious will be detectable not only in dreams, but also in the verbal and extra-verbal components of the patient's specific mode of communication. The extra-verbal components are the patient's "acting" – body posture and movements, facial expressions, how the patient presents him- or herself, dresses, etc. The infra-verbal component has to be grasped in the dual semantics of language, which give meaning to the patient's communications not simply as regards the content – the actual words – but in the tone, timbre and volume of the voice, and the rhythm, stresses, grammar and timing of the language.

The voice has special value as an experience of the self (Ogden, 2001), while at the same time expressing the self in the analytical relation. These are the "formal" aspects of communication that make up the music of the events in the session (Ogden, 1999), which I have called the "musical dimension" of the transference (Mancia, 2003a).

On this fascinating topic of music applied to psychoanalysis, meaning how to refine our analytical sensitivity so as to grasp in the present what cannot be said with words alone, Antonio Di Benedetto (2000) gives higher priority to the messages transmitted by the voice itself than to the content of the patient's speech, as a means of reaching the "unheard voices of the unconscious". We have to refine a certain type of auditory imagination while listening to the patient, that might be called *acoustic reverie* (Di Benedetto, 2003).

There are some interesting clinical examples to illustrate this: while treating an autistic child, Adele Ognibene (1999) used the sound and rhythmic elements produced by her patient Sara, who could not communicate with words. Sara modulated her voice to set up a sort of autistic self-protective barrier between her and her analyst, to defend herself against the anxiety of separation and the pain of anger. The analyst managed to "decode" Sara's primitive musical language, giving it meaning, and finding a way into her catastrophically distant emotional world.

If we put our analytical ears to the "musical dimension" of the transference, we can reach those deeper unconscious structures related to the patient's earliest and most significant relational experiences hidden away in the implicit memory as part of an unrepressed unconscious. If we pay attention solely to the contents of the narrative (Ferro, 1999, 2002) – however important for the purposes of construction (Di Chiara, 2003) – we risk losing the most significant aspects in the transference, linked to primary experiences (particularly to the mother's voice and language), unconscious fantasies and defenses which the patient cannot directly recall but which stimulate emotions and affects more directly in the analyst (Joseph, 1985) and facilitate the work of reconstruction.

Work on the musical form of the patient's communication permits a process which is both constructive and reconstructive: *constructive* to the extent that the forms of communication in the *hic et nunc* of the session bring to light in the present emotions dating back to affective events (linked to the musicality of the mother's voice) that the patient cannot recall, and whose meaning the patient cannot know; *reconstructive* in the sense that these same emotional experiences may turn out to be the most likely explanation – starting from early infancy – for the relational strategies in the current analytical situation.

When some authors speak of what is known but not thought,[2] such as Bollas (1987), or of a past unconscious (Sandler and Sandler, 1987), or of unanalyzed areas of the personality – of the patient or analyst (Russo, 1998), I think they are referring to the parts of the mind that have never been analyzed because they belong to an *unrepressed unconscious*. This escapes analysis because it does not manifest itself in the content of a narration or the recollection of an event from the autobiographic memory. It takes a "cryptic" or "implicit" form in speech, through the modalities of communication we have discussed, making up the formal, musical aspects of the transference, firmly anchored to the here and now of the session.

The musical dimension of the patient's transference conveys multiple sentiments. Often these are negative: anger, resentment, jealousy and envy, frustration, disappointment. The scene in the session shifts to an enactment with complaints, demands and boredom,[3] this latter sometimes becoming pivotal to the relation. A patient can combine boredom with complaints in "emotional missiles" he then chucks around with indecent violence; otherwise the boredom may be more underhand, aimed at the analyst to make her feel the patient's anger and resentment on her own skin, to make her live the impotence, exclusion, solitude and despair that the patient suffered as a child, with his parents.

Analysts too may have difficulty reaching this unrepressed unconscious core. When this happens – possibly more often than we are willing to admit – the situation of the analytical couple can influence the whole therapeutic process. Analysts' unrepressed unconscious, especially if it has evaded deep analysis, inevitably influences their ability to understand what their patients are communicating in verbal and extra-verbal terms; it will color analysts' choice of the most significant "fact" in the transference, the timing of their own interventions, but particularly how they speak to their patients, the tone and volume of their voice, the rhythm and musical dimension of their own speech.

Dreams, of course, are an indispensable tool for reaching the patient's unrepressed unconscious. On the one hand they have to be fitted into the analytical relation and analyzed as a "window" open onto the fantasies, defenses and sentiments of the transference (Mancia, 2000a). On the other, they can help in interpretation so the patient can be taken back emotionally to the earliest relational experiences – even traumatic – and the unconscious fantasies and defenses that cannot be directly remembered, but which, as part of the patient's unrepressed unconscious, carry on influencing his or her affective, cognitive, behavioral and sexual life even as an adult. These "earliest relational experiences" refer to the processes that, starting from the child's very first representations – proto-representations – lead, through imitation, identification and symbolization in their various forms, to the organization of the child's thought and personality (Mancia, 1996a).

Thus dreams offer images and emotions that analysts can exploit to offer their patients ideas about how their mind has developed, the traumas they have suffered but never thought about in their early relations with their mother, father and surroundings, the fantasies and defenses unconsciously organized to deal with the lack of containment and maternal reverie, or to cope with traumas, frustrations, separations and disappointments.

Work on dreams permits "construction" linked to the interpretations based on the transference (Mancia 2000a) and at the same time "reconstructions" that enable patients to "mentalize" fantasies, defenses and emotions dating back to when they were still incapable of symbolization or speech, and that they cannot recall because these are beyond reach, in the implicit memory. These are experiences that the patient could not think about, let alone render verbally, when they happened, but that the symbols employed in dreams can help make thinkable and even verbalizable.

In some analyses the patient offers scanty narratives with little significance, prolonged silences, communications made up of a slow, monotonous, repetitive, complaining language. The voice has no emotional tension, sentence construction appears laborious and the syntagmatic axis of the patient's discourse is excessively long. This form of communicating in the session puts the analyst in a position of "waiting" which may sometimes become exasperating. However, this very wait may conceal deeper unconscious signifiers in the transference: patients can keep their analysts "bound", and engage full attention, so they will not be abandoned. At other times the communication becomes so slow that it becomes difficult to remember a whole sentence; this may have the unconscious purpose of "distracting" analysts, attacking their memory and neutralizing their thought.

Conclusions

I have tried to show that the child's primary experiences, deposited in implicit memory to organize the unrepressed unconscious, can influence the very first creative task: that of forming the first representations (or proto-representations), positioning them in space and time, and constructing the self. The latter is the result of the encounter with reality of "innate pre-conceptions" or "presuppositions", analogous, as I suggested, to Kantian a priori principles. For Kant, these a priori forms are what permit *objective* knowledge of reality. For psychoanalysis, this relational knowledge is also *subjective* and therefore affective, emotional and cognitive.

Human creativity – poetic, musical, scientific or artistic – appears to be one of the aspects of the mind. It is always a form of re-creating, modeled on unrepressed unconscious fantasies and defenses that have marked the primary experiences, as the result of preconceptions encountering relational reality.

I have looked at the various unconscious instances in poetic, musical and transference language, with evidence to support the idea that these various languages all have roots in the unrepressed unconscious. They constitute the projection and integration of their *paradigmatic axis*, represented by the unconscious affective and emotional structure, on the *axis of the various languages* (syntagmatic, pentagrammatic, associative-narrative and artistic-iconic).

For the language of poetry, I have analyzed a line by an Italian poet where the musical rhythm, order and stress of the words reveals a *symmetry* related to the *symmetric logic* of the unconscious, as described by Matte-Blanco (1975) and more recently elaborated by myself. For the language of art I looked at the dual symmetric and asymmetric logic of one of Parmigianino's works, and for the language of music the affective oscillations in a piece by Schumann. For verbal-musical language, I took the surrealist compositions by Alberto Savinio and a young contemporary author, Paolo Castaldi.

On the clinical level, unrepressed unconscious elements represented by fantasies and defenses linked to primary experiences deposited in the implicit memory, and hence not recollectable, may emerge in the "musical dimension" of the transference. This dimension may be detectable in the patient's communications, particularly in the tone, timbre and volume of the voice, and in the rhythm, stresses, syntax and timing of the language.

Work on the musical form of the patient's communication permits construction linked to not only the here and now of the session, but also reconstruction. The latter enables the patient to re-experience emotionally, even without the actual recollection, the earliest childhood experiences, which were not known and certainly unthinkable at the start. Analysis of dreams may help further this reconstruction by offering images and emotions that enable the patient to symbolize, "mentalize" and make thinkable experiences that were not originally either symbolic or thinkable.

3

Therapeutic (f)actors in the theater of memory

The theater of memory and the unconscious

This chapter focuses on the convergence of two disciplines, neuro-psychology and psychoanalysis, with regard to the functions of memory, the concept of the unconscious and the role of dreams in the therapeutic process.[1]

The discovery of implicit memory raises new and interesting questions for clinical psychoanalysis. There is now a substantial body of literature in which the neonate's first relational experiences are seen as foundations of the emotional, affective and cognitive organization of the individual's personality and character (Stern, 1985; Mancia, 2000b). These experiences are preverbal and presymbolic, and are stored in implicit memory. Some of them may be traumatic, and these traumas may critically impair the child's attachment system (Bowlby, 1969) and reflective functions (Fonagy and Target, 1997), and constitute a threat to the formation of the self (Stern, 1985). Such early traumatic experiences will inevitably give rise to the organization of defenses, which, stored in implicit memory, will form part of an early *unconscious nucleus of the self*. This organization will condition the person's affects, emotions, cognition, behavior and character even as an adult.

The unconscious to which I am referring is not due to repression (Freud, 1915a, 1915b), but is the expression of storage operations that take place in preverbal and presymbolic form. It therefore remains outside consciousness and is not amenable to the assignment of meaning through language, even though it may express itself in a variety of other, extra- and infra-verbal ways. This concept of the unconscious has its roots in the implicit model of the mind and refers to experiences that do not undergo repression because the structures of explicit memory (particularly the hippocampus: Perner and Ruffman, 1995), necessary for repression, are not yet completely formed (Siegel, 1999).

This concept of non-repressed unconscious cannot emerge in the analytic relationship by narration alone (Schafer, 1983; Arrigoni and Barbieri, 1998; Ferro, 1999; Di Chiara, 2003), but may be expressed through various forms of extra- and infra-verbal communication, transference enactments and dream representations.

Freud (1915a, 1915b) was unable to postulate the existence of a non-repressed unconscious along these lines because implicit memory had not yet been discovered. His "dynamic" concept of the unconscious, based on repression, was grounded in autobiographical memory. However, he was curious about the amnesia to which the facts and experiences of the early years of infancy fall victim but never went beyond the concept of repression (original and proper).

What is therapeutic in work on memory?

I now come to the nub of my subject matter: what is it that makes the work on memory that we do with our patients therapeutic?

For Freud, the therapeutic effect of psychoanalysis is essentially bound up with a process of reconstruction mediated by work on the patient's auto-biographical memory. His concept of working through (1914b) has been seen as a process of recovering repressed experiences deposited in explicit memory and overcoming resistance to this process (Gill, 1982). This aspect of the therapeutic function of psychoanalysis, already criticized by some epistemologists (Grünbaum, 1993), has been the subject of a thorough-going reassessment by present-day psychoanalysis. A number of authors have sought the basis of the therapeutic effect of psychoanalysis in something other than the mere recovery of the memory of repressed infantile experiences (Winnicott, 1956; Loewald, 1960; Fonagy, 1999). Kleinian psychoanalysis (Klein, 1932) sets some store by the idea that the therapeutic action has primarily to do with the recovery of parts that have been projectively identified in the object and with the retrospective discovery, in the transference, of infantile experiences that made this possible (Steiner, 1989).

My own conception is based on an observational and interpretive position that focuses on the fantasies, representations and defenses stored in the patient's implicit memory. This position remains substantially *reconstructive*, but its starting point is nevertheless experience in the here and now of the session, so it is an essentially *constructive* process based on the transference and on dreams.

The transference is observed in its total relational dimension (Joseph, 1985), though basically in its extra- and infra-verbal components; the former refer to the patient's behavior in the analytical setting – posture, movements, style of dress and overall presentation to the analyst. The infra-verbal component regards the twofold semantics of language, marking the patient's form of communication, particularly the voice. In the psychoanalytical encounter, where speech is so important, the voice serves as a vehicle, in which the words create sound. In this sense the voice too is an "experience" of the self, that happens when one speaks (Ogden, 2001), but it is also an expression of the self in relation to the other party. I would add to these elements of communication the tone, rhythm, grammar and syntax and tempo of the language. This all combines in the "musical dimension" of the transference (Mancia, 2003a).

This is based on a conception of music as a language *sui generis*, whose symbolic structure is isomorphic with that of our emotional and affective world (Langer, 1942; Ognibene, 1999; Di Benedetto, 2000). This mode, rather than the content of the narration, is the transference metaphor of the affective and traumatic experiences that have characterized the implicit model of the patient's mind. It is capable of "pricking" the analyst's counter-transference skin (Joseph, 1985) more than any narrative content, because it is the formal, musical component of communication that conveys the parts of the self split off and projectively identified. It is the analyst's responsibility to pick up the unconscious meaning of this specific transference modality, particularly the quality of the affects that are split and projectively identified and to put it into words after giving it a symbolic sense.

Catching these complex manifestations in the transference is one of the most effective ways of gaining access to the most archaic parts of the patient's unconscious and of going back "reconstructively" to the patient's past. However, the reconstruction is *sui generis* given that the experiences stored in this memory system cannot be "remembered" as such. They can be emotionally relived and "acted out" only in the intersubjective relationship, or represented in dreams, which are the theatre par excellence of memory (both implicit and explicit), whose curtain rises on the transference (Mancia, 2000a; 2003a).

Dreams are often the best channel for grasping the fantasies, affects and defenses manifested in the transference, as well as the reconstructive moments connected with the preverbal and presymbolic experiences that characterize the implicit model of the patient's mind. One function of dreams is the pictographic and symbolic representation of originally presymbolic experiences. Interpreting them will facilitate the process of reconstruction the psyche needs to improve its own capacity to mentalize originally non-thinkable experiences and make them thinkable, even if not rememberable.

The critical component of the therapeutic action of psychoanalysis is thus the symbolic transformation of the implicit structures of the patient's mind so they can be rendered in words. This has to do with emotion-laden experiences rooted in the affective tone of the subject's earliest relations, rather than with remembering autobiographical memories dating from after the preverbal period. Making it possible to think the implicit structures of the mind and the unconscious ways it works means enabling the patient to retrieve the parts of his or her self that were defensively split and projected very early in the development of the patient's mind.

This does not imply that work on declarative memory has no place in reconstruction and therapy in analysis. In some circumstances excessive use of autobiographic recollections may serve the patient as a defense in the here and now, relating to painful experiences, hence as a form of resistance to analysis, but we must always bear in mind that the explicit memory is an integral part of the process of reconstruction. There is evidence that the two forms of memory can influence each other in the course of development (Siegel, 1999). Similarly, work on the implicit memory can influence learning and the explicit memory, and reconstruction using the autobiographic memory can help bring to the surface in the transference or in dreams the archaic experiences stored in implicit memory. Thus the same holds for declarative or non-declarative processes from the psychoanalytical perspective (Davis, 2001).

The case of E.

I shall now present a case history which seems to me to be relevant to these theoretical considerations and which demonstrates the presence of unconscious fantasies, emotions and defenses stored in implicit memory, which were able to emerge after many years of four-sessions-a-week analysis by way of specific transference manifestations and some dreams.

E. is the 40-year-old son of professional parents and has a brother four years his junior. He came into analysis at the age of 28 suffering from paralyzing anxiety accompanied by panic attacks and a blockage of thought that overcame him whenever he was separated from his parents. If they were away, even for a very short time, he would suffer severe fits of anxiety. When analysis began, the patient was still living with his parents. He had a good social life, albeit without a stable affective relationship. E. had just graduated in philosophy and had registered at the psychology faculty.

His mother had become pregnant with him at a time when she was facing great affective, social and economic hardship and his father was still married to another woman. She had seriously contemplated abortion. The pregnancy had, however, continued, but in difficult circumstances and in solitude. She had succumbed to a depression that had persisted for some years. The mother, then, was emotionally inadequate and too preoccupied by her own affective and economic situation to experience pregnancy and motherhood non-traumatically and non-conflictually. The mother's mental state must have caused little E. intense discomfort and suffering during his earliest years, which he spent alone with her.

The patient's father did not join the family until a few years later. He is described as an intelligent, sensitive and cultivated person and a hard worker. The younger brother was born after the father's arrival. From then on, E.'s family life had been regular and the family's economic circumstances were sound. There were apparently no conflicts with the brother, and the patient still seems very fond of him.

I shall discuss only the most significant aspects of E.'s transference. His defense against the anxieties resulting from his early experiences as a child alone with a depressed mother was to activate a sticky, querulous part of his personality and to intellectualize the relationship with me, doing his best to strip it of any affective element. His language was desperately monotonous and repetitive and he would often repeat the same sentence over and over again. The same manifestations affected his studies and paralyzed his thought.

An enveloping and heavy part of the patient was tangible in the counter-transference and had entered our vocabulary as his "spider" part. With it he wove a cocoon of words around himself to isolate him and protect him from any emotion. His mode of communication aroused in me a feeling of profound ennui and detachment that reminded me of his experiences as a small child in the care of a depressed and absent mother. Another function of the "spider" was to trap me in a sturdy web so as to control me and keep me tied to him by a thin but strong thread of ennui.

Elements of intense erotization also made their presence felt in the transference, manifested in certain dreams by *the appearance of female figures whom he penetrated anally, sometimes destroying them*. Such dreams and fantasies constituted an extreme defense against the fear of abandonment and fragmentation. However, they also represented an attempt to give himself the warmth and life that his internal depressed mother was unable to provide. In addition, a perverse nucleus held sway in the transference that made me feel cowed and humiliated, unable to formulate a clear thought. The penetrative effect of his intrusion was sometimes so powerful that I even imagined that I might go away and leave him alone with his masturbatory fantasies.

A discussion of the patient's frequent instances of acting out, especially in connection with separations, would take up too much space and would in any case be beyond the scope of this chapter. I shall simply outline the long sexual friendship he enjoyed with a woman who never inspired any real affection in him, but who was always available for a ritual they repeated obsessively: they sat on the couch, started talking, then he reached over to touch her legs, and got excited. She would masturbate him and sometimes let him penetrate her anally. His description of these encounters was always the same, aseptic and with no apparent affective involvement. In the countertransference I felt the compulsiveness, coldness and mechanical nature of their meetings.

Towards the end, the central problem of the relationship with E. concerned the termination of his analysis, as ending our relationship had until then been unthinkable. One reason for the difficulty in cutting the thread that joined us after twelve years was that he found it very hard to symbolize archaic experiences that were too traumatic to be thought, and to bring them to consciousness through words.

E. relived the fantasies and defenses associated with these early experiences in the transference, but was caught up by the "spider" in a kind of non-thought that contained him but at the same time held him captive in such a way that he was unaware of its defensive and paralyzing aspects. Only very recently, after it became possible for us to embark on the process of reconstructing the early relationship with his mother, both the acting out and the fear of a devastating abandon lessened and became amenable to working through. In parallel, his thought began to function and our relationship took on a more positive, "lighter" and more gratifying character.

At the same time E. was able to move out of his parents' house and to organize a life of his own, living together with a girlfriend with whom he seemed to enjoy a good affective and sexual relationship. At this point there appeared in the transference a father who was not only intellectual but also displayed emotions and was able to help him separate from and dis-identify with the entrapping figure of the internal mother and from myself in the transference.

The period when the most intense analytic work was done and the greatest transformation was achieved coincided with a series of singular dreams, of a kind never seen before during the course of this long analysis. Work on these dreams was crucial to set in motion a process of reconstruction linked to the earliest and most traumatic experiences, which he was only now able to represent pictorially in dream form and to conceive in thought, even though they could not by any means be remembered. At the end of this period of intense work on the dreams, we were finally able to set a date for the termination of the analysis, which the patient then kept to precisely.

The first dream of this last period of the analysis was as follows:

I am at my mother's house and there is a little mouse in a big hole in the wall. I want to put my wallet in the hole, but the mouse is in the way. But then the mouse falls to the floor, runs along the wall and finally hides in the rubbish bag. My mother says the mouse is all right in its refuge.

E. comments that the mouse was very small compared with the hole in the wall where it was at first, but it obviously had to leave its hole to make way for the larger wallet. He says he finds the dream hard to understand, but the rubbish bag is the right place for a mouse to end up in, as it can find the kind of things it needs there. He then recalls that he often goes to his mother's house to help her take out the rubbish bag, as she finds it difficult by herself.

In more specific transference terms, the dream represents the fantasy of penetrating me anally so as to use me as a refuge from his anxieties and fears about being left alone. Following up this line of thought, I suggest to him that the mouse might represent the small-child part of himself, identified with his penis which is too small to stay in the big hole of his mother's house/body, but which might feel comfortable in her rectum/rubbish bag. I do not mention the wallet that was supposed to take the mouse's place. E. describes insistent erotic fantasies about his mother's body, which he connects with the compulsive behavior that for years made him carry on the relationship with a woman who liked to be sodomized by him without any affective involvement.

Further elaborating the symbolism of the dream, I suggest the image of a little boy who cannot bear to be left alone, who enters into a sexualized mental dimension whereby he identifies with his small penis/mouse that penetrates the mother's body through the anus so as to be sure of taking control of it. In the erotization of the mother's body the boy finds a "psychic retreat" (Steiner, 1993) – a refuge from anxieties about separation and fragmentation of the self. The mother/analyst in the dream also seems prepared to acquiesce in his intentions.

A few weeks later, E. begins his session with another dream: "*My mother had written a poem containing the odd expression 'mazzi neri',*[2] *but she said that was fine*". E. immediately starts talking about the *mazzi*, which remind him of the flowers his mother likes, but wonders why they are black. I say nothing, thinking of the vulgar Italian usage of the word *mazzo* for backside. The patient continues: "You seem to be thinking of something else . . . but so am I . . . the expression '*ti faccio il mazzo*', but it's funny that it's black". I remind E. of the mouse dream and the work we did on it. E. admits his compulsive need to enter into women's "black *mazzo*", and I return to his infantile fear of being left alone and his fantasy of wanting to get into his mother's "black *mazzo*" so as to defend against these painful feelings of loneliness and fragmentation. At the same time I draw attention to his wish, expressed in the dream, that the mother/analyst should consent, as she did in the mouse dream.

On the following Monday he brings another dream:

I am in a car with you and someone else; you are at the wheel. We arrive at a church and go inside. But I leave again immediately and bump into a "hairy caterpillar" going the other way. I take the opportunity of following him back into the church and notice that all the people who had gone in before have been turned into animals, some of them even four-legged.

He at once tells me of his dissatisfaction with his girlfriend, who restricts his freedom.

I connect the "hairy caterpillar" entering the church with the mouse going into the rubbish bag, but point out that I too am conspicuously hairy and that he seems to be following me back into the church. E. first complains that the analysis, instead of increasing his sexual freedom, has restricted it; then he tells me that he has heard about a children's story I had published which recounts the adventures of a hairy snake. I now link this dream to the previous ones and to the fantasy of penetrating the mother's body/church so as to fuse with her and not separate. I also remind him of his transference fantasies of penetrating me anally, which are well known to us. At this point E. mentions an analysis/car that enables him to identify with a hairy me in order to fulfil the old fantasy of entering his mother's body.

These and other similar dreams that followed ultimately allowed E. to recover and think about the fantasies and defenses connected with archaic experiences that had hitherto been neither representable nor thinkable. This was a demonstration of the specific function of dreams as the royal road to the unconscious (Freud, 1900). However, this is not only a "dynamic" unconscious due to repression, but also a non-repressed unconscious stored in implicit memory. Through pictographic representation, dreams are thus the "main road" to the symbolization even of presymbolic events. By taking this "road", one can bring an event that is in itself lost to memory back into the relational present and reconstructively recover for thinkability the most archaic affective and emotional experiences even if they cannot be remembered.

The case of F.

F. is a 40-year-old man, married, with adolescent children. His mother is successful, wealthy, efficient, active, enterprising, seductive, bossy, aggressive, easy to anger, and dominant in the family. His father is a professional man, totally taken up with his work, absent and detached from family questions. F. has one sister a few years older than him, and one younger; he used to say he was "squeezed between two sisters and a mother". F. is himself a successful, shrewd businessman, tyrannical and competitive at work. He came for analysis because his wife was threatening to leave him and had fallen in love with another man, and he felt inferior to her, seeing her as livelier, more intelligent and more cultured. He suffered occasional episodes of impotence and frequent premature ejaculation.

At our very first meetings it became evident that he was highly uncomfortable with his competitive, authoritarian and enterprising wife who, like his mother, made him feel like a clueless child, but also impotent and unable to satisfy her sexually and emotionally. F. felt he was a sort of second-rate citizen at home, and his two adolescent daughters did not hold him in high esteem, whereas they seemed caught up in their mother's fascinating web.

F.'s transference was immediately marked by intense competitivity towards me, intolerance of the state of dependence, resentment and anger at the asymmetry of the relationship, and a feeling of being like a poor, powerless child, about to be abandoned, unable to manage his own emotions. He set up defenses in the form of organizing an arrogant, competitive part of the personality, towards me and towards his colleagues at work; he became pushy and overbearing in business, and would not put up with frustration or dependence. But at the same time the fear of being abandoned set in motion a childish part in him; this petulant, anxious and repetitive part, often boring, was projected into me as the expression of control over my thoughts and defense against separation.

I was particularly struck by the way F. communicated, and used his voice in the sessions, especially after a weekend or long holidays. His voice was usually deep but it became nasal and his normally lively communication, that kept my attention, became monotonous and boring. One Monday he told me he had had a strange weekend. He had been excited and had masturbated repeatedly. Then he started talking in an expressionless voice, with no rhythm, like a spoilt, bored child whining. As the session continued I felt my concentration waning so I interrupted him and pointed out how he was speaking, his tone of voice unconsciously aimed at blunting my attention, possibly because he felt like an angry child resentful at having been left alone for the weekend. F. did not reply and maintained a hostile silence for the rest of the session, not responding to my attempts at understanding him, and finally obliging me to say no more.

The next day he wanted to talk about the previous session. He said he was very irritated and angry at me. He didn't know why – perhaps because of my silence. Then he talked about his mother and her indifference towards him, and how his mother's silences had made him despair, and finally he hated her. This enabled us to connect his acting in the previous day's session, his complaining, whining and obstinate silence, with his fantasies and defenses as a small boy responding to his mother with angry silence, projecting his resentment onto her and creating a vicious circle of heavy, persecutory silence.

At other times he spoke quite differently. For example in one session after a long separation, F. started talking in a completely unusual way. The words tumbled out, practically falling over themselves as if fleeing something. He never stopped and such was the maniacal torrent of words that I had trouble grasping his meaning. There seemed to be no emotion in his speech – he just shifted from one topic to another in a semi-mechanical motor exercise compulsively activating his language system. Finally I broke in and asked him if this way of communicating was perhaps due to his need to fill a "void" he felt inside himself, that he was projecting into the space of our relation, a way of "self-containment" through language. I also painted a picture of a tiny child who felt abandoned by me/mother and who had to contain himself using the muscles that served to produce sound/words, as if he were talking to himself to defend himself from depending on me, and from the pain of separation, which felt like abandon. F. accepted this interpretation and in fact he himself linked this hurried speech to his hasty ejaculations, as if ejaculating quickly was one way of filling a void that caused anxiety, and abandoning the object (wife/mother/analyst) to his own unfulfilled wishes was a defense against the fear of being abandoned.

F. produced numerous dreams during his analysis and most of our work concentrated around the associations and emotions these evoked. His dreams revealed his fear of being a dependent, powerless child, prepared even for sexual abuse. In one of these dreams, *he is with his wife, but their roles are inverted: he has become a little child who is frightened of being penetrated by her, and she is the dominant partner.* Evident in this dream was the eroticized transference anxiety brought on by the asymmetry and the psychoanalytic setting.

Separations often produced dreams containing marked persecutory anxiety. Fierce, aggressive, man-eating beasts appeared – sharks, leopards, lions, animals of all sorts that terrified him and attacked the world. In one such dream *there was a parrot – which talked aimlessly – and an elephant which was heavy and vindictive.* These represented parts of his self split off (the parts he used to fill the void, and those with no lightness) trying to live together but in actual fact in conflict. In another dream *there is a bothersome little yappy dog* that he identifies with as a child "blackmailed" by his wife/analyst who threatens to leave him. He reports fantasies and dreams of symmetry between the two of us as a defense against the asymmetry of our relationship, which he finds humiliating and unbearable. He complains that his relationship with his wife is emotionally and intellectually asymmetrical, and he is trying to turn it round in the dreams.

In some dreams his internal mother is strongly erotic, excited but frustrated because his father neglects her sexually, but her blatant desire inhibits him and turns him into an impotent little child. In another dream he is *a little boy with his mother, whose breast is like his wife's. In the dream he wets himself with pee.* This dream enabled the patient to realize he was using his "child's ureter" aggressively against his wife/mother and to contemplate the possibility that his premature ejaculation might be a somatization of his impotent anger at this internal figure.

In the transference his hostility manifested itself in extreme competitivity with me and in the whining, complaining nasal voice he used to communicate. At the same time he frequently attacked me with hostile silence or parried my interpretations. He was very worried that analysis might cut down his arrogance and occasional unscrupulous dealings in business. One day we spent the whole session on a contract he wanted his business partner to sign; it was clearly one-sided and the partner had to take him at his word, whereas he did not trust the partner the same way. I pointed out that his insistence on this type of contract – to his own advantage – might be a sort of defensive reversal of the asymmetry he found so hard to tolerate with me. I added too that this attitude, due to his domineering part, seemed unethical, because he was trying to intimidate his partner. F. disagreed and fell into a leaden silence for the rest of the session, absolutely unresponsive to my attempts to lighten the atmosphere and grasp his true meaning.

The next day, going back to this silence, he told me had felt terribly anxious when I failed to agree with him. He recalled a period in his childhood when his mother frustrated his wishes by contradicting him and made him fall into angry silences, to which she replied with equal silence, which only fueled his anxiety. It was thus possible to reconstruct the link between his aggressive use of silence, emotionally relived in the transference and projectively identified in me, with the early defenses of his youth when his mother frustrated and disappointed him.

F.'s father appeared only later in the transference and in dreams. He gradually took on the role of an increasingly strong and reliable figure who could help F. dis-identify/separate from mother/me in the transference, so he slowly acquired a separate identity. This significant shift from identifying with the exciting, intrusive but confusing internal mother to a free father, capable of accepting separations, marked a decisive step in F.'s psychoanalytical path. It coincided with his wife deciding she would sleep in a separate room. This set up intense anxiety in F., with various interesting dreams. In one *he is with his father who is cleaning the carpet at home with a powerful vacuum cleaner. The machine works well but there are old spots that won't come out. He tucks them under the bed but all of a sudden the bed-head becomes convex like a magic mirror.* Evidently even the efficient machine/analysis run by the internal father/analyst was not able to clean off the old spots – left-overs of old maternal trauma stored in the implicit memory?

– which when tucked away under the analyst's couch turn his [bed]-head and consequently distort his thoughts and emotions.

As examples it is worth looking at two paradigmatic dreams with a long interval between them, during which we had worked to enable F. to transform the dynamics of his internal objects so as to progress from the paranoid-schizoid to the depressive position. In the first dream,

> *F. is in a train, stopped at a station. He gets off the train and goes to the underpass. He sees a wall with two guards, as if there were some great secret behind it that had to be kept hidden. At a certain stage, then, the wall dissolves and shapeless zombies appear: they are aggressive and he is frightened. The guards disappear with the wall and he is left on his own to face the zombies. But he thinks that surely someone will magically appear to save him.*

He tells me that during the weekend he had been on his own because his wife was away with the children, and he had felt he missed analysis. He notes immediately that the zombies represent parts of him that set up persecution and anxiety. He recalls that the previous Friday he had been in Rome and had felt very anxious because he had decided to close his firm but the Ministry would not give him the necessary permit. He associates the train with analysis and the station with the stopover for the weekend.

I note that the analytical train, stopping for the weekend, had enabled him to go down into his armored vaults where he hides away his secrets. F. agrees. I suggest that the underground wall might represent his memory, defended by two guards (his and mine), that allowed the zombies to emerge as it fell. This had woken his memory up from its long sleep that had let the monsters act in the transference and afflict in reality his emotions, affects and even his sexuality.

After a certain period of intense "constructive" and "reconstructive" work on the transference and various dreams,[3] one Monday F. starts the session by complaining of particularly strong anxiety over the weekend, which surprised him considering his social and financial success in this period. Then he described this dream:

> *I am at a house where there is a military base. I am on my own looking at a pool with a small tortoise still and alone on the bottom. I am undecided whether to reach in and bring it up to the surface, or leave it there.*

I point out that the tortoise is calm and slow-moving, and needs to breathe to survive. He recalls a tortoise from his childhood that lived in the garden of the house where he was born, where he took his first steps and where his parents often left him alone. I remind him of the earlier dream where he was in the station underpass with the train stopped at the weekend, and how the wall dissolved and threatening, persecutory zombies appeared. I also remind him of the difference between a zombie and a tortoise, as two parts of himself filed away in a memory that has come to light in the two dreams.

F. is visibly moved and picks up my communication by confirming that the zombies in the older dream were intimidating, while the tortoise in this dream was a lovable little thing, like his childhood pet. He says:

> *The tortoise makes me think of solitude. It is a good animal, but spends a lot of time on its own. When I was afraid my wife was going to leave me I went back to the garden of my childhood home and wanted to see if the tortoise was still there. There was a tortoise, and I was very excited, but the porter told me it was not the same one as in my childhood – that one had probably died – but someone had brought this one for the garden recently. I was moved all the same and thought about my solitude once more.*

I point out his ambivalence about whether or not to pick up the tortoise from the bottom of the pool, as a metaphor of his uncertainty whether or not to push further into his oldest memory and retrieve the nicer, solitary parts of his self linked to the emotions of infancy. F. ended the session, saying: "I know I have to go to the bottom of the pool to recuperate the more patient, slower part of myself. That tortoise, like the one I knew as a child, has to breathe."

In the years that followed this dream the transformation F. achieved by working with me changed his relationship with his wife. Various events offered opportunities to tackle the painful theme of separation from his internal mother, who trapped him, transforming his persecutory zombies in more tolerant objects, more in line with the "depressive capacity" (Fédida, 2002) he had acquired. We finally reached a stage where he could usefully work through his feelings about his wife, and the potential separation from me in analysis.

One day, however, F. arrived with a very troubled expression. He told me he was especially sad because he had just read a book called *Le parole che non ho detto* (*Words I Didn't Say*) in which the main character's wife dies and he is left on his own, maniacally attached to a picture of his dead wife. He writes letters to her and can't free himself of her ghost. He cannot even contemplate relations with other women. Finally he meets a woman with whom he tries to establish a relationship, but she eventually leaves him, as she feels he is absent, still too tied to the ghost of his dead wife. He takes out his boat, leaving a message of despair in a bottle, and drowns at sea.

F. had been deeply struck by this book and said he lived the story as if in a dream where he had had trouble accepting a relationship with his wife different from how they had always been, when love meant "fusing" totally one in the other. That was the only way to love, in his mind. Now his wife wanted independence and a separate bedroom and would no longer put up with this "con-fused" way of loving. I completed his tale by pointing out that his wife wanted to live with him in a different way now, and that the claustrophobic ghost of his mother seemed to be transformed. I noted, however, that he still seemed unwilling to give it up, because he was afraid he could not go through with the grief for separation from this internal figure. He would prefer, like the character in his book, to die con-fused with the mother/sea (la *mère/mer* in French).

A few days later F. talked about the film *Pane e tulipani*, where the main character wants her freedom and decides to leave her husband and set off for Venice. The husband cannot understand this, and is not willing to live through the mourning for the separation. The woman then feels she is not understood and seeks a relation with a man who will respect her need for a separate identity. As he comments on the film, he says he has recognized the woman as his wife, and has understood that if he doesn't want to lose her he will have to accept the grief at separating. He has therefore to accept that he will suffer – he says: "With your help, but with the anxiety because shortly we shall separate" – so as not to die at sea like the character in the book he had read. Then he talks about love, and the fact that for so long he had been convinced love meant "fusion" with the loved one. He admits that this con-fusion with the wife-mother was the cause of his premature ejaculation. He now acknowledges, regretfully, that things are not like that and that since he has been working with me on the subject and has understood things better, his ejaculation is no longer so rapid either and his sex life is more satisfying.

Then he says that a few days earlier he had dreamt that *a friend's baby boy was crying because he had been left alone, but he had comforted him and helped him accept the situation*. He concludes the session saying: "How much time have I wasted questioning your interpretations and trying to correct our asymmetry, reversing our roles . . . Now I realize there is a basic difference between us and my dependence was necessary if I was ever to understand!"

Discussion

Despite their different personal histories and feelings in the transference, these two clinical cases both illustrate the importance of early childhood experiences as a cause of relational pathology much later. E. felt unwanted in childhood and was not contained by his mother, who was going through a difficult stage, with depression and anxiety about her own existence and ambivalence about the pregnancy. E. suffered the traumatic experience of not feeling loved and being threatened with abandon in an early phase of development. These experiences can be stored only in implicit memory. The same holds for his defenses against anxiety at the threats of abandon, separation and fragmentation of the self, that have influenced his adult life. E.'s earliest defense was to sexualize the fantasy of penetrating his mother's body so as to deny all attempts at separation from her and to control a desperate death anxiety.

The three dreams he brought seemed a reconstructive representation of these defenses. Their interpretation was facilitated by the particularly close and moving "moments of encounter" between the patient and me, which enabled us to build a bridge, as it were, between the constructive here and now of the session and the reconstructive "there and then" of his mind's future development. I linked his fantasy of anal penetration (his mother's rubbish bag in the first dream) with his desire to enter his mother's body and become one with her, like in a refuge for the mind (Steiner, 1993). His parallel urge for anal masturbation was for consolation and reassurance that he could control his mother's breast, "geographically" confused with the buttocks (Meltzer, 1966).

The same need to defend himself against feelings of solitude and fragmentation dictated his fantasy, in the second dream, of entering his mother's *mazzo nero* and, by extension, that of the women with whom he had purely sexual relations, with no emotional involvement.

In the third dream the patient is following a caterpillar/analyst into the mother/church body, again to become one with it, denying separation and identifying himself with the various quadrupeds that copulate "from behind".

The transference/countertransference evidence built up during this long analysis was the basis for my interpretation of these three dreams, essentially bearing in mind their *reconstructive potential*, besides the actual elements in the transference observed in the here and now of the session.

F.'s story was completely different. Born into a more solid setting than E., he had a highly active, intrusive, seductive, authoritarian mother, and a detached, absent father. His most pressing relational disorder was competitivity at work and at home, which manifested itself for a long time in the transference as intolerance of dependence on me, and the asymmetry of the relationship. The other problem, connected to the relational difficulties, involved his sexuality, which was tormented by frequent episodes of premature ejaculation.

An important feature of F.'s transference was his way of communicating, in particular how he used his voice and formulated his speech. These transference modalities provided a key to the feelings of his early childhood, which enabled him to reconstruct the emotions and affects dominating his primary relation with his mother, and the significance of his silences and anxieties. This reconstruction led to a lasting transformation of his intrapsychic and intersubjective dynamics.

Dreams formed the real, constant theater in which the analytical couple was able to deal with F.'s main themes: defense against asymmetry, ambivalence about the maternal figure, eroticized transference anxiety, the significance of silence. F.'s father came into analysis only after some years, and helped the patient dis-identify/separate himself from his internal mother, and from me in the transference. This led to an improvement in his relations with his wife, and overcame, or at least reduced, his problem of premature ejaculation.

Two highly indicative dreams described after lengthy work enabled F. to become aware of parts of his self that were greedy and persecutory and to transform them. This was the prelude to his achieving a "depressive position", from which to make far-reaching changes in his personality. He started to take a more mature attitude to his wife and to love as a whole, which he had always viewed as total fusion with the object, but now he became more tolerant of separation and more respectful of his partner's need for freedom.

PART TWO

The dream: between neuroscience and psychoanalysis

This part looks at dreams from the neuroscientific and psychoanalytic viewpoints. Freud's *Interpretation of Dreams* (1900) marked the moment when the dream made its appearance on the psychological stage, and enabled him to guess at the concept of the unconscious, just as the discovery of REM sleep in the 1950s opened the doors of the dream to the neurosciences.

The epistemologic and methodological differences between the neurosciences and psychoanalysis means that research on the dream differs completely in quality and other aspects. Neurophysiology investigates the basic functional mechanisms of the different phases of sleep, involving neocortical synchronization and desynchronization. Psychophysiology looks into the various phases of sleep to see how mental processes are organized within them, including dreams. Neuropsychology, using bioimaging techniques, investigates the cortical and subcortical areas and circuits involved in the organization of dreams. This discipline also looks at the brain's functional characteristics involved in dream formation, distinguishing them from those responsible for the architecture of sleep. Clinical work teaches us that some structures and circuits, such as the dopaminergic system, are essential for dreaming, and lesions cause a disconnection syndrome.

Psychoanalysis is the only discipline interested in the meaning of dreams, and how they can bring repressed and unrepressed unconscious experiences to the surface. It makes use of the dream to attain access, through symbolization, to the patient's earliest unconscious presymbolic areas, making them thinkable and verbalizable. Work on dreams also enables the analyst to reconstruct a person's affective and emotional history, building a bridge between what is actually happening in the transference and the traumatic experiences of the earliest relations.

4

The labyrinth of the night: biology, poetry and theology

You sometimes hear it said that the night brings rest, or that sleep brings counsel. A closer glance at the neurobiology of the night, though, immediately shows that the brain does not rest while the body is asleep. If we go on to look at the mental proceedings during the various phases of sleep, we find a very strange form of activity, certainly not what we might expect to bring counsel!

The night's neurobiological activity starts with falling asleep and ends with waking. A complex series of steps leads to sleep, involving many variables and "organizers". For example, in lower animals the fading evening light induces the biological changes of the night, with slowing of the activity of the hypothalamic suprachiasmatic nucleus, whose oscillations govern circadian rhythms.

In humans things are a bit different because cultural factors, habits and conditioning all overlap and interfere with biological circadian patterns. Even so, the marvelous passage from waking to sleep, from reality to unreality, still involves a surprising number of relational and vegetative functions.

Neurophysiologists work on the basis of variables serving as the electrical equivalents of the behavior and mental activities that get organized during sleep. The variables are the electrical waves recorded in the brain (the electroencephalogram – EEG); muscle electrical activity; eye movements; and recordings of the heart, respiration and basic autonomic functions.

When we fall asleep our cortical electrical rhythms slow down gradually, muscle tone weakens and eye movements disappear; breathing becomes progressively more rhythmic and regular, and the body's cardiovascular and heat-regulation systems run smoothly. During sleep at night our biological system works like a tightly closed circuit, concentrating on homeostasis, requiring constant control and regulation of various autonomic functions.

Since the slow cortical waves indicate the activation of circuits different from those governing the rapid waves of waking, we can only assume that our cells do not need rest, but only a change of "work shift" for some groups of neurons. Others simply switch to another language – the "language of the night", made up of bursts of activity and intervals of silence. In some of the brain's systems night-time seems to transform a continuous activity mostly responding to sensory inputs into a discontinuous, oscillating activity, mainly involving the thalamo-cortical integrative system (Mancia, 1980a, 1996b). The "re-entry" of information into this system can be considered responsible for the "differentiated consciousness" (or higher-order consciousness).

Moving on during the night, we find ourselves faced with the mystery of the different phases of sleep and see how, as it becomes deeper and deeper, the oscillating systems that generate the great brain waves become increasingly active. In parallel, the field of consciousness shrinks, finally disappearing altogether. This is the moment when individuals are actively, perceptibly isolated from the world around them, with inhibitory processes operating on all the sensory pathways.

For about an hour and a half after falling asleep our brain employs a special night-time language so its neurons can organize its activity. But quite regularly at the end of this period, the brain's functions change dramatically, often in the space of a few seconds. The systems that were oscillating change their language once again; the cerebral cortex's electrical activity speeds up, as if in waking; and our eyes start moving rapidly, while our muscles are totally paralyzed. This is the "rapid eye movement" phase: REM sleep. When asleep, people have vivid visions or hallucinations, as if they were at the theater, but cannot take any active part in whatever is going on because they are immobilized in their seat.

Autonomic systems also go through a stormy moment: the heart's rhythms, and the sleeper's breathing, become irregular. Blood pressure rises or drops; heat regulation is put on hold and all the autonomic control systems that until now were closed and homeostatically perfect open up, their control lost! This storm blows over in a few minutes, leaving the way open to slow-wave sleep. Another cycle gets under way, leading to another episode of fast-wave, REM sleep, the rhythms alternating until the person wakes in the morning (Mancia and Smirne, 1985; Mancia, 1996b).

Ethologists have long been fascinated by the importance of sleep for animals. Psychologists too recognize its importance in the "economy" of the human mind. In recent years a theory has been gaining ground that sleep should leave the realm of physiology and move into the areas of ethology and psychology, as representing a true *instinct*, on a par with hunger and sexual urges. Ethology, as the study of behavior in natural surroundings, might potentially act as the bridge between physiology and behavior. Tinbergen (1951) was the first to suggest that sleep, in all its complexity, might be an instinct. Moruzzi (1969), picking up Tinbergen's idea, analyzed the various phases of sleep and the preparation for it; he concluded that preparatory behavior for sleep could be viewed as the "appetitive" phase of this instinctive behavior, and all the actual stages of sleep constituted its "consummatory" phase.

Further work on this concept led to the notion that the "appetitive" phase was limited to non-REM sleep, while the "consummatory" component of the sleep instinct was governed by the REM phases (Mancia, 1974). Since it is in REM sleep that the most vivid and bizarre dreams take place, it seemed logical, in the light of Freudian theory (Freud, 1900), to assume that the instinctual drive is fulfilled in this "consummation". Psychoanalysis takes us directly into the realm of human wishes and their fulfillment with the complicity of the night. In this sense psychoanalysis is thus the science of the night par excellence, conjuring up mysteries and knowledge.

Our industrialized world has tried to cut the bonds between human daytime and night-time halves – as Roger Bastide (1975) sustained – splitting open the links between dream and culture that were a prerogative of primitive societies. The dream has been relegated to a purely subjective position, with no social value or functions, because it falls outside the area of productive work. Psychoanalysis has repaired this tear and rebuilt the bridge between daytime and night-time in individual lives, so the dream returns to its original mythical, religious dimension: it connects up with people's inner world, with those figures that have "sacred" connotations for individuals, representing the affective experiences that govern their behavior and give meaning to their actions (Mancia, 1987, 1988).

While westernized societies have tried to deprive the dream of its social purpose, declaring it purely subjective, psychoanalysis – by recuperating that subjective component – has restored the social function: human beings need to dream and the dream enables them to gain knowledge of their internal objects and those belonging to outside reality.

Now, through the dream, the memory enters the stage of our night-time theater. Our main job as actors involves what we might call being "mythically condemned" to relive the past, in different forms, so that our implicit and explicit memory can serve as the bridge between our experiences today and those of our infancy. The dream is therefore the *pontifex* of the night, helping tie the bonds between past and present (Mancia, 1987). This past is filed not only in the explicit memory, from which it can be recalled, but also in implicit memory – where it is not available for recall but can stimulate the reconstruction of a person's emotional and affective history (Mancia, 2000b, 2003a).

This is another function where the night holds court in our life-story (ontogenetic, phylogenetic and anthropologic), taking us back to the "hot" societies that write things down, and the "cold" ones where everything is committed to memory (Lévi-Strauss, 1964). In the cold societies, where memory is so important, the distinction between past and present is less marked than in hot societies. This leads to the suggestion that "wild" thinking (and, by analogy, night-time "thought") establishes a special relation between past and present. Just as myths, in Le Goff's (1977) opinion, upheld by memory, bring the past up to the present while at the same time allowing the present to be shifted back into the past, so dreams too – which emerge from implicit memory – bring the past up into the present (in the transference); this permits a reconstruction that makes it possible to move the present back into the past.

If we carry on from anthropology to psychology, we can visualize memory as carrying us from the "hot" daytime culture to the "cold" culture of the night; in a dream memory fills in the gaps between current reality and the childhood experiences that have left the most memorable affective mark, combining in a single emotional pathway the adult's object world, built up during a person's life, with the childhood object world.

Seen in this light dreaming, the "hit show" of the night, can be defined the "historic event" par excellence. In this moment of rare privilege the worn traces of time, misshapen and torn, acquire new meaning by being combined in a series of relations that bring us up to the present. The night's job is therefore a "work of history", presenting as current – meaning *synchronic* – affects dug up from the depths of time in our distant memory – meaning *diachronic*. But at the same time it is *metastoric* in that it recuperates emotions from the past tucked away in implicit memory, bringing them to the surface so they can be used for reconstruction, even if they cannot actually be recalled.

The night is the *organizer of a private theater*, unique, unrepeatable and unrivalled, where our interior world is played out in the immediate present; this present is linked to the past and the past enables us to build up a metaphorical space where the complex relations are played out between internal objects and internalized parental figures – the ancestors of primitive societies – in continuous dynamic interactions and with the self. These are pivotal in a person's affective life, governing relationships with reality.

This is what led me to suggest that dreaming could be considered a *religion of the mind:* in analogy with Durkheim's (1912) sociological theories, dreams are part of a general system of the internal world, serving to represent a person's "sacred things", i.e. those internal figures that have acquired theological value for him. These are the bases of our moral values and our vision of the world (Mancia, 1987, 1988).

The night is therefore like a *liturgy* that leads to an *apotheosis* of the internal world. And like in religion "the essential precedes the actual" (Eliade, 1948) in the dream too, the internalized parental objects, originally made sacred, precede the real external history. So in going back to the origins we live these objects, essential to our mind as parts of our own personal theology.

In this theological model symbol formation is always an *internal* function, never *external*, linked to reality. Just as a myth narrates a sacred tale that is "true" besides being exemplary and significant – to paraphrase Eliade – precisely because it is sacred, our own personal myth of the night, represented in dreams, will also hold "truth" in the sense that it is meaningful, actually generating meaning.

The meaning a dream can give to real objects is directly linked to its hierophantic capacity, meaning its ability to reveal things sacred and its symbolic potential. Symbolization becomes one of the night's main, most significant tasks, the dream highlighting the close relations with hierophancy. The symbol can not only prolong the hierophancy but also – if necessary – actually become it. During the night a person's wish to prolong the "hierophanization" of the world infinitely, giving significance to objects that transcend his or her own existence, is fulfilled. This alone is surely enough to justify our need to dream!

In dreams, objects from real life, sometimes left over from the day, become actors in the theater of the night, representing something different, losing their own qualities and meanings; thus, out of their usual context, they can carry multiple meanings. This work of the night has many points in common with artistic creation: it too is a work of *transformation*. But as dreaming implies supplying a basic tool of knowledge, the night becomes an "epistemological site" par excellence where knowledge acquired in the dream contributes to mental growth, enabling us to know and recognize our internal and external objects.

Night also meets individuals' need to dramatize their inner world and work out how to assemble their thoughts. Current psychoanalysis has reflected on the symbol while at the same time investigating thought (Bion, 1962). Freud (1900) did not consider the dream a thought process, but as a sort of distortion that could be decoded by interpretation. This revealed a tendency to separate the work of the night from that of the day. We now are more likely to consider that the dream expresses its own truth, without distortion, and that this thought process is a continuation of our thinking while awake. We therefore tend to combine the night and day as a single form of thought.

But the question remains: how can the mind work like this during the night? It has been suggested that dreaming is one way of thinking an emotional experience and transforming it to a representation using a symbolic and metaphorical language very close to the language of poetry. But careful! It is a *poietic* operation that structures our dreams, giving formal shape to the affects and passions marking our experience.

Today we are in a position to extend the concept of language, adding value by combining with the simple verbal form various preverbal modes of communication, such as the musicality, rhythm and syntax that are the carriers of multiple specific affects and emotions. This is based on the assumption that music can be considered a language *sui generis*, that does not use words, but employs symbols corresponding to our emotional and affective unconscious (Langer, 1942). Therefore, poetic, musical and spoken language in the transference follow the same laws as the unconscious, and have similar structures.

From this angle the night becomes a *place of poetry* where the dream is an *internal language*, or a poetic language describing the inner world (Meltzer, 1984). If the language of poetry is a primary experience harking back to the child's language as he or she stares at the mother's face while she nourishes her child at her breast, it is also related to the unconscious fantasy that employs projective identification as an old, preverbal means of communicating a person's feelings and affective experience. How many similarities can we find between this language and dreams, in that special moment when a person's infantile part exploits the preverbal parts of inner language to communicate his or her state of mind!

The language of the night is therefore a *language of poetry*: symbolization and narration, condensation and displacement, the use of metaphors and metonymy, synecdoche and alliteration (Freeman-Sharp, 1937), and plays on similarity and symmetry (Matte-Blanco, 1975; Mancia, 2003c) bring the work of dreaming very close to the active process of poetry. Narration of a dream may sometimes seem poor and less refined than a poem, but they seem to use very much the same rules of communication. Thus, in the wake of this magic preverbal form of affective communication known as projective identification, both dream and poem look like a communication inside the self, that can convert an emotive experience into one representing a state of mind.

The roots of this preverbal language date from childhood, when the infant was consumed by an uneasy dependency and dedication; the mother-tongue that children used to nourish themselves was the same as the language to which poets entrust themselves, without boundaries, merging with but reflecting the mother and the world. This language serves as a container from which to project a person's specific *paradigmatic axis* that holds unconscious, unrepressed affects and emotions, onto the *syntagmatic axis* that serves for speaking (see Chapter 2).

This experience has its own beauty which in the dream – like in poetry – proposes a truth connected with the person's internal world and its sacred values and signifiers. An appropriate phrase comes to mind to close this chapter: *in nocte veritas!*

5

The dream:
between neuroscience and psychoanalysis

The contribution of neuroscience to dreams

At the beginning of the twentieth century, when Freud (1900) had already published his *Interpretation of Dreams*, European psychology seemed more interested in sleep than dreaming.[1] At that time Henry Pieron (1913) defined sleep as a physiological state that was periodically necessary, its cyclic pattern relatively independent of outside conditions, during which there was a complete break in the complex sensory and motor relations between the subject and his environment. This past century has in fact seen great steps forward in understanding the neurophysiology of sleep, which Pavlov (1915) pioneeringly proposed was an *active* form of cortical inhibition, though later it was again considered a *passive* event induced either by sensory deafferentation (Bremer, 1935), or functional disactivation of the ascending reticular system (Moruzzi and Magoun, 1949; Moruzzi, 1972). However, there were evidences that it was an *active* state produced by sleep-inducing caudal reticular systems (Batini et al., 1959; Cordeau and Mancia, 1959), or by preoptic basal forebrain structures (Sterman and Clemente, 1962).

It was only in 1953 that neurophysiologists started taking any real interest in the mental aspects of sleep. This was when Aserinsky and Kleitman (1953) observed a paradoxical phase, which we now know as REM sleep, opening the gates of dreams to physiologists and experimental psychologists. These researchers noted that children sleeping deeply presented eye movements visible under their eyelids, with twitching of the limbs, and a desynchronized EEG tracing like during waking. This phase therefore became known as paradoxical, usually referred to by the abbreviation for *rapid eye movements – REM.*

Neurophysiological research in the 1960s (Jouvet, 1962) clarified the electrophysiological parameters and structures responsible for REM sleep, distinguishing it from the non–REM phases: EEG desynchronization, atony of postural muscles, rapid eye movements, monophase waves in the visual system, known as ponto-geniculo-occipital (PGO) waves, and neuro-vegetative turbulence, involving respiratory and cardiac arrhythmias and changes in blood pressure. The endocrine system too showed significant changes during REM sleep. The cholinergic reticular organization of the pons was found to be responsible for the ascending and descending events of this important phase, and is therefore the *deus ex machina* of REM sleep.

Around the same time Kleitman's group (Dement and Kleitman, 1957; Dement, 1965) studied mental activity during sleep in healthy volunteers, waking them during REM or non-REM phases. When they were woken at the end of a REM episode they often reported an experience that it seemed logical to classify as a dream, with rich perceptive-hallucinatory detail and strong emotional participation of the dreamer, with self-representations. When they were woken outside the REM phases, their mental activity consisted only of fragments of reality and thought, not organized like in a dream.

The physiological basis was thus laid for a dichotomous REM/non-REM model as the electrical equivalent of different types of mental activity. Subsequently the duration of each REM episode was correlated with the amount of "dream material" narrated (Wolpert and Trosman, 1958), the amount of eye movements with the content of the dream (Dement and Wolpert, 1958), and the specific direction of the eye movements with the spatial organization of events in the dream (Dement, 1965; Molinari and Foulkes, 1969).

These psycho-physiological investigations led to the idea that REM sleep was the neurophysiological basis, or "neurobiological frame" within which dreams could be organized. The EEG desynchronization itself reflects neocortical activation that is a basis for perceptive and cognitive activity and for activation of memory, all events common to dreaming. The eye movements were interpreted as the motor equivalent of hallucinatory activity that would be enough to create a dream-space. The monophase PGO waves recorded in the visual system were considered to be the electrical reflection of a form of decoding and reading information arising within the nervous system, which the dreamer then lived as visual hallucinations (see Mancia, 1996b).

Psychophysiological research during REM sleep subsequently showed that the geometric-spatial and emotional aspects of the dream are mainly organized in the right hemisphere (Antrobus et al., 1983; Bertini and

Violani, 1984), while the left hemisphere is involved more in its narration. More sophisticated observations, taking account of the experimental setting, the dreamers' expectations, and how they narrated their dreams on waking, showed psychophysiologists that there was complex mental activity not only in the REM phase, but also while falling asleep and in non-REM sleep. The different results reflect methodological differences but also how the dream is interpreted. Starting out from an extremely broad definition like that given by Fromm (1951), according to which any mental activity during sleep can be considered a dream, to more restrictive ones such as that proposed by Bosinelli and Franzini (1986) who describe a dream as a mental experience involving estrangement and unreality, vivid perception, personal participation of the dreamer but inability to examine reality, and loss of voluntary control of the thought process.

If you ask young sleep volunteers to tell you everything that passed through their mind just before waking, a high percentage of those woken in either REM or non-REM sleep describe an experience that we hardly hesitate to call a dream. While falling asleep too, one goes through a hallucinatory state with the same sort of mental images as in other sleep phases. Thought becomes fragmented as voluntary control of reality is gradually lost. This allows bizarre, regressive contents to intrude, laying the foundations for dreams. These contents grow into the visual and auditory images that build up the hypnagogic hallucinations amply described in the literature (Bosinelli, 1991).

An analysis of the mental activities that go on as you fall asleep, however, finds differences from those in other sleep phases: the spatial structuring of the dream-like state is different, and so is the level of the dreamer's personal participation. Antrobus (1983) suggested that the number of words used to narrate the dream(s) might be the most efficient basis for analyzing the psychological differences in the two phases, REM and non-REM sleep. Another might be the number of representations of the dreamers themselves in REM sleep compared to the falling asleep stage (Bosinelli et al., 1974).

Current psychophysiological findings confirm that the human mind produces dream-like experiences in all phases of sleep, the characteristics and contents in the REM or non-REM phases depending more on the length of the "story", hence the number of words needed to narrate it, than on the quality of the happenings. Antrobus (1986) too agreed that people dream in all phases of sleep, though only REM sleep offers the conditions of cortical activation that guarantee enough recovery of memory for long narrations of the scenarios. The rapid cortical activity found in REM sleep (40 Hz) (Llinas and Ribary, 1993) suggests there may be more room in this phase for cognitive activity. Descriptions from volunteers who have been woken up also present a higher degree of linguistic organization after REM sleep than after the other phases.

It does appear, therefore, that the lower level of cortical activation in non-REM sleep leads to dreams with less capacity for elaborating on material stored in the memory, and the dreamer has less capacity for narrating them. This research shows up differences in cognitive functions during sleep: people are more able to remember and describe the experiences of REM sleep; they use more words to tell the dreams, whose content tends to be stranger and more bizarre. Cognitivists such as Antrobus (1983), Foulkes (1985) and Cavallero (1991) consequently consider REM sleep as the phase most likely to produce dreams, for several reasons: first, the cerebral cortex is strongly activated, like in waking, so it can recuperate memories more easily; second, the associative cortex participates in the symbolic organization of the experiences typical of dreams; third, the activated brain is capable of generating "multimedial" happenings, like during waking.

However, since people dream in REM and non-REM sleep – though to different extents – Bosinelli's group suggested the brain may have a single system for dream production active, in different measure, in all phases, from falling asleep to waking up. This theory, however, has its opponents who insist there are *qualitative* differences, in the level of bizarreness and the more emotional aspects, between dreams in the various phases of sleep; they suggest that dreams are generated by two mechanisms that operate separately in the brain in REM or non-REM sleep. This brings us back to the old REM/non-REM dichotomy, though in a blander form. There is also a third idea, according to which "undetected" REM-like processes are active in non-REM sleep, producing dreams (see Nielsen, 2003).

It is clear in any event that our mind does not rest, even during sleep. The mental activity changes, basically because the dreamer's self has a different relation with reality. Perceptive reality is replaced with hallucinatory reality, with self-representations and strong emotional participation in the dream events. Although there is no substantial difference between mental events during the stages of falling asleep, REM and non-REM sleep, psycho-physiological research confirms that dream-activity in REM sleep is more lively, with greater reference to the contents of the memory, more bizarre imagery and a longer narration than in the other biological frames of sleep.

In view of the greater role of REM sleep in dream organization, Hobson and McCarley (1977) and Hobson et al. (1998) proposed what they called *activation-synthesis* hypothesis as a brain mechanism for producing dreams. They suggested that in REM sleep the brain is actually a generator of the dream state; the motor is the pons, which stimulates the brain from inside, producing information that is projected to the forebrain and limbic system, which then elaborate it to recover recollections stored in the explicit memory, so as to build the plot of the dream and ensure the dreamer's emotional participation.

This theory implies that, first, the primary energy responsible for the dream is physiological, produced internally by the pontine generator, determined genotypically rather than psychologically; second, elaboration of the information from the pons (*deus ex machina* of the dream) and its synthesis is done by the forebrain, aimed at organizing the perception in the form of a hallucination, self-representation, the emotions these elicit, recovery of experiences from memory, and the cognitive elaboration typical of dreams; third, the brain in REM sleep can be compared to a sophisticated computer looking for key words, to integrate phenotypic data obtained through experience with genotypic stimuli; fourth, the content of the dream that makes its way through our consciousness is neither unconscious nor deformed by censorship, as Freud would have had us believe, but is a *chaotic process* of self-activation starting from the pons, where the content of the dream originates, with all its bizarreness, and the other features Freud called the work of dreams.

Hobson et al. (2003) have now suggested that, first, visual hallucinations are due to self-activation of the visual part of the brain, due to output from the pons which also activates the parietal cortex needed for spatial organization of the dream; second, the emotions in a dream are due to activation of the amygdala which involves other limbic and paralimbic structures; third, oneiric delirium, loss of self-awareness, and the illogical experiences of a dream are due to aminergic de-modulation and inhibition of the dorsolateral frontal cortex. This led Hobson et al. (2003) to radicalize this concept, stating that the mind during dreaming is simply the self-activated brain.

* * *

Bioimaging has supplied interesting information on the activation of various brain areas during REM sleep. On the assumption that this was the phase when people dreamed most, some researchers directly correlated activation and inhibition in certain brain areas with the production of dreams. This resulted in a significant neuropsychological contribution that has cast light on the brain areas and structures involved in dream organization. In humans, positron emission tomography (PET) shows the following areas activated during REM sleep: the pontine tegmentum, the amygdaloid nuclei on both sides, the left thalamus, the cingulate cortex and the right parietal operculum, this last region being important for spatial construction; limbic activation might be the neurophysiological substrate for the emotional components of the dream (Maquet et al., 1996).

Earlier, Braun et al. (1997) had helped make a structural distinction between the mechanisms of waking and of REM sleep, confirming the activation in REM sleep of limbic and paralimbic areas, including the insula, the cingulate cortex and that of the medial temporal lobe. Later, the same group (Braun et al., 1998) observed increased activity during REM sleep in the hippocampus and parahippocampal gyrus, and the extra-striatal cortex. The dorsolateral prefrontal cortex, striatum and orbital cortex are all disactivated during this phase of sleep.

In a study to demonstrate the importance of REM sleep in the process of memorization, Maquet et al. (2000) noted that waking experiences influenced specific brain areas during subsequent sleep. In particular, the brain areas activated during a waking-hour task were significantly more active during REM sleep, indicating that memory traces are processed during this phase in humans. However, Huber et al. (2004) sustained that specific areas of the cerebral cortex were able to memorize a sensory-motor experience from the daytime waking hours also during that night's synchronous sleep. This suggests that while dreaming, in REM or other phases of sleep, a person can recover from memory events from his or her waking hours. This is what Freud (1900) called daytime residues.

These results are particularly interesting when compared with more recent findings from Anderson et al. (2004). They found that *voluntarily forgetting* mental experiences, a process comparable to Freudian repression,[2] is accompanied by increased activity in the dorsolateral prefrontal areas and a parallel reduction in hippocampal activity. This pattern is the opposite of that in dreaming, where hippocampal activity increases and dorsolateral frontal activity diminishes (Braun et al., 1998).

This picture holds out hope that neuropsychology using bioimaging will provide some satisfactory explanation for repression (Freud, 1915a), which sets up the dynamic unconscious (Freud, 1915b), and of the opposite process, "return of the repressed" which, as lost material is dug out of the memory, permits dreams to surface.

★ ★ ★

Neuropsychological investigations using bioimaging on patients with brain lesions (Solms, 1995) found that dreams and REM sleep develop in separate parts of the brain: dream organizers are not regulated only by the pons, since patients with extensive lesions to this region still dream. However, lesions to the forebrain and corresponding associative cortices prevent dreams. People with lesions to the temporo-occipital associative cortex still dream, though with some loss of the hallucinatory component, while patients with damage to the limbic structures cannot distinguish between dreams and reality, and may live a virtually continuous dream-like existence. Solms (1999) suggested there may be a dissociation between dreams and various brain activation states. People do in fact dream when dopaminergic circuits in the ventro-medial anterior brain are activated, which might explain the genital reactions in males and females during REM sleep (see Mancia, 1996b).

In a summary of various clinical experiments, Solms (2003) stated that, first, dreams and REM sleep can be dissociated as dreaming is linked to forebrain mechanisms that do not govern REM sleep; second, the forebrain structures responsible for dreaming are the anterior and lateral hypothal-amic areas, the amygdaloid complex, the subventral striatal areas and the cortical areas of the occipito-frontal limbic system, the anterior cingulum and the insula; third, the primary visual areas and the dorsolateral prefrontal cortex are disactivated during dreaming in REM sleep; fourth, dream imagery is not due to chaotic activation of the pons, but to forebrain organ-ization that builds up the cognitive process. This mechanism is generated by a dopaminergic circuit that can be activated in any phase of sleep. Bischof and Bassetti (2004) described the total abolition of dreaming in a 73-year-old woman with focal lesions to the temporo-occipital areas, more severe in the right hemisphere.

These findings suggest that disruption of the dopaminergic circuit involving temporo-occipital areas, particularly in the right hemisphere, may abolish sleep; this would be an expression of a disconnection syndrome (Geschwind, 1965).

The dream in psychoanalysis

Dreams in Freud's time

In 1895, a period of great changes in Freud's scientific thinking, he shifted away from the exact sciences approach to venture on the sands of the universe of the mind. This move paralleled a shift in personal identification: from Breuer, strict guardian of the scientific method, to Fliess, whose approach was less tightly bound to scientific rigor. The *Project for a Scientific Psychology* (1895) bears witness to this, as does the mind–brain relation model Freud set up as the foundation for his concept of the dream – to which he returned, modifying it, in Chapter 7 of *The Interpretation of Dreams* (1900).

Figure 3 summarizes Freud's progress between 1895 and 1900 on the topic of the organization of memory and the unconscious, and the role of the latter in the production of dreams. There is the φ system, responsible for perception; the ψ system, containing memory and instincts; and the ω system, representing reality. On the right-hand axis Freud puts movement (M) and the perception-consciousness system (P-C). Outside stimuli reaching the gateway of perception (φ) run along the abscissa, reaching movement according to the reflex scheme drawn up by Sherrington (1906); at the same time, however, they are deposited in the memory, where they integrate themselves with the world of instincts to create the unconscious psychic system (ψ). In the waking state, reality (ω) guides progress along this path. In sleep, however, with the inhibition of movements and loss of contact with reality, the psychic energy built up in the ψ system cannot proceed towards M, and is obliged to regress towards the gateway of perception (φ) which, pushed from inside as it were, sets up a perception with no external object, i.e. hallucination. Through this regressive path the hallucination can satisfy the repressed desire. On the basis of this model Freud formulated his definition of the *dream as a hallucinatory satisfaction of a desire repressed in infancy*.

In Chapter 7 of *The Interpretation of Dreams* Freud elaborates the model further with ordinates for the memory, the unconscious and the censorship. Dreams not only provide hallucinatory satisfaction of a repressed desire, but

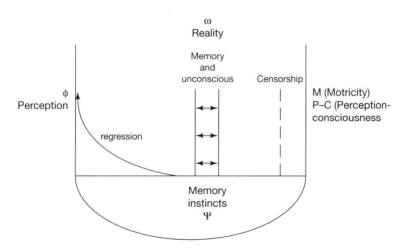

Figure 3 Drawing representing the synthesis of the two models for the brain–mind relationship proposed by Freud in the *Project for a Scientific Psychology* (1895) and *The Interpretation of Dreams* (1900). For explanation, see the text.

also enable the unconscious to pick its way through censorship to reach the P-C system. But to manifest itself to the conscious mind, the unconscious has to undergo the distortions and transformations imposed by the censorship. This is what causes the *rhetoric* of dreams, meaning the difference between its manifest and latent contents.

The censorship executes the main work of dreaming, preventing the unconscious gaining direct access to the conscious mind. Censorship not only creates a dream as the primary event, but also makes us forget it. The primary event cannot be known as such, but we can gain access to the secondary event through narration which transforms the representations of the dream into a system with linguistic significance. Censorship, however, always has the main job in the work of dreams: condensation, displacement, symbolization and dramatization (for a full description of these functions of censorship, see Mancia 1996b).

The work of the dream is permeated with affectivity and builds a bridge to the events of infancy, making it possible to transcribe the contents of memory from the child's earliest affective experiences. Freud defines this emotional recovery of memories *Nachträglichkeit* – a "rewriter of memory". The concept stretches to implicit memory too and its specific transcription of experiences forming the structure of the unrepressed unconscious (Mancia, 2003a, 2004c). We shall come back to these points further on.

Freud's concept of *Nachträglichkeit* embodies what he considered the aim of work on dreams: to transcribe the history of traumatic events from a patient's childhood, that might explain a neurosis. Thus, Freud proposes using the dream to rewrite the patient's true life story, as faithfully as possible. This meant he could base his dream-reconstruction work on the historical, autobiographic memory, and the events from the past irrupting in the analytical relation, even if in *Screen Memories* (1899) he cast doubts on whether we have precise recollections of our infancy, or more likely "recollections" constructed on what we remember of it. He comes close here to the more recent idea of implicit memory (Mancia, 2000b, 2003a), from which we cannot recall events and which therefore cannot hide anything repressed. This is another point we shall come back to.

In *Constructions in Analysis*, Freud (1937b) goes back to the past surviving into the present as the basis for the analytical relation and the work of (re)construction of things forgotten, starting from the traces they have left behind. In the 1930s, then, he shifted back to his original definition of the dream – thirty years earlier in 1895–1900 – as the hallucinatory satisfaction of a desire repressed in infancy – though with some exceptions. His theory is still valid as a whole, but two conditions need reconsidering: dreams referring to traumatic experiences, and those evoking painful recollections of infancy. He thus admits that his theory may need modification, to permit the dream to be seen as an *attempt* at fulfilling a repressed desire. His theory is safe but cannot stand up to the evidence produced by advances in psychoanalytical thought.

Dreams after Freud

In the 1930s, Melanie Klein (1932) radically transformed Freud's instinctual energy model, replacing it with a relational model. This metapsychological change of the mind wrought far-reaching changes in the concept of the dream and how it could be worked on in analysis. The importance of affective relations, linked primarily to primary experiences, suggested repression was no longer the trigger that put our mind to work in dreams, but more likely a dynamic relation between affective representations (internal objects) that have precipitated and layered themselves in the unconscious in early infancy but manifest themselves through the primary processes of splitting and projective and introjective identification.

Though not explicitly, the Kleinian unconscious that manifests itself in dreams is therefore linked no longer to repression but to the splitting and projective identification that Klein introduced into clinical work, and is one of the most important features of current psychoanalysis. Klein is also credited with giving the dream a major part in the economy of the mind, where it represents the various stages of development, that can surface in the transference.

Thus the dream becomes an internal theater (Resnik, 1982) where the human mind is represented by people relating among themselves (the intrapsychic dimension) who give rise to a meaning that is then carried out into the outside world and external relations (the intersubjective dimension) (Meltzer, 1984).

The theory of internal objects has had considerable heuristic utility, bringing values into the psychoanalytical dimension of the mind, making individuals responsible for the state of their internal and external objects, giving new meaning – basically relational – to the concept of unconscious fantasy, hence to the deepest significance of dreams. This shift at the top constituted an important movement in psychoanalytical thought, replacing Freud's instinctual energy model based on desire and its repression with a relational model based on more complex modalities in the organization of the personality and the mind's unconscious functions. From this starting point, work on dreams implies finding out the state of the patients' internal objects, their conflicts and defenses.

The theoretical model of the mind has thus been transformed and enriched, and the dream has acquired a new purpose, studied by the latest generation of analysts (Bion, 1962; Money-Kyrle, 1978): it has become a basic tool of knowledge. The proposed model can be considered *epistemological* and is based on an elegant statement by Money-Kyrle (1961), who said that if man is his representation of the world, and this is identified with his conoscitive dimension, the dream – representing the human inner world – is itself a source of knowledge.

In 1962 Bion formulated a task for the dream, executed by the *alpha* function: this was to transform sensory, emotive and emotional experiences reaching the mind during waking hours in the form of beta elements into thoughts in the dream. This turned the dream into a tool the mind uses to work over sensory experiences and convert them to thought. This permitted a valuable continuity of mental functions in the passage from waking (dominated by fantasies) to sleep (dominated by dreams). Bion (1962) overturned Freud's relation between dreams and unconscious, maintaining that censorship and personal resistances in the dream were not the product of the unconscious, but tools dreams use to create and distinguish the conscious from the unconscious.

This epistemologic aspect of the dream raises the question of the human *need* to dream. If dreaming is essential for knowing oneself and one's objects, the mind needs these to mobilize itself and grow. One of the purposes of the dream might therefore be to produce knowledge through the world of representations. Freud (1900) had guessed this when he compared dreams to a newspaper under a dictatorship: it has to come out every night but, as it is not allowed to tell the truth directly, it has to mask it between the lines. We can use the same metaphor, except that for us the dream that comes out every night has to tell the truth even if it is distorted, to show the dreamer's affective state; this is connected – as if by a bridge – to individuals' early experiences, but at the same time reflects their relationship with their analyst as regards the patient's mind and his or her objects, and the analyst's mind with his or her own personal and countertransferential affects. Today, therefore, we can consider the dream a real experience that represents the dreamer's inner world in the immediate present, and therefore expresses the whole of the transference.

The analyst can use the dream to recognize the splits, identifications, denials, idealizations, fears and defenses, aggressions and seductions activated by the patient, and can employ them in work on the dream. This work involves various parts: interpretation, decoding the manifest and translating it to the latent, exploring, hypotheses, second thoughts, reworking, moves and waiting like in chess: all with the aim of gaining knowledge – and making the patient gain knowledge – of the internal objects and their dynamics in relation to the patient's earliest experiences, the defenses set up in response to the pressures of the transference, and action towards the outside world. This complex work on dreams is possible thanks to the relational context that has its part in the organization of the dream.

Taken in the right context and viewed in the here and now of the analytical setting, the dream is a most valuable aid for grasping a given moment in the transference, selecting the emerging affects and assembling the pieces of the relational mosaic into a *construction* on which to attempt an interpretation. At the same time, however, dreaming makes it possible to bring early experiences to the surface and give them new meaning to "update" them to the present. Thus the dream can be seen as the most creditable and reliable tool in what Freud called *Nachträglichkeit*, referring to reassigning significance to some past experience, even if it was preverbal and presymbolic, by rewriting memory (with or without the actual recollection). This is the true work of *reconstruction* on dreams (Mancia, 2003a, 2004a).

Dreams in psychoanalysis today

The discovery of implicit memory and the unrepressed early unconscious (Mancia, 2003a) and their connections with the experiences of early infancy – sometimes traumatic – has given the dream another, particularly valuable, dimension in theory and clinical practice.

The dream is so important because, besides the various modalities of transference that rely on the patient's voice and language (which I call the "musical dimension" of the transference: Mancia, 2004a), it renders symbolic experiences that were originally presymbolic and preverbal, so they can be expressed verbally and thought about. To this extent the dream, through its representations, can create psychic figurability (Botella and Botella, 2001), helping fill the representation gap of the unrepressed unconscious.

This new function of the dream not only opens up the transference in the immediate present, helping with the work of *construction* in analysis, but also allows a *reconstruction* that enables patients to transcribe their life story, as it relates to their identity, and to recuperate the "history" of their unconscious from their earliest significant preverbal and presymbolic experiences, which they could never recollect.[3] This involves some broadening of Freud's *Nachträglichkeit*, which he conceived as a "transcription" of the memory of events in the distant past connected to the patient's life story, hence to the patient's explicit memory. This therefore involved reconstruction of an event that had really taken place, brought to the surface through the recollection, using the dream, which is the best possible means of de-repression.

We are now in a position to extend this concept of *Nachträglichkeit* to implicit memory too, hence to a process of transcription of unrepressed emotional experiences that cannot be recalled but have marked the infant from its very first encounters with its mother. In this light, *Nachträglichkeit* includes the early events that Freud (1915a) wrongly believed were subject to primary repression but that today we consider as laying the groundwork, together with fantasies and defenses, for an early, unrepressed unconscious that can influence the infant's mind and subsequent processes of repression (Mancia, 2003a, 2004a).

Therefore, psychoanalysis currently sees the dream not only as a window open onto the transference (Mancia, 2000a), or as a real experience that represents the dreamer's inner world in the immediate present, thus expressing the transference as a whole (Joseph, 1985; Mancia, 2004a), but also as a symbolic transformation of a presymbolic happening that the patient can relive emotionally in analysis, even without the actual recollection. In addition, the dream creates images, mentally compensating for the lack of figurative coverage, filling the gaps in the dreamer's affective and emotional history linked to his or her earliest experiences, filed away in implicit memory.

6

The dream:
a window onto the transference

Freud's definition of the dream as the hallucinatory fulfillment of a wish repressed in infancy was first seen in his *Project for a Scientific Psychology* (1895): during sleep the ψ system, the archive of instinct and memory for repressed experiences, moves towards the φ gates of perception and, pushing them from inside, creates a perception with no object – this is a hallucination, by which to satisfy the repressed wish. This operation is made possible by the fact that the ω system, which represents reality, is non-operative during sleep, and movement is inhibited.[1]

The *Project* also saw the birth of the concept of regression in dreams (topical, temporal and formal) and explains part of the dream work produced by censorship. This is the source of the *rhetoric* of dream, meaning the gap between latent and manifest content, hence the deformation and distortion the dream undergoes as it takes form. The oneiric modalities concentrated in these three regressions, allow the dreamer to relive the most meaningful emotions and experiences of his or her ontogenesis.

This implies that dreaming involves a process centered on the memory, consolidating the present and past and building a bridge between current emotive and affective experiences and those from far back, stored in the memory but deeply buried in temporary forgetfulness. This becomes clear in the analytical process, based on the *transference* which helps these old, repressed recollections re-emerge.

However, when he wrote *The Interpretation of Dreams*, Freud (1900) had no way of foreseeing the value of the transference for helping patients. He still had to experience the negative therapeutic reaction of Dora (Freud, 1901) to see how important the transference was, and how its interpretation was the key to continuing treatment. He could therefore not guess that the dream was such a valuable "detective tool" for the analyst. He preferred the link to *ontogenetic* fantasy to infer another mechanism operative in dreams: phylogenetic fantasy, from the development of the human race. This in turn is related to the regression Freud brings up in *The Interpretation of Dreams* and can be considered a variation on the major theme of *Totem and Taboo* (1912–1913): *ontogenesis recapitulates phylogenesis*. In their dreams, therefore, individuals employ modalities that are phylogenetically pre-human and ontogenetically preverbal. But this was the definition Money-Kyrle (1978) put forward for the *projective identification* Klein (1946) had already advanced that we now understand operates in various relational situations, particularly in dreams.

Freud, early in the twentieth century, not only failed to appreciate the value of the transference, but actually viewed it with some diffidence, as a disturbance and an obstacle to continuation of the analytical process. Rather than aiming at what we today might call *construction* work on the transference (Mancia, 1991), Freud tended more to seek the repressed elements in dreams and associations that enabled him to *reconstruct* what was essentially a history of the traumatic events that might have caused the patient's neurosis. Thus, on the basis of the dream Freud proposed rewriting the patient's autobiography, as closely as possible to what had really happened. The part the dream might play in the representation of the transference in the immediate present remained to be established. This enabled Freud to entrust the reconstruction solely to the historical memory and to the events from the past re-emerging in the relationship. He summarized this idea in the *Nachträglichkeit*, meaning re-living an event from the past through retranscription from the memory.[2]

The ambiguity about the historical memory operating in dreams seems to run right through Freud's (1937b) work, when in *Constructions in Analysis* he returned to the past surviving in the present as the basis of the analytical relation, and the work of *construction* of forgotten material starting from the traces it had left behind.[3]

In 1932, in his *New Introductory Lectures on Psycho-Analysis*, Freud returned to the concepts of the *Project*: all dreams are wishful, this instinct finding satisfaction in regression towards the gates of perception. Even dreams of punishment and anxiety are wishes originating in at least part of the Ego (the Super-Ego), which is critical and punitive towards the rest of the Ego.

Freud's idea that all dreams regard satisfaction of a repressed wish was widely accepted by the first generation of psychoanalysts. For instance, Ferenczi (1909) offered numerous clinical examples confirming Freud's hypothesis. However, the second and third generations (Fairbairn, 1952) raised serious objections. Klein (1932) herself contributed to major changes in the interpretation of dreams, by changing the metapsychological conception of the mind. No longer was what was repressed the only thing that stimulated our mind to work in dreams, but there was a dynamic interaction between internal objects, precipitating in layers in early infancy, forming an unrepressed unconscious marked by the primary processes of splitting and projective and introjective identification. The relational model thus takes its place in metapsychology opposite the Freudian instincts model. These objects remain in a dynamic relationship throughout life, based on the fundamental affects that marked the child's early relations with its parents and played their part in forming its personality and character.

Klein was the one who gave the dream its pivotal position in the economy of the mind: it represents the mind's various phases of development, as they can be captured in the transference. In line with the new metapsychological model, dream interpretation thus becomes *theological*, in that it serves as the link to a person's internal objects, meaning the parental figures that have become "sacred" to the individual, becoming the gods and devils of his mental universe (Mancia, 1987, 1988, 1994). Fifty years after Klein's ground-breaking work, Umberto Eco (1981) suggested that behind every strategy of the symbolic world there is a theology to legitimize it. This legitimation was what led me to seek analogies and common ground for dreams and religion (Mancia, 1987, 1988).

The internal objects theory has substantial heuristic value because it introduces "values" into the psychoanalytical dimension of the mind; it puts the responsibility on human beings for the condition of their objects – internal and external – and gives a new meaning, essentially relational, to the idea of unconscious fantasy, hence to the meaning of dreams. This is the step that goes beyond Freud's instincts paradigm, essentially grounded in the wish and its repression.

The theological model of the mind and the dream was further shifted and enriched by the latest generation of analysts (Bion, 1962; Money-Kyrle, 1978) who assigned a further function to the dream: as a fundamental instrument of knowledge. The dream thus gives origin to a theory of knowledge that makes it the basis of a model we can call *epistemological*.

Bion (1962) proposes the dream serves to transform our waking emotive and sensory-motor experiences into dream thought, and gives continuity to mental life as we pass from the waking state, dominated by fantasies, to sleep, dominated by dreams. This overturns Freud's original relationship between the dream and the unconscious. Bion maintains that the censor and resistances in dreams are not products of the unconscious, but are the tools by which the dream creates and differentiates the conscious from the unconscious. Bion's concept, the *contact barrier*, has important clinical implications. This fluid barrier is what enables us to sense from the dream, before anywhere else, significant changes taking place in the patient and his or her relationship with us, besides lending some scientific consistency to the saying that the patient's dreams fall into line with the analyst's thought.

If we understand these workings of the dream, through analysis of the transference, we can start to grasp the deeper aspects – including defensive ones – of people's mental organization; we can peek into the basic modalities (splitting, projective identification, denial and idealization) and the affects that influenced their development as infants. We assume here that the child–parent relationship is recreated, not identically but with similar anxieties and defenses, in the patient–analyst encounter.

This latter dimension of the dream is understandably *epistemological* as we see the mind developing as it gains knowledge of itself and its objects – internal and external. As both knowledge and mental growth depend on the will and ability of these objects, we have to conclude that the mind's cognitive function is tightly bound to its *theology*. We can therefore consider the dream as a "real experience" that, representing the internal world in the immediate present, expresses the transference in its entirety.

However, there is of course more to the dream than that: it has other jobs too! For example, it constitutes a specific communication from the patient to the analyst; it is also the fulfillment of a wish or, as the ancients might have said (Mancia, 1998a), a premonition or even a form of acting out in the session. For instance, a patient may quite frequently describe large numbers of dreams just to fill the analytical space with material that cannot in anyway serve for construction.

Every analyst knows how important it is to observe how patients use dreams: how they communicate dreams, select them, the associations they may attach to their dreams, the willingness – or not – to work on a dream, depending on the anxiety it arouses. Whatever the circumstances, however, the dream always has an active role in the process brought to light in the transference of dramatization of the relation, and the work done to build up a line of thought shared by both partners.

If we agree with the definition of the transference as a total relational situation (Joseph, 1985), shifted from the past to the present, that enables patients to communicate and represent the current state of their internal objects in relation to the analyst, and their links to the past, we understand that the analyst is expected to see how splitting and identification, denial and idealization, fear and defenses, attacks and seduction are operative in the dream. The analyst uses work on the dream, which obviously consists not only of interpretation and translation of the manifest to the latent, but also of exploration, waiting, hypotheses, second thoughts and elaboration, to achieve – and help the patient achieve – insight onto the affects behind the internal objects, onto the defenses raised in response to stimuli in the transference, and onto actions towards the outside world.

It is worth insisting here that it is through the transference that the patient can represent his or her own internal objects in their *intrapsychic dimension*, like in a private theater where parts of the self split off and projectively identified with the various characters in the dream can work out and express their affects and conflicts. Naturally, these objects can also be projectively identified with the analyst (the intersubjective dimension), but my own clinical experience leads me to attribute more importance than I once did to the intrapsychic dimension of the dream, where the split parts of the self come on stage, playing out their wishes, affects, fantasies, conflicts and defenses. In order to foster insight, it is important that the work on dreams makes patients aware of their private theater, and these unconscious modalities involving their internal world, that sometimes only the dream can unveil.

All this is possible against the relational backdrop involved in producing the dream. In agreement with Meltzer (1984), I feel it is stimulating to view the dream as drawing on the mental life of both participants in analysis; it is not just a symbol belonging to the patient, which the analyst interprets, but is a process of symbolization born out of the meeting of the two parties, that permits the creation of new, shared meaning (Meltzer, 1986; but see also Nissim-Momigliano and Robutti, 1992). The dream can therefore be considered an experience narrating the current and future relation of the couple.

The dream must obviously be brought into the here and now of the relation; it is a precious aid to construction, meaning the selection and working through of the material in the transference, whether or not it lends itself to interpretation. But the dream also sets old emotions in motion again and symbolizes old experiences – especially traumatic ones – with all the associated fantasies and defenses. Deposited in implicit memory, these form the *unrepressed unconscious*, on which true reconstruction can be done (Mancia, 2003a, 2006a).

Neuroscientific findings pertinent to implicit memory and unrepressed unconscious have extended and added complexity to the question of dreams and their relation to *construction* and *reconstruction* (Mancia, 1990). Besides serving as a "window onto the transference", through which construction can be achieved, the dream is also a mental function that, through symbolization, offers the items needed for *reconstruction* of significant emotional and affective experiences, even if they cannot be recalled. Work on the dream thus becomes much more of a "transformation" of old experiences filed away in the implicit memory. This is what makes it possible to think and talk about experiences that originally could not even be brought to the level of thought.

On a more clinical note, Freud did not place enough emphasis on the use of the dream in analytical *working through*, and how it was transformed in the process. Today analysts consider this a central point. Dreams undergo continual changes in relation to how patients themselves change while working with us. For example, my experience is that many dreams, especially early in analysis, show strongly persecutory components during analytic separations. This can almost be considered a *psychic constant*, which is defensive since in the most painful separations the patient prefers an object that is present, even if persecutory, to an absent one.

Dreams therefore change in analysis, as the patient changes. Clearly, so many affective variables are represented in a dream that it is impossible to classify them rigidly. For the very fact that the patient has brought them to the session even the most desperately evacuative dreams lend themselves to working through. However, the fundamental events in the encounter – separations, fear, frustration, envy and jealousy, dependence, humiliation, the asymmetry of the relation – all lead to the organization of dreams representing the patient's fantasies and defenses in the face of the painful feelings awoken in the transference.

As work proceeds and the patient, while clearly still oscillating between the paranoid-schizoid and depressive positions, succeeds in transforming these feelings and moves gradually closer to the threshold of the depressive position, the dream's symbolic functions become ever richer, while work on the dream and its use become simpler for the analyst and the patient.

It is thanks to this wide-spanning transformation achieved by analytical work on dreams that representations often start to appear symbolically referring to experiences from early infancy, with the fantasies and defenses held in implicit memory. Like an unrepressed unconscious core, these have influenced how the person's whole personality is organized, and how he or she relates to the world. The dream can therefore make hypothetical reconstruction easier even without the recollection. To this extent, therefore, the patient becomes able to think about and even talk about sometimes traumatic experiences that originally were unthinkable, let alone verbalizable.

Constant work on the dream leads also to an attenuation of censorship while analysis is proceeding. As Freud noted, it is the censor that causes the deformation of dreams (what I called its *rhetoric* earlier), so clearly any attenuation will close up the gap between the latent and manifest contents; in the resulting representation the characters and their roles are related more logically, like in a complete, organic *allegory*, meaning, as Umberto Eco

(1981) suggested, a visual or verbal text that proceeds by separate images that can be interpreted literally. This makes it somewhat easier to read meaning into the dream, and may even suggest interpretations based solely on its manifest content. It may therefore directly represent the patient's feelings, fantasies and defenses in that precise moment of the transference.

On a clinical level, we can allow the dream numerous functions, all traceable to the transference and the context of the analytical relation. The dream is consequently often the first sign of a patient's resistance; it may be an early marker of standstill, or even of a negative therapeutic reaction. It may involve the analyst (countertransference dreams) as an expression of his or her mental distress (Barale and Ferro, 1987) or else it may – in my own experience at least – reflect moments when it is hard to understand the patient's material, and analysis stagnates.

When worked through properly the dream can serve as a useful antidote to a patient's acting out. It can help both parties gain awareness of the meaning of certain of the patient's psychosomatic manifestations, situations or behaviors relating to his reality. It can act as a sensitive thermometer to measure the patient's "temperature" in the transference; and it can also tell us what the patient is not managing to say in words. Examples include not only anal masturbation (Meltzer, 1966), but also early experiences dating back to the presymbolic stages of the child's development.

However you look at it, the deepest meaning of the dream in analysis lies in its ability to represent the transference in the present, and to give us an X-ray view of the parts of the self in play, and the affects dominating the "analytical space" at that fleeting moment in the relation.

The case of A.

A young woman doctor had recently started analysis with me on a basis of three sessions a week. A. was very worried about something that was happening at the time, and fearful of her identity as a doctor. Fairly early in analysis she described a dream:

> She is at the port, about to take a ferry, but someone points out that she is in the arrivals area, not the departures. To reach the departure area she has to take a longer way round, through Customs. She is a bit worried about passing Customs and having to show her papers.

The patient associates the ferries with the boats going to the Aeolian islands and remembers having seen me on the wharf at Naples, many years ago, waiting to take one. The Customs reminds her of her father – who is not Italian – who had obtained a passport for her from his own country, but then she had felt a conflict when, as an adult, she had decided to opt for Italian nationality. I comment that the dream seems to show she is worried about starting this trip with me, so she presents herself at the arrivals instead of the departures – as if the trip were already over – and that she seems somewhat anxious about her own identity.

The patient did not reply but at our next encounter, the last of that week, she recounted another dream:

> She is about to leave for a boat trip with a skipper but before departing she has to go and fetch some water. Further inland she finds a well, with a wooden lid, and with the help of the skipper, who in the mean time has joined her, they manage to open it and make sure they can reach the water.

The patient's comment is that the dream reminds her of the one she had described earlier, where there was a ferry about to set out to sea; she notes that water is indispensable for traveling and also that her search for water seems like a preparation for travel. My own comment referred to her associations, with the idea of the equivalence of water/milk and her need for "reassurance" about taking off on a trip with me without the guarantees she felt were needed.

Then comes the weekend, in an uneasy state of affection that a dream she brought at the beginning of the next week helped clarify: *she is playing with her brother on a balcony at home, with things hanging over the edge. Her brother drops a golf-club, which falls on a person below, killing him.* She says the dream was extremely worrying and she woke up in a state of anxiety, and tells me it goes back to an event that really took place when she was 5 or 6 years old. She was playing on the balcony at home, on the seventh floor, and dropped a heavy object, which landed close to a person below – it could have killed him!

Then she tells me about her brother, who is distracted and has no sense of responsibility towards his family. One of his children nearly died because of his carelessness. Then she starts talking about golf, which she plays passionately every weekend. This last association takes me back in a flash to the weekend and our separation, to her feelings expressed in her dreams, and the associations of the past week's sessions. I comment that her brother, easily distracted and irresponsible (perhaps a part of herself), seems in her dream to have the task of taking revenge on someone by dropping the golf-club on his head – which after all is the very center of thought! I suggested that person might be someone who means something to her – maybe her analyst who was being punished for leaving her on her own over the weekend.

A. thought for a moment, then said: "I'm not surprised that my hostility and ambivalence toward you come out in my dreams", thus admitting these feelings that she had been denying for several months. I started then to wonder whether the irresponsible brother might also be me, leaving her over the weekend without worrying about her, and whether the dream possibly revealed a fantasy of "killing" our relationship, which caused her such painful asymmetry, dependence and frustration. I said nothing of this to the patient.

A few weeks later she arrived one Monday and told me that while she had been at the golf course over the weekend she had decided to stop analysis, even though the decision was painful. It was too much of a commitment, emotionally and financially. I merely pointed out that these ideas that had come to her on the golf course reminded me of an earlier dream in which a significant person had been killed, and that during the weekend she seemed to have decided to act out the fantasy and the dream by "killing" our relation. A. seemed fascinated by this remark, and at the same time relieved. She then agreed to a "compromise" that I suggested: she would continue analysis in order to clarify the nature of her resistances and ambivalence, which she was acknowledging for the first time.

At the next session, which was much calmer, she described this dream:

I am with Stefano (an old boyfriend), who is telling me about his father, who has a tumor. Then we end up in bed, and Stefano asks whether I would be willing to keep the baby if I became pregnant. I reassure him, but I cannot resist remarking slightly jealously that who knows how many babies he has around the world.

My comment is that the Stefano of her dream might be me, for whom she feels an erotic attraction and contemplates having a child, but then other feelings come to the surface: her jealousy, and a feeling that me/Stefano is not reliable because I must have sexual relations with lots of women, leaving children all over the place. I point out that Stefano's father's tumor recalls the fantasies of death that might reflect the fantasy of ending the relation with me. Several sessions later, the topic of death surfaces once more, in a dream she had had before the weekend: *she was with a woman friend who was desperate because a man she had met in church was doomed to die.* She herself commented this short dream: "I was the desperate friend, desperate because I had to tell you I wanted to stop analysis. Part of me was still unwilling, and I am grateful that we have been able to reach a compromise."

But the compromise I had proposed did not last long. She was too fearful for her identity as a doctor and the worry about the asymmetry of the relation and her dependence on me set up death anxieties when we were separated. After only a few days, the young doctor – visibly ill at ease – informed me she did not intend to continue analysis. She had felt exceedingly anxious over the weekend and her golf game had not been enough to contain it. So she stopped analysis, acting out the killing of the relation that she had seen in her last few dreams: were they premonitory?

The case of R.

Like at the start of analysis, at its end too a dream can serve as a reliable pointer on how to decide with the patient when and how to terminate the process (see De Simone, 1994). Naturally, the dream can reveal all the anxiety, the ambivalence, worries and disagreements surrounding the decision to conclude analysis, besides the anger and resentment some patients manifest because they feel the decision was not theirs – despite the dreams on which it was based.

R. was a 50-year-old patient of mine, in the seventh year of four-times weekly analysis, which he had requested because he believed his sexuality was not satisfactory. R. described two dreams, fairly close together, a few months before his analysis ended. In one of these

> *He left someone he cared about in the house of friends, while he left for the airport to depart on a trip. In the second dream he was in the lift going up to the second floor (my rooms are on the second floor) with an estate agent who is telling him that the apartment on the second floor is very valuable, but he suddenly realizes – almost with astonishment – that it is his own.*

He associates the two dreams with the forthcoming end of analysis and recalls a fragment of a dream in which his friend Beppe died. He comments that possibly the person he is leaving behind is the analyst, and he is on his way to the airport for a final separation. The second dream he explains by the fact that he is having work done on his own apartment, which is also on the second floor, and that he has acquired his current emotional state through analysis. He says nothing about Beppe's death. I make the brief comment that his departure will leave me alone but that he does recognize that he has gained something of value from me (the second-floor apartment). The session ends on this note, but the patient promptly disappeared with no explanation and missed all four of the next week's sessions, without letting me know he would not be there.

When he returned he described this dream:

> *I walk into a fine old building – similar to this one – and on the stairs see someone carrying a lamp, a bit like the one on this table. When I ask what is going on the person replies that he has to change the lamps, moving the*

indoor one outside and the one on the stairway inside. But the lamps are actually the same, one simply being more powerful. Then, in the same building, I see a stretcher with someone lying on it, and a person – or assistant – sitting next to it. [He adds that the assistant resembles me.] *The patient and assistant are reproduced to infinity in the dream, like in a series of mirrors, but the patient seems to change: first he has a beard, then he hasn't, and his expression changes profoundly.*

R. associates the indoor (internal) lamp with what he has gained from analysis and has now to take outside, doing the work on his own, as we have decided to terminate analysis. I point out that the first part of the dream seems to involve a change not so much in quality as in the power of the lamp, possibly alluding to his sexual potency – the symptom that brought him to analysis. R. agrees and in fact the change should correspond to his desire for sexual potency which, he says, "analysis has not achieved though in other ways there have been far-reaching changes in my life". I point out that there is also a change in the second part of the dream, regarding his identity as a person. R. acknowledges that in the dream the assistant remained the same from beginning to end, whereas the "patient's" facial expressions indicated various moods, including despair.

R.'s lack of satisfaction that the analysis which was about to end had not achieved what he wanted – more sexual potency – had set up strongly ambivalent feelings in him about the therapy, causing him to consider it worth less than he had originally thought. His response was to skip various sessions, with the excuse that his business appointments were more important than our encounters.

After a week's absence, he brought this dream, apologizing for not having paid what was due for the previous month.

There was a white bear [the patient is big and tall, with a long white beard and hair that does make him look a bit like a bear!]. *The bear was not dangerous – in fact it was quite friendly – and stayed mainly in a "kennel" outside the house, coming in only occasionally. I am with a friend and we watch the bear, who seems to have two white "boxes" under his belly. In the dream I am thinking that if it was a she-bear the boxes might have milk in them, but as he is a male they might serve for collecting his dung. My friend helps me to remove the boxes from beneath the bear and we find two large black turds, like two sausages, on top of them.*

He says the sausages remind him of food, which he likes, especially "black pudding" (sausages made with blood) which are widely appreciated in his home town. He was a bit put out that in the dream they were actually feces.

I comment very simply, without excessive emphasis, that the big friendly white bear makes me think of him, with his white beard and long hair. He says:

"I hadn't thought about that but it's true – it was a bear that looked like me. How strange, though, because it stayed partly in the house but mostly outside." I interrupt him: "A bit like you with me – sometimes you come in for sessions but mostly you are out and about." He replies: "You are right – I have missed quite a few sessions recently, and in the dream those strings of excrement might be a sign of hostility." I note that the hostility might well be related to the fact that our analysis is very shortly due to end, even though he does not entirely agree.

He tells me that he has another dream to describe, from last night: *I was going into my grandmother's house to talk to her, but I found a young woman who had hanged herself in the bathroom, wearing a red sweater.* He comments: "How strange, this violent death by hanging. My grandmother was a strong, determined woman, who would never have killed herself . . . but the girl in the red sweater reminds me of Rossella." I note that Rossella, with whom he seems to identify himself in the dream, and who undergoes a violent death/separation, was the witness of the start of his analysis and is now called in to witness the conclusion. R. himself continues, suggesting that Rossella's violent death might be a metaphor for the end of our relationship!

PART 3

Further reflections on narcissism and other clinical topics

This part concentrates mainly on clinical work. It aims to link the theories discussed in the previous chapters with the analyst's work with the patient, in the transference and countertransference. The complex theoretical and clinical aspects of narcissism are discussed. The case of a borderline patient provides an opportunity to talk about the defensive narcissistic organization of the personality, with its conflicting parts, and the destructive part's "propagandistic", seductive efforts against the patient's healthy libidinal part. The meaning of dreams in narcissistic patients is assessed, considering that they so often contrast openly with what comes to light in the transference and with the dreamer's behavior.

My approach to my work with patients is dissected, explaining why I consider it important to listen to their tone of voice and the prosody – the stresses and accents – and timing of their language. My own voice and the structure and tempo of my language are equally important. Countertransferential emotions can be put to good use in grasping the patient's most significant childhood items through the transference.

Transference love, sexuality, happiness and mental pain are all reviewed, in the light of recent discoveries on implicit memory and the unrepressed early unconscious. Besides the mother as a "traumatic object", the father emerges, in a dimension different from Freud's Oedipal picture, as a cause of distortion in how the child's unrepressed unconscious becomes organized. Clinical work indicates it as a potential source of pathology and mental suffering in the adult.

7

Further historical/critical and clinical reflections on narcissism

The background

I shall deal here with narcissism, a psychopathological category that has held center on the internal psychoanalytical stage for many years, and its relations with mental illness (neurosis, psychosis and borderline personality).

Freud introduced the concept of narcissism in 1914, and since then it has undergone far-reaching changes that have influenced the psychopathology of psychosis and borderline patients. Freud's approach was essentially theoretical, although the example of the ameba as a metaphor for a narcissistic situation led him to discuss the role of this modality in psychosis, particularly schizophrenia, which was considered the "queen of psychoses" at that time.

Freud's approach to narcissism can be summarized in five stages, described very briefly here (for an exegesis of the concept of narcissism, see Mancia 1990). The first stage coincided with the publication of *Leonardo da Vinci and a Memory of his Childhood* (1910) then the "Clinical case of President Schreber" (1911), where narcissism is seen in relation to the etiological role of homosexual drives in paranoia.

Narcissism is defined here as a sexual preference for one's own body; this idea appears in *Instincts and their Vicissitudes* (1915c) where love is considered originally narcissistic as the Ego satisfies its own instincts through autoerotism (sexual pleasure using its own body).

The second stage dates from 1914 with *On Narcissism: An Introduction*, where Freud (1914a) examines the relation between the Ego and the outside world, and the role of narcissism in this relation and in the development of sexuality. This work lays the groundwork for a theory of the libido (distinguishing Ego-libido from object-libido) that later found its place in the instincts theory.

From our point of view, the interest of *On Narcissism: An Introduction* lies in the fact that Freud, for the first time, links the idea of narcissism to the *dementia praecox* introduced by Kraepelin (or Bleuler's *schizophrenia*); he interprets it as the result of the object–libido withdrawing into the Ego, an interpretation dating back to Abraham (1908). The notion of the withdrawal of the libido was illustrated using the metaphor of the ameba, which draws in its pseudopods according to the energy constancy principle – used by Freud in his *Project for a Scientific Psychology* (1895) – when the Ego-libido increases the object–libido diminishes, and vice versa.

Freud (1914a) also specified two "normal" conditions in which the libido is withdrawn from the object and narcissistically invested in the Ego: organic disease, and sleep. The growing child invests his or her libido in the first love object – the mother. This is primary narcissism, when the child feels "at one" with the mother, and sees her as a part of him- or herself. As the Ego develops, the distance from primary narcissism gradually grows. But this very process sets in motion a movement in the opposite direction, tending to take the Ego back towards the Eden of primary narcissism when the Ego-libido and object–libido were indistinguishable. This is *secondary narcissism* when the libido, with all its erotic potential, is withdrawn from the object and again directed towards the Ego.

In *Mourning and Melancholia* (1915d) Freud links narcissism with loss of the object. When this happens the libido has nothing to invest in, and turns to its own Ego, which it thus identifies with the lost object. This intuition led Freud very close to the concept of *projective identification* that Klein actually described in 1946. Freud called it *narcissistic identification*, and was the first to note the connection – subsequently elaborated by Klein – between narcissism and projective identification. The idea of narcissistic identification that Freud set out in *Mourning and Melancholia*, according to which part of the Ego identifies with the lost object, can, I believe, be considered a forerunner of *intrapsychic projective identification*. This involves splitting off parts of the self identified with various internal objects, but this identification remains inside the person's psychic world. Paula Heimann (1950) later applied this concept in clinical practice, working on it and discussing it.

The third stage dates from *Beyond the Pleasure Principle*, in 1920, when Freud returned to the idea of narcissism in relation to instincts. The Ego, at the start of mental life, contains its instincts, this being its narcissistic condition, and can satisfy them (this being the moment of auto-eroticism). The auto-erotic instinct defines the pleasure-Ego, the non-auto-erotic instinct the reality-Ego. Love, according to Freud, is originally narcissistic and dependent on auto-erotic satisfaction. This is why hate is older than love, because it comes from refusal of the outside world by the Ego's primary narcissism.

In this third stage, Freud introduces a two-faceted view of mental life: the instincts work to restore a very early state of events – that of the inorganic world. Basic biological considerations convince Freud that humankind contains a force that leads people to destruction and death: this is the *death instinct* or *Thanatos*. Its counterpart is an instinct towards preservation and life, *Eros*, which combines the object-libido (aimed at preservation of the species) and the Ego-libido (which resembles the narcissistic Ego, and whose aim is self-preservation).

In the fourth stage, in *The Ego and the Id* (1922) Freud reworks his dual instincts theory. The Id – no longer the Ego – becomes the container for the libido that reaches maximum power in the Id, and can invest objects. Primary narcissism is the condition needed for object investments, and also involves the Ego to the extent that it is not yet differentiated from the Id. Once the Ego has been formed, part of the libido turns towards it, thus forming *secondary narcissism*, in which the libido withdrawn from objects appears desexualized and sublimated.

In that book Freud has the Super-Ego absorb the Ego ideal as a residue of identification with the parental figures. This process cancels out the concept of the Ego ideal as an ideal internal object serving to uphold the personality, with cognitive, esthetic and moral values on which to lean, and use as inspiration in life. It is a reference object for working out the frustrations, disappointments and trauma that reality serves up to each of us in our lifetime. This somewhat pessimistic turn in Freud's thinking has, of course, effects on the theory of the mind, the concept of narcissism itself, and for clinical applications of the death instinct.

After *The Ego and the Id* comes a fifth stage, in which narcissism is gradually extended and dynamically linked to the death instinct, which thus enters clinical practice with *The Economic Problem of Masochism* (Freud 1924a). Freud connects narcissism and masochism as it has developed from the death instinct, sustaining that in masochism the destructiveness returning from the outside world is subsumed by the Super-Ego, which thus increases its sadism against the Ego. The Super-Ego's sadism and the Ego's masochism complete each other. Clearly in this work Freud was influenced by his earlier thinking in *The Ego and the Id* of 1922. The Ego-ideal too, which should have been able to oppose the Super-Ego's sadistic and prohibitory tendencies, becomes part of the Super-Ego, making the Ego the victim of its persecution, with no possibility of appeal.

In *Analysis Terminable and Interminable* (1937a), one of Freud's most significant spiritual testaments, the death instinct becomes the key to any clinical

reading. It is held responsible for resistance to analysis (the negative therapeutic reaction), for masochism, unconscious guilt feelings and narcissistic
neurosis (in other words psychosis).

Narcissism and the death instinct are also part of our mental life, as
pleasure is identified with narcissism, while *pain* can be identified with the
object relation. Mental pain is therefore the result of renouncing narcissistic
pleasure and auto-erotic satisfaction.

In his last few years, Freud suggested a link between the narcissistic stage
– as a source of pleasure – and hatred and destructiveness against the outside
object, as a source of pain, i.e. between narcissism and the death instinct.
The outline of this idea still constitutes an outstanding cultural offering that
helps explain much of humankind's hatred and destructiveness throughout
the world in the twentieth century. It also explains mental illnesses ranging
from neurosis to the then-unexplored field of psychosis. I shall return
to the question of Freud's contribution, with all his reservations, to the
treatment of psychosis.

Although his aim was clearly to see how narcissism came into clinical
situations, Freud left behind him a concept that was ambiguous and dotted
with question marks. Many authors have since maintained that from the
beginning of life the Ego has to invest the outside world. Federn (1925) was
one of the first who did not fully agree with Freud. Then Balint (1937)
decided that the earliest phases of an object relation were not narcissistic,
bringing clinical examples to support this and pointing out that narcissistic
patients are excessively sensitive and vulnerable precisely when it comes to
relations.

Years earlier, Abraham (1919) had noted from his clinical work that some
relational modalities seemed to express a form of narcissism fueled by envy
of the analyst, and this tended to make the encounter fail, to belittle the
analyst, enfeebling him and rendering him impotent.

Klein too looked back to Abraham when, already in 1932, she decided
to reject the idea of primary narcissism as an "objectless" stage when the
libido is withdrawn into the Ego; she too holds that the child's relation
with its mother is centered on the breast from its very earliest days, with
all the ingredients of an object relation: love, hate, fantasies, anxiety and
defenses. Klein (1932) shifts narcissism from this objectless state, making it
a way of relating to the object, with specific modalities such as splitting,
projective identification, denial and idealization, all participating in the
organization of the child's (unconscious) personality that is still operating
in the adult.

It is clear that Klein (with help from the other authors mentioned) chips
away at Freud's instincts model, replacing it partly but significantly with her

relational model that assigns prime importance to the object: the mother, father and the growing child's environment. This Kleinian "paradox", for we can hardly call it anything else, has left its mark on much of the theoretical and clinical psychoanalysis since the mid 1950s. Although she preferred the relational, object-centered, non-narcissistic model to Freud's instincts model, Klein remained faithful to the idea of the death instinct. This "paradox" has influenced many Kleinian – and other – analysts of the latest and the previous generation.

The "paradox" also helped transform our idea of the unconscious. In place of repression as the pivot around which the unconscious revolved (Freud, 1915a, 1915b), Klein (1946) put the concept of splitting and projective identification. These have nothing to do with repression. However, Klein did not go into the question of the unrepressed unconscious which, on the basis of today's neuroscientific findings regarding the implicit memory, is now attracting the interest of psychoanalytical research (Mancia, 2000b, 2003a, 2006a).

Klein's unwillingness to dissent from Freud's line of thought extended to the Oedipus complex, the hinge on which Freud's theory of the mind hung. In 1928, even while introducing the concept of the unconscious fantasy of children in their first months of life, and their dyadic relation with the mother, Klein still hangs onto the Freudian triadic conception, mentioning an early Oedipus, even though the child's fantasies concern not only the father's penis but also the presence of other babies in the mother's belly.

We have to credit Klein, however, for having noted the fundamental importance of the child's first relations with the mother, and the preverbal and presymbolic experiences marking the paranoid-schizoid and depressive positions. These experiences are now believed to help form the structure of the unrepressed unconscious, stored in the child's implicit memory. Through these primary relational experiences – sometimes traumatic – the child's personality becomes organized; the aim of analysis of the transference and of dreams is to reach back to these primary emotions.

On the topic of narcissism, Klein (1946) introduced a difference into psychoanalytical theory between narcissistic *states* and narcissistic *object relations*. The first are produced by projective identification of one's own Ego-ideal onto the object that is loved and admired as it contains one's best parts. Narcissistic object relations, on the other hand, are structurally linked to projective identification of disturbing parts of one's self – envious, sadistic, hostile, avid and aggressive – onto the object. In normal conditions these relational modalities enable children to grasp their mothers' capacity for *rêverie*, her tolerance and ability to contain. Through these, infants acquire their first knowledge of the world. If mothers can metabolize and make good their children's anxieties, and make them feel loved, they will be able to introject a good ideal object, protective and reassuring. Children will then be able to assemble an Ego-ideal that will light their way and smooth their relations with the world, while letting them believe in object love. However, the mother may be anxious and depressed, with no capacity for containment and *rêverie*, and unable to satisfy her child's wishes, or to accept and elaborate affectionately and tolerantly the parts that are projected into her, and return them in good shape for introjection; worse, she may use the child for projective identification of her own depressive anxiety (a reversal of projective identification). In this case the child will introject a bad, anxious and depressed object, and will be obliged to get rid of it in fantasy using splitting and projective identification. The child will also use this strategy to control the object, to deny separation from it, and make it feel the distress and mental pain that he or she suffers. These implicit defenses will mark narcissistic object relations even in the adult.

Failure of the primary relation forms the *original trauma* (and the mother will be the *trauma-object*) that will oblige the child to organize fantasies and pathological defenses, many of which will remain unconscious. The first are splitting and projective identification, used on a massive scale. As this latter is considered a defense against envy and avidity too, these painful feelings will dominate the narcissistic object relation.

The outcome will be that the Ego, disappointed and frustrated by the "trauma-object", will be led to organize a narcissistic personality; it will destructively attack the Ego-ideal and turn it into a Super-Ego which will feel hostility and hatred toward the whole world – internal and external. The projective identification of these parts of the self, with their heavy burden of aggression, will create bizarre, persecutory objects that, in turn, will produce psychotic anxiety.

The Ego's unfailing defense at this stage will be to create omnipotent objects to satisfy its wishes. These objects will be far removed from reality and will deny it; they will be artificial substitutes, created by the Ego to compensate the lack of affection, the relational failure, and the emotional catastrophe, and to cope with feelings of powerlessness, exclusion, solitude, inadequacy and inability to face reality and the world. The resulting *delusional narcissistic structure* grandiosely takes the place of reality. We find this in one of Dostoevsky's heroes who says: "If God does not exist, then I can act in his place. I shall therefore become the example that makes people believe in God. I shall therefore be God by proxy."

These defensive modalities that lead the psychotic patient so far from reality surface in full force in the transference, and, as they form the "negative" parts of the personality, they will end up dominating it.

Before starting to describe the "negative" personality, I want to note that the concept of narcissism I have outlined here follows a historical path running from Freud, through the whole of Klein's work, up to the post-Kleinian authors who have focused particularly on this state of mind and have applied their conclusions clinically, especially in psychotic and border-line patients. But narcissism over the years has attracted the attention of many authors (Ciani, 1983) who have interpreted it in their various different ways and used it differently in clinical practice (for a review: Mancia, 1990). Here I shall simply mention Kohut, who in "Forms and transformations of narcissism" (1978a) defines this state of mind as a libidinal investment of the self that cannot be considered pathological; it reflects an attempt to deal with "irregular" maturational situations arising inevitably during a child's development, tending to idealize the parental *imago*. Kohut (1978a) sustains that this latter operation is what produces the love and admiration that mark the Ego-ideal, whose task is to manage the world of instincts. The "God" of Kohut's mythology, so to speak, is therefore the interiorization of this idealized object containing the idealized image of the self and the self-objects.

Giorgio Sassanelli (1982, 1989) picks up Kohut's ideas, considering narcissism as the dimension of a cohesive area of the personality involved in setting up an "organizational network", or "psychic connector" to support and contain human mental experiences. Naturally, parallel to this "cohesive" structuring, a "symbiotic", parasitic organization may develop in the child, causing defensive, antilibidinal forms of narcissism that find an outlet in humankind's sadism and destructiveness.

Otto Kernberg (1984) makes a distinction between *normal* and *patho-logic* narcissism. The first reflects a libidinal investment of the self which allows integration of libidinal and aggressive components. The second reflects a libidinal investment of a grandiose pathological structure of the self, pervaded with aggression, which explains the malignant nature of narcissism.

Narcissism was significantly "revisited" by André Green (1982) in *Life Narcissism, Death Narcissism* where the traditional concept is compared with a second one that he calls *negative* or *of death*.

The negative personality

André Green (1993) first introduced the idea of a "negative personality", which he defined as caused by the "lack" of the object, which thus becomes a worthless trauma-object, which is interiorized and gives rise to a "negative knowledge" based on what Money-Kyrle (1978) called "primary misunderstanding".

Green sustains that the negativity arises out of separation, which is, however, necessary for the Ego to acquire its own subjectivity and distinct identity. Emerging from the "negative knowledge" will be feelings like hatred, hostility and envy. Envy in particular makes the person see others as equals, thus denying the possibility of anything positive different from him- or herself: this eliminates the asymmetry in the relation (particularly with the analyst where asymmetry is intrinsic).

Green stresses the fact that in the field of relations, especially in psycho-analysis, Freudian pessimism leaves little space for the "desperate undertakings of negativity", with its attachment to compulsive repetition. Negativity is therefore a challenge to rational thought. It is in fact rooted in the common conscious and lacks rational dynamics. Its task is to relate the intrapsychic polarity and intersubjectiveness using splitting and projective identification.

My own conception of a negative personality goes further than Green, as it is less anchored to Hegelian philosophy and is founded anthropo-logically more on clinical experience. I believe the negative areas of the personality are dominated by envy, competitivity, delusional jealousy, hatred, sadism, greed, dishonesty, systematic lying, violence, cruelty and refusal of the rules of community living, to the point of various forms of destructiveness.

Research into the psychology of development (Bowlby, 1969; Stern, 1985; Fonagy and Target, 1997) suggests that the origins of this negativity are to be sought in an infant's growth period and its first object relations, when the child's wish bumps into reality. Children's "internal equipment" will either enable them to tolerate the inevitable trauma, frustration and disappointment reality will deal out to them, or else will oblige them to set up pathological defenses. The child's environment, particularly the maternal object – also as it relates to the father – will induce a process of trauma, a trauma-object.

Severe trauma, such as the loss of both parents, or their separation while the child is still small, physical or psychological violence – sometimes sexual abuse – may cause the child's attachment system (Bowlby, 1969), or its reflexive functions (Fonagy and Target, 1997) to fail, and will make it affectively "out of tune" (Stern, 1985).

Less severe, but continuous or repeated trauma may also cause a child serious mental suffering; these might be lack of understanding or misunder-standing, prejudice, parents who are violent, or lack moral substance, or cannot understand the child's real needs, but also the lack of cultural, moral and even esthetic substance in the environment. Such situations will pro-duce pathological defenses involving the child's whole personality, which will carry over in their affective-emotional and cognitive dimensions even through adult life.

Internalization of these models of violence and destructiveness will ensure this "negative" patrimony is passed on from one generation to the next. These models have a strong cross-generational potential which starts to operate early; they are deposited in the child's implicit memory and form part of an unrepressed unconscious that influences the person even as an adult, affecting his or her relations with the world, and surfacing again and again, generation after generation.

Apart from trauma, the "natural" separation from the object also plays a specific role, and can create intense anxiety and pathological defenses in the child. The ontogenetic paradox arises from the negativity that comes from separation anxiety which, however, is indispensable if children are to grow and establish their own adult identity. The negative will in that case be causally related not only to children's inability to work through their grief at the separation from the object, and to tolerate adequately the disruption of their attachment system, but also to their specific response to frustration and disappointment at the unfulfilled, all-engulfing wish.

The "negative" therefore not only is hidden in the wish for the other, but also may be facilitated by the environment, its cultural and moral confusion, by parental and social models that show devastating gaps, ignorance, arrogance and violence.

The development of mental illness, from neurosis to psychosis and borderline personality, from hypochondria to psychosomatic disorders, can thus be seen as the sum of a combination of factors pushing a child to set up pathological defenses; this happens mainly in the pre-Oedipal stage, though Oedipal sentiments can later play their part in the pathological organization of the personality.

The defenses include the construction of prosthesic and autarchic internal objects, to take the place of the real objects which are painful and unacceptable because of their violence and rottenness. These defenses and internal objects will therefore be delusional and may settle in the unrepressed unconscious, influencing the person throughout his or her life. Naturally we must not overlook the genetic heritage that is passed on to every individual and that dictates the internal equipment governing how the child specifically responds and adapts to reality.

These numerous, complex aspects of the negative personality will emerge in the analytical relation, forming essential elements in the *negative transference*.

On a strictly clinical level, Hanna Segal (1957), one of the first analysts, with Herbert Rosenfeld, to deal with schizophrenia, and who went thoroughly into the question of the relations between narcissism and psychosis, considers the negative transference as requiring more specific interpretation in these patients. This interpretation should focus more on the sense of splitting and projective identification than on the actual material repressed, so as to help patients work through their underlying feelings – above all envy – and the defenses raised against them.

Analysis of the negative transference will make it easier to progress from the paranoid-schizoid to the depressive position; this will involve closer integration of the split-off parts of the self, reducing omnipotence and projective identification, and making for closer contact with reality.

Herbert Rosenfeld (1965, 1987) was the first to establish the concept of *malignant* or *destructive narcissism* as a relational modality for psychotic and borderline personalities; they display omnipotence and omniscience, envy, greed and jealousy, with large-scale splitting and projective identification that tend to belittle the analyst's work and make him or her feel powerless, inadequate, humiliated, but also bored and unable to think. Rosenfeld describes this state of mind with an evocative metaphor: he calls it a *mafia* or *Nazi-like* organization, made up of bandits who use internal propaganda to attack the self's libidinal parts and back each other up in their criminal enterprises. This sort of metaphor is useful to understand – and help patients understand – how the inner theater of their mind is organized and works: the intrapsychic object dynamics that govern patients' affective, emotional and cognitive spheres, and govern their behavior towards reality.

Current post-Kleinian psychoanalysis holds that every psychotic or borderline personality contains libidinal and destructive aspects which merge to varying extents, and are often conflicting. If in this conflict the destructive part attacks the thinking Ego, using projective identification to empty out parts of the self, the result will be *psychosis*. If the attack is directed at the soma-Ego, through projective identification into the body of destructive, suffering parts of the self, the result will be a *psychosomatic illness* (Mancia, 1994). If this is then followed by re-introjection of the object-body, projectively invaded with suffering, the result will be a *hypochondriac condition*. In psychotic or borderline personalities the destructive part of the self acts against its own internal objects – particularly against a trauma-object of the primary relation – against the analytical relation, which is connected to the trauma-object through the transference, and against the self, which is the result of these primary relations.

The attack on the analyst will be designed to oust him or her from the setting, and make it impossible for the analyst to think. This is how patients will try to defend themselves against the unbearable feelings of envy and anger at the analyst, who uses the work of interpretation to break down the patient's defenses. The psychotic or borderline patient's transference can therefore be even more intense than a neurotic's. Even more than the neurotic transference, it can arouse intense feelings in the analyst too (which may be linked to unrepressed unconscious areas of the analyst's own personality); the analyst will have to manage and use these countertransferential shifts to ensure he or she understands the patient's transference properly, and to avoid dangerous counter-actings and projective counter-identifications (Grinberg, 1962).

Wilfred Bion (1967), in his work on the development of schizophrenia, returned to Klein's idea that violent anxiety plays a major part in projective identification in schizophrenia. The Ego is obliged to break up itself and the objects introjected, so its internal relations end up in small pieces. It therefore uses projection to toss out this psychic reality and create "bizarre objects". The result, according to Bion, is that the patient lives in hatred of reality, thus justifying his or her massive projective identification which in turn drenches his or her objects in hostility, making reality even more aggressive and dangerous, thus impeding re-introjection. The outcome is that the patient increasingly refuses reality, putting objects with delusional features in its place.

Bion sustains that schizophrenic disorders originate from the interaction of the environment with the personality which is dominated by destructive impulses and hatred of reality – external and internal. This causes a constant threat of annihilation that makes the schizophrenic personality particularly fragile.[1] Its transference is prompt and precipitous, marked by heavy dependency, and dominated by excessive projective identification centered on the analyst. This attacks the analyst's conscious apparatus and confuses him or her. The excessive splitting causes the self to break up, creating an identity crisis.

There is also a specific process in which an outside object is swallowed by a fragment of the schizophrenic personality. If these parts of the self are intended to become words, the words become the same thing as the object swallowed. Bion (1967) says this makes the patient treat words as if they were the same as the object they represent creating the "symbolic equations" described so well by Segal (1957).

An excessive use of projective identification sets up conditions in which the patient can no longer introject, which makes the analyst's work particularly frustrating, with little success for the patient, who lives the analysis day by day, with no memory of it and without ever managing to build it up into a "history". In such cases Bion finds it essential to analyze patients' attack on their memory and the libidinal parts of the self, and clarify the substitution they are achieving of projective identification for repression and introjection.

Bion (1957) later suggested making a distinction between the psychotic and neurotic personalities, stressing the fragmentation of the self in the psychotic that influences his perception of external and internal reality. He also returns to Freud's *Neurosis and Psychosis* (1923b) which notes that while in neurosis the Ego represses the instincts by acting on the Id, in the psychotic the Ego is at the service of the Id, withdrawing from reality.

A closer reading of Freud, especially his later writings, in the light of Kleinian and post-Kleinian ideas, leads to some interesting considerations on what he had to say about psychosis. Although he believed it was impossible to analyze psychotics because they were not capable of forming a transference, Freud returned to the question in 1938, specifying that for therapy to be effective the analyst must find an ally in the patient's Ego. But the problem is that a psychotic Ego is not a good ally, and, as Freud might have said, cannot keep faith with such a contract.

Despite this pessimism, Freud (1915c) already showed an interest in psychosis taking it as an instinctual conflict dominated by narcissistic modalities, among which the mechanism of projection stands out. But projection implies splitting, and Freud only took to this concept later, in 1939, in relation to the mechanisms of the Ego necessary for psychosis. In his *An Outline of Psycho-Analysis* (1938) he writes:

> We have repeatedly had to insist on the fact that the ego owes its origin as well as the most important of its acquired characteristics to its relation to the real external world. We are thus prepared to assume that the Ego's pathological states, in which it most approximates once again to the id, are founded on a cessation or slackening of that relation to the external world. This tallies very well with what we learn from clinical experience – namely, that the precipitating cause of the outbreak of a psychosis is either that reality has became intolerably painful or that the instincts have become extraordinarily intensified. . . . The problem of psychoses would be simple and perspicuous if the ego's detachment from reality could be carried through completely. But that seems to happen only rarely or perhaps never. Even in a state so far removed from the reality of the external world as one of hallucinatory confusion,[2] one learns from patients after their recovery that at the time in some corner of their mind (as they put it) there was a normal person hidden, who, like a detached spectator, watched the hubbub of illness go past him.
>
> (Freud, 1938: 201–202)

In a quick clinical glance at a patient suffering delusions of jealousy, Freud continues:

> We may probably take it as being generally true that what occurs in all these cases is a psychical *split*. Two psychical attitudes have been formed

instead of a single one – one, the normal one, which takes account of reality, and another which under the influence of the instincts detaches the ego from reality, The two exist alongside of each other. The issue depends on their relative strength. If the second is or becomes the stronger, the necessary precondition for a psychosis is present. If the relation is reversed, then there is an apparent cure of the delusional disorder.

(Freud, 1938: 202)

These ideas set out late in Freud's life were put into clinical practice only many years after his death. From this viewpoint narcissism becomes a form of resistance the psychotic patient uses as an extreme means of opposing any change. A similar situation was described by Abraham (1919). He had detached himself from Freud on the question of manic–depressive psychosis and *dementia praecox* which he treated by the analytical method up until 1912, connecting the schizophrenic's psychosexual behavior with the auto-erotic and narcissistic stage.

Federn (1925) was another who put a distance between himself and Freud because he was struck by the fact that his psychotic patients wanted to establish a transference, and made an effort to involve both the sick and the healthy parts of their personality; this proved pivotal to the therapeutic approach.

Nearer our times, Rosenfeld (1987) went back to Freud's ideas, rightly noting that his description of the Ego splitting into a normal and a psychotic part is still fundamental to understanding the psychopathology of this disorder, although in Freud's day the main conflict in psychosis was believed to be between the Ego and reality, rather than between parts of the self (an *intrapsychic conflict*) which, as a secondary effect, created a secondary conflict between the Ego and reality.

Kleinian authors such as Segal, Rosenfeld and the early Bion always considered psychosis as expressing a death instinct working in the organization of narcissistic parts of the personality, acquiring the features of a *mafia* or *Nazi-like* organization designed to bring pain and death in outside reality but also in internal reality by attacking the libidinal parts of the self.

I have already expressed my reservations on this theory (Mancia, 1994) and in place of this death-dealing instincts model I prefer the reality of the negative personality. The latter expresses an early relational failure that prevented the mother – or both parents – from fulfilling the child's wishes, leaving him or her frustrated and disappointed, or with varying degrees of trauma that oblige the child to set up pathological defenses. Naturally we cannot overlook the child's internal equipment, largely innate, for dealing with this primary failure and the mental pain arising from separation from the object, which destabilizes the child's attachment system and his or her affective "tuning".

When I speak of internal equipment I am not referring to an instinct, but to a *mental function* depending on the child's genetic equipment, its affective, emotional and cognitive components being essential to deal with reality. When this equipment is inadequate, the object is particularly frustrating and traumatic, and the environment violent and destructive, the whole thing forms a trauma-object par excellence. The child can thus introject only evil, violent, persecutory internal objects, setting up pathological defenses which will include the creation of replacement internal objects that are simultaneously autarchic, violent and fragile – like Cervantes' delicate, glass-like *Licenciado Vidriera* – but anyway split from reality.

This whole process can be considered an extreme defense against fragmentation of the self, but at the same time a specific form of (pathological) adaptation to the pain and trauma of reality.

This tortuous path through the child's development will largely be stored in the implicit memory, where it will form part of the unrepressed unconscious that will contain the child's fantasies and pathological defenses. It will be the defenses that form the delusions that can burst out at any time if traumatic situations arise during adolescence or in adult life that mirror the specific affective and emotional features of the original trauma-object buried in the unrepressed unconscious.

Highly pertinent to any discussion of the psychopathology of narcissism is Meltzer's (1992) description in *The Claustrum* of the evidence of projective identification as an intruder in some narcissistic patients; it can work on the "internal mother", or on parts of this, subsequently fueling a masturbatory paradise where genital masturbation can serve various defensive functions. It can appear in the transference as insistent acting out. However, anal masturbation too can respond to the patient's omnipotent wish to deny separation and reality. Often even extreme greed can do this too.

Other ways of attacking the bond involve belittling the object (the analyst in the transference) and make patients feel they can manage alone, without the analyst's help. This enables them to defend themselves against the pain of dependence, and from the often catastrophic feelings related to the separation. Getting by on their own includes interpreting their own dreams in the session, attaching scant significance to the analyst's interpretations, and erasing from their memory everything that is said and done between them. All this points to massive defense against introjection.

The case of G.

The clinical case I should like to describe here falls under the heading of destructive narcissism, mentioned earlier. G. was a 40-year-old solicitor when he started analysis, with three sessions per week. For many years he has been living a completely split life. He appears elegant and polished, with nice refined manners; he is the typical professional, always dressed in grey double-breasted suits, who arrives punctually for his appointment and checks how long it lasts with the same precision. However, alongside this personality is another which prevents G. forming affective relations with anyone; it leaves him in a constant state of anger, particularly at women, and sexually impotent, while obliging him to masturbate compulsively and hide behind magic, pre-logical thought forms. He lives a life of almost complete affective solitude, broken only by occasional trips to France where he has a good command of the language. He sees France as a sort of magical paradise where he feels contained and protected and can masturbate to his heart's content, with the complicity of TV porn.

G. has a younger sister and describes himself as a victim of their parents. Mother was a "crude" woman, a bigoted Catholic and a centralizer; she considered money very important, had no culture whatsoever, and was an affective "blackmailer". She was obsessed with religion and terrified of sex. She was jealous of any relation her son set up and was convinced that all women were dishonest, or at any rate not worthy of her boy. Her ideal was to keep G. as an eternal child, stopping him growing up and filling him with fears about his sexual impulses. His father was completely under his mother's thumb, psychologically absent, possibly depressed but violent and authoritative towards his young son. His father was himself the victim of a brutish father who had frustrated and humiliated him, beating him and punishing him by making him sleep in the dog-kennel.

At our very first meeting G. tells me about his isolated, miserable life. He had just spent his Christmas holidays alone in France, keeping company with a bunch of homeless men in Grenoble, and eating with them in a canteen for the poor. Then he talked about his life, confused with that of his parents, since he had never managed to separate himself from them; in particular he spoke about his mother, for whom he had intensely ambivalent feelings. His confusion with his internal mother figure (as described in Meltzer's *Claustrum*, 1992) had always been central to his affective and emotional life. She naturally turned up immediately in the transference. At the very first session he described this dream:

He was prisoner in a church, and armed men patrolled the exits. But with the help of a friend he managed to evade their control and escape. Once out he climbs into a ski-lift but instead of taking him upwards it goes down towards the center of the earth.

The associations with this dream revolve around his main problem: he is too bound to his mother to go and live on his own in a house his parents would like to give him. Even his secretary depends on his mother, who hired her for him, and when she finishes her office duties she comes to work as his mother's maid. Through the secretary/maid his mother could keep an eye on every facet of his life, at work and at home. After telling me about this dream, G. started to show off a feature I was to see in every session for years to come: he was a very skilled patient, who certainly didn't need me to understand his dreams and fantasies. He would interpret it all himself, in long monologues that often bored me to tears, and blunted my ability to think.

He told me he had already been in therapy with two other analysts, but both had failed. One had not understood his problems, and this was enough to stop analysis. The other analyst was exasperated by the failure and stalemate, and had decided to give up trying. G. found it hard to conceal his triumph when he talked about the previous analyses, and occasionally gave a derisive sardonic smile, belittling the two analysts, but also warning me that the task ahead was hard and he would in any event remain at the helm.

For a long time in our sessions G. followed a behavioral stereotype: he usually brought one or more dreams and immediately started interpreting them himself, showing considerable experience and ability, but cutting me out completely and not allowing me to intervene in any way. He spoke of the events in his dreams and the affects involved as if they concerned someone else, without showing any willingness to take responsibility for his own parts in play.

In the first dream I described above, for instance, I tried to explain his confusion/intrusion and ensnarement with the mother/church, and how the father figure, represented by the guards, stopped him escaping from this identificatory situation. G. had no trouble accepting my suggestion and seeing the figure of the analyst in the friend who helped him escape from the church. When I then proposed that the situation he found outside the church (the ski-lift might well represent analysis) took him down into the mother/earth instead of up and away, he thoroughly agreed, but expressed himself in a way that gave me reason to think he was not absorbing what I was saying, and was not able to consider his parts and affects played out in the dream. From the outset this laid a heavy cloud over his possibilities of achieving change.

Another detail of G.'s transference, which aimed to make me feel impotent and often bored, was that he always had a "story" for whatever he described in the session; this repetitive narration was like a record that had got stuck, but was meant to make me stuck too, to paralyze my thoughts and stop me working constructively with him. At the end of each acting-narrative, G. would get up triumphantly from the couch and leave, apparently satisfied. At our next appointment, however, he was ready to complain that he had not been understood or helped, and had the feeling I was distracted. He complained that I was exactly like his earlier analysts: he could not entrust himself to me so all he could do was moan. These complaints were delivered in a monotonous, boring voice that sent me even further away, and increased our isolation from each other, the stagnation and dissatisfaction at our work as a couple, but which he reckoned justified his disgruntlement.

Our separations gave rise for a long time to furious masturbatory acting-out, in which he combined compulsiveness with anger and destructive feelings towards real people and towards me in the transference. The dominant fantasy at weekends was to attack me, to flatten my head (where I kept my thoughts, which bothered him), and hurt me in various ways. He had no friends to spend time with at weekends, because in his megalomaniac arrogance he found none who were up to his level. He would go alone to some cinema to watch violent, sadistic films, identifying with the personages. If he accepted an invitation it was from people in whom he projectively identified his bizarre, decidedly mad parts.

After two years of analysis, G. showed some interest in a woman we shall call C. who, however, lived with another man. His relation with C. was in fact purely one-sided and virtual, as it was based on his telephone calls to her; he could not bring himself to meet her physically because he was overcome with fear and anger that led him to want to attack and destroy her. His jealousy reached a peak during our separations when C. became the metaphor for his violent transferential feelings, object of his greed and oral destructiveness. He confessed one day after a weekend: "I want to gobble her up in one mouthful". But he also had perverse, sadistic fantasies: "I would like to be a crocodile and sadistically munch up the legs, arms, and genitals of a female colleague of mine".

It soon became evident in the transference how deep the split in his personality was, and this was what enabled him defensively not to break down and burst in a psychotic crisis. This meant he could consider analysis a safe place rather than a place for working through and transforming – a bathroom where he could evacuate his complaints and the learned do-it-yourself interpretations of his dreams.

He kept the most destructive parts of his self in an emblematic figure he himself called the *energumen* – a sort of inner demon, a person possessed. This figure was in reality the powerful "mafia-like" organization of his personality that kept a constant, dominating rein on his libidinal part, often involving it in perverse happenings. After an anxiety-ridden weekend, full of fear, anger, masturbations and a dangerous drive down the motorway, G. says he holds me responsible for the last session of the previous week, which had not worked, he tells me, and had made him the victim of a mad demon. Over the weekend he had dreamt the following:

He was with his weird alter-Ego and a boy they had to look after. A blood-thirsty robber with a hammer hanging from his belt passed by. The two of them, with the boy, set off for his mother's house, but soon realize there is also a band of bandits led by a Nazi skinhead, also aiming for that house, followed by the robber. G. and his alter-Ego are overcome with anxiety because they are all going to the same house. This was rapidly becoming the most dangerous place possible for them and for the child entrusted to their care.

G. associates his misfortunes over the weekend with the dream. He had thought about a French woman – another friend with whom he has an "idealized" relation, completely unrelated to reality. He had masturbated, but it had given him no pleasure, just to relieve his anger and tension. Then he had intended to sleep alone in his house, but he could not get the heating going, so in the middle of the night he had gone back to his parents' home, waking his mother. Then he had got angry with her and masturbated again.

I comment that the hammer-penis in his dream, hanging from the robber's belt, as an expression of the mad, violent part of his self that makes him impotent; his masturbation when he thought about the French girl released his separation anxiety and in a way expressed his excitement at his identification with his mother. I also stress that his internal "possessed" person heading a band of Nazi skinheads is dangerous, and creates a risky place for the couple (the two of us in analysis) and for the child (part of his self) in the house of an internal mother where his mad parts seem trapped. As usual G. appreciates my interpretation but carries on as if the dream itself and the work done on it had nothing to do with him.

After another weekend, G. starts the session by talking about C., who seems affectionate and willing to be with him. But he was frightened, and felt blocked and paralyzed, not just sexually, but also about being close to her, and touching or kissing her. He then describes a dream:

He is in a car with a beautiful woman who provokes him by showing off her legs. He goes up with her into her house, but the girl turns into an ugly woman. She comes up to him and he shows her his tongue split in two, that he is holding in one hand, while another tongue is growing in his mouth. He realizes that the cut tongue in his hand has three holes in it.

G. associates the tongue with love, kisses and other pleasurable things he could do with his tongue. But then he tells me of his terrible fear about being with women. He associates the three holes with his three sessions weekly, and admits that analysis has at least partially enabled him to grasp the nature of his fears, but for the first time he also mentions his father who threatens him, and his castration anxiety lived in the dream like in real life.

The most effective defense against these anxieties is for his mad destructive part to debase me in analysis and C. in reality. These strategies are especially evident in the periods of separation when his intolerant part, identified with the demon, takes over and threatens his libidinal part which would like to have friendly relations with me and with C. In this period, he has a dream:

> He is in a big hotel with a group of people threatened by a kidnapper. Helped by a Spanish hostess, he goes to the lift which takes him up to a leafy paradise of a terrace. But two well-dressed killers come over and shoot him in the testicles, blasting them off.

As usual G. interprets the dream by himself, noting the risk of being kidnapped by his possessed person, acknowledging the help from the Spanish girl – which presumably refers to me on account of my surname – but also the danger, once he had reached "paradise" on the terrace (which clearly refers to his masturbation) of losing his virility.

For a series of sessions, over a long period, I felt pitifully powerless to penetrate his armor and help him, as G. projected his own impotence and inability to accept help. He had a dream in one orgy of masturbation which gave him no pleasure but merely showed to himself and me that analysis was no use:

> There was Chirac, an important president but who is a bit mad and destructive [associating the atomic bomb tested with the French President's approval] and Patrizia [a crazy drug-addict friend of his] who is criticizing Chirac, saying he is mad and impotent and has a daughter with mental problems.

This dream gave me an opportunity to explain to G. the perverse loop in which his mind, dominated by the "inner demon", had locked our relation, investing me/Chirac with his destructive folly and impotence, but then identifying with Patrizia who attacks me/Chirac for the impotence and projected folly; this gave him the justification – in his own eyes – for the complaints and disappointment and the utter boredom he aroused in the session.

As often happened, G. fully agreed with my interpretation, but he saw it from outside, as it were, as if the inner demon who we had discussed, and his projective identifications, belonged to another person – the topic of a purely academic discussion. He could not by any measure introject my words and realize he was responsible for them. This was his most disarming defense: his compulsive repetition fueled his negative transference and cancelled out all my attempts to understand and help him. I was transformed into an object into which he could evacuate his impotence and despair.

In the countertransference I felt exactly like G. unconsciously wanted me to feel: frustrated and powerless, invaded by his dissatisfied observations, thoroughly bored and obliged to contain the massive projective identifications of his frustrated and impotent parts, without being able to transform them. G.'s impotence was in fact the expression of a death-dealing part of his self which even attacked his penis, causing him a case of castration anxiety. Like in this dream:

> G. is in a dark, muddy street. From a lighted window a cage is tossed down into the street, and there is a dead bird in it. He goes to look at the cage and finds that part of it is like a trap, that had caught and cut one of the bird's feet.

He explains that the cage is his deadly internal part that has killed the bird and is therefore the cause of his impotence. I comment that even if it comes from a well-lit house/analysis the cage might represent his internal mother, who ensnares and castrates him, with whom his death-dealing part that makes his penis die seems to be identified. But the dream also shows a sharp-edged father-trap, the part of the mother-cage that castrates him. G. returns to the main theme of his difficulties separating himself from his mother and the heartfelt intolerance of his "possessed" part which pushes him to act during the separations (the dangerous fast driving, his masturbatory flight to France).

During analysis it became evident that G.'s narcissistic "inner demon" was a violent, perverse mafia-type organization in which his parents were the prime "godfathers": his mother in particular – seductive and intrusive but castrating and a pious humbug – and his weak father, totally at the service of his wife's most sadistic and punitive parts. G. recalled his father beating him brutally as a child, trying to transfer onto him the terror and violence – which he played out on his dog too – that he as a child had suffered from his own father. This internal situation had set up a conflict that left G. like a young lad at the mafia's beck and call especially when, during our separations, his libidinal part felt the lack of the analyst's support. Then he would use the phone to appeal for help. He had only to hear my voice to calm down and rest the negative siren-songs of his internal propaganda, which diminished the analyst and analysis, laying the blame on them for his malaise and anxiety.

In a dramatic dream in the fifth year of analysis, *G. is anxiously watching a young Englishman having intercourse with his mother. But the Yugoslav police arrive and stop him, separating the lovers.* G. associates the Yugoslav police's sadism during the Balkan conflicts, and says the young Englishman is himself, in an incestuous relation. But incest is severely prohibited, and punished by the Yugoslav police. Evidently, from this dream and from work we had done in that period, G. was the victim of an internal organization where his mother played a dominant role, erotically seducing him while at the same time obliging him to vilify and attack the object of his desire. It was as if G. saw a mother figure in every woman, stimulating his desire but at the same time punishing him with fear, attacking his penis which lost its sensitivity, and striking at his testicles (like in that earlier dream). This intrapsychic conflict was like a war causing psychotic anxiety that annihilated his libidinal part, urging him to compulsive masturbation.

On the phone the woman he claimed he was in love with aroused tender, affectionate feelings. But as soon as he became close to her physically, he humiliated her and scorned her, because he was tormented by an internal propaganda that told him she was a whore to be chased away, treated sadistically or destroyed.

These anxious conflicts and actings were always followed by a monotonous narration of what had happened, and complaints that analysis was not helping, and the analyst could never understand his drama, or at any rate was no use to him. The complaint was laced with hatred and anger aimed at anesthetizing the session and boring me,[3] and he would leave my rooms triumphant but increasingly desperate.

This was a typical session, especially on Mondays. Generally, even if the session had gone differently and had been useful, and I had managed to make him understand that his "inner demon" was using wicked propaganda against his libidinal self and against me, G. still could not introject, and regularly "erased" all the work achieved. Once he had left my room, he systematically forgot the interpretations I had offered him but then at the next session he would fret about his bad memory.

At one Monday appointment he told me that he had found the previous session very useful, but could not remember anything we had said. Then he had tried to reach C. but her fiancé FC had replied angrily, telling him he was the one who called the shots in the relation with FC, then described a dream:

> *He is with a colleague, R. [who really is a good-for-nothing] who becomes a good lad, rolling up his sleeves in a sincere effort to help his poor parents, who have gone bankrupt. In the dream R.'s sister is also there; she is cute and G. starts to make advances. FC also turns up but G. kicks him out.*

Having told me about it, G. says he is satisfied with the dream, which he considers very positive, because finally R., which is a part of him – that arrogant, restless person he is in reality – has become a good fellow who even helps his parents. I comment his usual habit of interpreting his dreams on his own, to cut me out, and to underline the change in R. which, however, does not sound authentic to me. I tell him that the dream defensively reverses our roles: his poor parents – the analyst in the transference – are incompetent and fail, while he turns up to save them.

This causes G. to burst out in sardonic laughter, admitting that I am probably right. Then he adds that in the dream he himself had chased out FC, who represents his arrogant inner demon. I point out that his omnipotent, megalomaniac part had defensively overturned the roles in this case too, with FC actually showing him the door and making him jealous. G. replies immediately that that was exactly what had happened: yesterday FC had kicked him out and made him angry and jealous.

G. was heavily influenced by "magic". When he was on holiday in France this was how he acted things out: everything was just fine and he was always in a good mood, which changed for the worse as soon as he passed the border into Italy. In his home town, or Milan, if he saw a car with French number plates he felt reassured and this would have a positive influence on our session. His decisions whether or not do things were all based on outside signs, which he believed were vitally important.

One day he turned up for his appointment in a state of severe anxiety. He had just bought a used car, which was in excellent condition, but had been owned by a funeral parlor director. He knew who was selling the car, but had not paid too much attention. However, as soon as he had signed the contract, his beautiful, perfect car had immediately turned into a "hearse", a funeral vehicle that could transport only death. With his head full of these worries he had only just managed to avoid a serious accident on the motorway, in which he could really have died. For many days after that, he spent time his regretting his mistake and projectively identified his deadly part in the car and its previous owner, as a metaphor in the transference of his death-dealing analysis and the analyst.

* * *

In analysis in subsequent years he continuously oscillated between moments of utmost anxiety when his negative, persecutory internal propaganda got the best of him, and moments when he showed confidence in analysis and good relations with C., even though this relationship remained on the "virtual" level, and was conducted purely by telephone.

G. carried on using analysis as a safety outlet, or like a toilet bowl into which he could evacuate his anxieties, more than a place for learning and change. His good moments when work went well alternated with periods when he lost confidence and became destructive about our work, his own profession and the relation with C. The oscillations in analysis and the internal splitting that explained them seem to be depicted well in this dream: *He is in the kitchen in his childhood home. There is an abandoned hen with a broken leg, but there are also two little dogs which seem well looked after.* The three animals could be traced back to three sessions when he felt I had not always cared for him properly. G. immediately recognized that the hen and the dogs represented his various parts and his different reactions during our sessions.

Another interesting feature of G.'s analytical path was the sometimes striking contrast between the quality of the dreams he recounted in our sessions and the feelings he lived with me in the transference and in outside reality. These dreams, to borrow from Quinodoz (2001), *do not* turn the page. In his book entitled *Dreams that Turn over a Page: Paradoxical Dreams in Psychoanalysis*, Quinodoz discusses paradoxical situations that can arise in analysis. For instance, some dreams may have a manifest regressive content that often alarms the patient and contrasts with the progress made through the transference. However, thorough analysis may suggest that the regressive content is linked to a change in the psychic processes governing the transference. The regressive dream can help retrospectively clear up the nature of the change and set the process of working through in motion again.

It is as if the patient had reached a good level of working through and a good relation with the analyst, and finally manages to express in the dream his oldest suffering parts that until then had eluded representation. These parts, possibly connected to an unrepressed unconscious, therefore dating back to very early, presymbolic and preverbal, traumatic experiences and defenses, can finally be rendered symbolically through the figures in the dream, and reach a certain level of thought and verbal expression.

The case of G. was exactly the opposite. Most of his dreams showed considerable gains in insight for a long period. They represented his mafia-like, crazy, criminal parts of the self, but there was nevertheless a healthy part that managed to control and manage them and render them harmless. For instance, in one of these dreams:

> G. is with a slightly mad long-haired friend, in a fenced area where their freedom is limited. He manages, however, to cut a hole in the fence, and he and the hairy friend get out.

G. recognizes the hairy character as his "inner demon" that ensnares and limits the freedom of his healthier part. He has no problem acknowledging that his healthy part is strong enough to break out through the fence of his folly to regain full freedom. But he is untouched by the message of the dream and in reality does not want freedom. He feels this part of the dream does not belong to him.

In another more recent dream:

He is with his buddy B., an old school mate, who is not particularly clever but did well at school, in his life and with women! A menacing black animal approaches them. The friend is carrying a rifle and keeps the black beast at a distance so it is not a real threat.

Once again G. recognizes that his companion represents his mature part, which enjoys good relations with other people, especially women; he has no trouble acknowledging that this part can manage his internal persecution, in the form of the black beast. But he remains untouched by the dream, as if it were not his, and keeps up his complaints about the "inner demon" who threatens him and makes him so anxious. He admits that it might be possible to transform his folly and distress, but will not take the dreams into consideration because they would put excessive responsibility on him, asking too much.

In his everyday life, outside the session, he goes back to being prey to his mafia-like organization as if he had never had the dream and we had not worked on it. The black beast immediately takes charge of his mind and he is once more trapped by paralyzing fear that stops him relating normally to the world and its women, and, of course, to me. Back in his home town he displays his madness by identifying with outlandish, perverse people. There is no trace of his healthy, responsible part. At subsequent encounters, he complains that his dreams seem to have said one thing, but he is living just the opposite. The dream is therefore depicting some progress in analysis but his perverse part is denying it in the transference. Unlike Quinodoz's dreams that turn the page, G.'s dreams seem *not* to turn it. They delude the analyst the patient's healthy part that they can achieve a transformation, and gain freedom that the patient cannot – or does not want to – reach.

When G. notes the contrast between his dreams that say one thing and his transference and life something completely different, he often gives himself away with that sardonic smile as if the progressive dreams brought to analysis were one way of pretending to fulfill my expectations of change; but at the same time they enable him to remain at a standstill while continuing to use analysis as a safety outlet or place for evacuation, rather than as a cognitive experience and an opportunity for real change.

Throughout many sessions G. obsessively grilled himself on whether to act as advocate for his internal terrorist or defender of our relation. A solution was suggested in two dreams from that period: *in one he is a lawyer defending a mafia criminal. In another he loses the defense documents for a Milanese couple.* His choice is clear: he wants to defend his sick part (the mafia boss), since he is rather fond of him, but can't be too bothered about the two of us in Milan, and in fact mislays the trial papers (by forgetting all the interpretations that might help him take responsibility for his disturbed parts).

He often insists firmly that analysis cannot work for him. In his eyes this justifies his complaints, that make me so bored I lose my motivation and feel powerless to help him. This perverse circle comes through in a dream in which *he is in church and his mother is officiating, giving him little bits of host that he, however, refuses.* This was a period when G. was making poor use of analysis and continually blamed me for it. After several months of work on his difficulties taking responsibility for the megalomaniac, omnipotent parts of his personality, G. described another dream in which *he killed Prime Minister Berlusconi with five pistol shots to the head.* He recognizes Berlusconi as his dishonest, omnipotent, megalomaniac part, that the healthy part is out to kill. He is surprised that the dream says something that does not match his own reality, as he had always considered Berlusconi someone to envy and imitate, with his overbearing, arrogant and all-powerful style (apart from the fact that he is his mother's idol). This was why he had voted for him at the last election. But he has to admit that something about Berlusconi is not right, just like his own mind is not working properly, making him fearful and unable to establish a decent relation with a woman.

Another dream, a few days later, offers an opportunity to look closer at his intrapsychic dynamics and their bonds with his perverse parts:

> There is this strange, long-haired, scruffy type who wants to "pretend". He is gesticulating wildly, trying to convince his supervisor that he is a poor fellow who never has any luck with women, but the truth is that he gets on famously with the girls, and knows all their erogenous zones. But he wants to trick the supervisor so as to make sure he survives and doesn't go mad.

His associations take him back to Berlusconi as an internal object that tells lies, tricks other people, is unreliable and wants to look different from what he really is: a poor scruffy fake who has to lie to survive and escape madness, but who in reality knows how to please women, and how to turn them on. However, he prefers fooling the supervisor/analyst so as not to have to take responsibility for the work done in analysis, and the growth of his healthy part.

A dream some days later brings us to the question of the relations between sexuality and the narcissistic parts of G.'s personality:

> In my mother's house at B., with relatives, I am in the bedroom next to my mother's with a beautiful nude woman. I touch her sex and am on the point of penetration when someone calls and stops us going any further. Then there is a woman with her who measures my penis and says it's all right – it's just what's needed for pleasing a woman.

"It was a nice dream," says G., "but it frightens me and I can't consider it mine." G. is still not able to transform his internal mother, who condemns all women, and is frightened of them. They excite him but he feels they are too much of a danger. This causes conflict between libidinal parts, smoothed over by analysis, that want to open up again to his genital sexuality and the narcissistic parts confused with his internal mother and her prohibitions, that set up fear and anxiety around his genitality.

The internal mother's decisive role in the organization of G.'s narcissistic part, prohibiting love and sexuality and relegating them to an icy "dungeon", is clear from this dramatic dream a few days after the previous one:

> G. had been let down by a woman and had returned to his parents' home. He climbs into their double bed and is horrified to see first an arm, then his mother's whole body, frozen solid as if hibernated. He flees, disgusted.

I suggest to G. the image of a newborn baby who would be disgusted at being held by a mother whose arms and body were cold, "hibernated", incapable of warmth and affection. The imagery in the dream reflects the emotions of an old traumatic experience, which G. cannot actually remember but which has colored his relations with women, and his fear of physical contact with them. This phantom has followed him and he cannot manage to transform it, as suggested in this further dream:

> I am in my mother's house at B. and a ghost is chasing me. I have a small pistol and the ghost is within range, but I dither and he fades away.

He associates the ghost with his internal "inner demon" who has governed his relational and affective life, but also with his inability to take responsibility for changing, his dithering around that leaves him surviving in precarious equilibrium where he can only just keep his most disturbed parts under control without going crazy.

The following dream illustrates clearly the conflict between these parts of the self that hole him up in the maternal dungeon while at the same time exciting him so he becomes a voyeur, but risk killing off his libidinal parts:

> I am trapped in a cathedral and tied up with strips of foam. There is a nude woman inside the cathedral, closed in a transparent plastic bag but she has no air in the bag and risks dying.

G. recalled the first dream he brought to analysis, when he was trapped in a church similar to the cathedral of this dream. He says that C. has been looking for him but he is afraid of her. He comments that the "foam" in the dream reminds him of soured milk that traps you rather than nourishing you and helping you grow. The nude woman in the transparent bag excites his voyeurism, but protects him from physical contact, which would be dangerous. The woman, who risks suffocating, represents his death-dealing internal object that is unable to give pleasure.

Some final considerations

I have looked through the historical/critical literature on the topic of narcissism, focusing particularly on Freud's ideas and the far-reaching changes brought about by Melanie Klein and the last generation of her followers, most of whom are no longer with us.

Freud's relations with narcissism date from his classic work of 1914 and carry on through the main stages marked by *Mourning and Melancholia* (1915d) and *Beyond the Pleasure Principle* (1920). I have discussed the major shift presented in *The Ego and the Id* (1922), in which the theory of the absorption of the Ego-ideal into the Super-Ego influenced not only Freud's theory of the mind but also the whole approach of clinical psychoanalysis. The removal of the Ego-ideal from the horizon and the importance acquired by the Super-Ego, with its sadistic, punitive and persecutory features, helped the death instinct take root in psychoanalytical thinking, and made it easier to fit it into Klein's model of the mind, with its seeds of the relational model.

As this model gained ground the concept of narcissism changed radically. It no longer expressed an objectless relation but more a specific object relation, making massive use of splitting and projective identification, denial and idealization. It was Rosenfeld who compared the narcissistic personality to a mafia-like grouping or a Nazi-fascist regime that obliged the Ego to defend itself by setting up artificial substitution objects; these are delusional in the sense that they take no account of reality and their task is merely to compensate the affective lack, and emotional coldness (Resnik, 1999) produced by a mother incapable of *rêverie*. This relational failure reflected traumatic experiences in the child's earliest and most significant relations.

This organization becomes the center-pin of the *negative personality*, with its envy, competitivity, delusional jealousy, violence, cruelty and sadism, omnipotence, arrogance, anxiety, ignorance, dishonesty and refusal of the normal rules of civil living. One possible cause lies in the child's earliest traumatic experiences, tucked away in the implicit memory, where they form an unrepressed, unconscious nucleus of the self that influences the person's emotional, cognitive and sexual life even as an adult. Separation, starting from weaning, is pivotal in this process.

When the negative personality forms the transference it can cause negative therapeutic reactions that cast light on the most destructive aspects of the patient's narcissistic organization. The patient will try to boycott the analyst by refusing his or her help, emptying and boring the analyst, with sadistic attempts to chase him or her out of the setting and goading the analyst to act. The patient will use the analyst as a container for the most destructive, provocative, jealous and envious parts of his or her personality, with the aim of erasing the analyst's attempts at breaking down the patient's defenses.

One consequence of the negative therapeutic reaction is that the patient gives scant credibility to even the most progressive dreams. The patient neglects them or forgets them, as they cast spanners into the works of his or her narcissistic defense system, which is fueled solely by diminishing the analyst's work and refusing any introjection of the positive parts of the self.

I referred earlier to a type of narcissism trapped in a "dungeon" consisting of the internal mother whose perverse characteristics are those the patient identifies with. The patient's defenses against dis-identification and separation from this mother figure are the main obstacle on the analytical path, impeding the transformation the patient might otherwise achieve.

The father too may have an important part in the separation; originally absent and inadequate he may, with the introjection of the analyst, ease the painful work of separation and help the patient make significant changes in his or her self.

I have described here part of the long analytical road of a borderline patient with psychotic parts of the personality, obliging him to split the self, which housed a serious professional person but also an autistic part that forced him into isolation and made it impossible for him to make close affective or sexual contact with a woman.

A series of dreams during this long analysis, and the features of his transference, led us to recognize that this patient's personality contained a malignant narcissistic organization that he himself identified as an "inner demon", like a mafia band that dominated his healthy part and forced him to stoop to repeated compromises.

His dominant internal objects were the omnipotent, intrusive, sex-phobic, superstitious, ignorant, bigoted and castrating mother, and a weak but violent father, totally at the beck and call of his wife. G. was the pathetic lad whose libidinal part and penis were attacked by the mafia, forcing him into isolation, impotence and masturbation.

In the transference the internal "inner demon" stopped him listening to the analyst's interpretations and pushed him to interpret his dreams on his own, communicating in the sessions in long monotonous monologues, whose aim was to blunt and anesthetize the encounter, making any attempt at introjection hopeless.

During these years of analysis evidence surfaced, especially from dreams, that his narcissistic organization was closed inside a *maternal dungeon*, so every real woman held hidden inside her a mother figure that invited him but repulsed him, seduced him but punished him, excited him but frightened him, making him sexually impotent but fueling at the same time his imaginary but deathly masturbatory paradise.

One very interesting clinical feature of this patient was his dreams that did *not* turn a page. This is a play on the title of Quinodoz's (2001) book in which he described dreams that are apparently regressive in relation to progress in the transference. He sees these as expressing progress nevertheless, as the patient is able to represent old emotions and defenses that he could not bring up to the surface until then.

G.'s dreams described here never did actually manage to turn the page because they had exactly the opposite characteristics: they were very progressive, in marked contrast with the regression and failure to learn in the transference. Unlike the dreams Quinodoz describes, these lent themselves to interpretation as expressing the patient's seductive desire to satisfy the analyst's therapeutic wishes, more than providing a basis for learning. G. himself remained skeptical about the message contained in these "progressive" dreams, and tended not to believe the truths they offered. This enabled him to keep the analysis at a standstill and to live it as a safety valve for his psychotic anxiety and fear of going mad, or often merely as a pot into which he could evacuate his complaints, rather than an emotional and cognitive experience to achieve transformation.

8

Being with the patient:
four clinical cases

In this chapter I want to describe my way of being with a patient, my style of listening, the attention I pay to the transference and countertransference. My clinical work is inevitably influenced by the theoretical model I have built up in long years of analytical experience and work in other disciplines (neurosciences, philosophy, musicology) which have all contributed to my professional training.

The discovery of implicit memory and its relations with the early unrepressed unconscious, and with a patient's childhood traumas, has had a far-reaching impact on my attitude to the analytical relationship, and the quality of how I listen to the "formal" and "musical" aspects of what patients are communicating. It has also influenced my way of speaking to them, offering comments, recalling and interpreting whatever has been brought into the analysis.

I have always paid special attention to dreams, which are the patient's only means of symbolically representing presymbolic experiences, and giving figurative form to emotional situations to compensate the lack of representation of the unrepressed unconscious.

The brief *tranches* of the analysis of the four clinical cases I have selected here offer significant insight into the emotions underlying these encounters and how they can achieve transformations of the patient's personality, changing their attitude towards me in the analytic relation.

Luisa

Luisa is in her fifties, the next-to-last of five children.[1] She is suffering from breast cancer, which had been operated on years earlier. Luisa had already been in analysis with a colleague, but was not satisfied, and wanted another consultation. Her state of depressive anxiety and fears about dying disrupted even her family relationships. During analysis (four sessions a week) she received various cycles of chemotherapy.

Her transference was marked from the start by her strange way of speaking. Her language was slow, fragmented, quiet, and broken by long silences. She created an atmosphere of waiting for her words and made me uneasy but at the same time bored at the monotonous tone of voice and the feeling of distance in her language. This form of expression conveyed a continuous, despairing lament, apparently impossible to work through.

Her concern for her health – justified as it happened – concealed resentment at a fate that had destined her to represent suffering and anxiety at leaving the world. But she saw this fate as representing her mother and in the transference she poured out her anger and resentment onto me for that inadequate mother who was unfair to her, who showed love only for her brother, and who had made her feel like a poor little Cinderella, cast aside and misunderstood; she was wretched, sick and full of hard feelings.

She also expressed anger and resentment towards her husband. He did not do enough for her, had too few interests and was boring, didn't understand her and expected sexual performances that she felt were absolutely beyond her. The husband, of course, was the object onto which she shifted her child-part's dissatisfaction and resentment at her mother, who she felt was unable to look after her, and naturally onto me in the transference.

It was my task to interpret these negative aspects of the transference that invaded our relation, and the deeper significance of her complaints and boredom. In the early phases of analysis, this attitude was her way of keeping me at a distance, reflecting her mistrust and fear about this unknown primary relational object that she felt was not welcoming, and unreliable. Subsequently the complaining became the channel through which Luisa transmitted her anger and discontent to me in the form of a massive projective identification that obliged me to contain her with patience, silence, and short remarks intended to make her understand the underlying significance of her complaints and the leaden atmosphere they created in the session.

Work on this dimension of the transference made it possible to grasp some facets of her unrepressed unconscious, linked to her earliest relations with her inadequate and frustrating mother. These experiences, emotionally relived in the transference but beyond actual recollection, explained her fantasies and feelings in the *hic et nunc* of the session, and her defenses consisting of splitting and intense projective identification. For a long time the resentment and attacks obliging me to provide containment, and my interpretations, were how we carried on together. We did tackle the problem of sexuality, and how she felt the penis was not a gratifying object – possibly the expression of an internal father who could not help his child detach her identity from her mother, and foster a positive identification with him.

Despite this constant, patient work, sometimes obstacled by her negative transference and problems with her illness, I felt we were still not getting down to the deepest parts of her unconscious. Our analysis had not yet reached the oldest events in her highly dysfunctional relation with her mother which could quite likely explain – beyond the memory – the reasons for her feelings in the transference: anxiety, hate, mistrust, anger and resentment.

Several years of analysis were needed to transform this nucleus of the patient's personality. This did, however, help her reach back to her oldest unconscious emotions, which came to light in some dreams. Work on these dreams suggested some "reconstructive" hypotheses which helped Luisa relive emotionally some of the events she had never even thought about, and rewrite, as it were, her early relational history. It was work on dreams that made it possible for her to think about the possibility of ending analysis. Before this came about just mentioning the possibility – which surfaced all the same in some of her dreams – created an intense negative therapeutic reaction.

Some of the dreams described here helped her achieve significant transformations during the course of analysis. In one of them, *Luisa is lying on the couch talking, while I am behind a curtain. But when the curtain is drawn back, I am no longer there.* After listening to the dream, I wondered whether I was momentarily absent, or had never been close to my patient at all. On the level of the transference the question seemed justified. I answered the first point by recalling that in fact she was at times so complaining and boring that I dreamt of going out into the open air to lighten the atmosphere of our meetings. So I offered her an interpretation in the transference (a constructive one linked to the here and now).

The second part of my question took me back to Luisa's childhood, her loneliness, her despair at feeling her mother was incapable of affection and reverie, perhaps depressed and distant. I therefore offered her an interpretation in the shape of a reconstructive hypothesis relating to an absent mother, too busy with her other children to cope with her too, who left her alone and angry, resentful at not being properly loved and nourished. I also proposed the image of her as a newborn who did not feel contained physically by her mother, who kept her at a distance, and who never gave her the warm, reassuring feeling of contact. Luisa did not reply.

The next day, however, she brought this dream:

> *Luisa is at the computer with her husband, but there is a heavy rug over the keyboard that stops her feeling the keys. She tries to make the rug lighter but it is still not possible to feel the keyboard.*

146

Her associations relate to her real problems with her husband, who she feels is distant, and her worry that I may get fed up with her complaints and abandon her. This enabled me to link the dream to a "sensory" fantasy: that of not feeling mother/me emotionally close and physically in contact with her, therefore of not feeling firmly contained, and risking being left alone in her despair.

Luisa tells me about a painful separation from a woman friend, that has created a distance between them. Then, after a lengthy silence, she says: "I had a catastrophic fantasy – I wondered how far you would be willing to stay close to me if things got really bad." She was clearly referring to her tumor which in the mean time had become metastatic.

The fear of being abandoned and of dying activated very regressive defenses in Luisa. In a nightmarish dream two days after the previous session, *she feels transformed into a sort of pre-human vegetable with branches on her head instead of hair*. Chemotherapy in that period had made her lose her hair and she used to wear a wig, which she felt was an attack on her identity. At the same time, the progression of the cancer had accentuated her anxieties of death with fantasies of disappearing as a human being. However, I suggested that the dream might refer to much older experiences, tucked away in her implicit memory, and might represent a transformation of her self into a cold, insensitive vegetable, with branches on her head, emotions without thoughts, as a form of defense against an unthinkable pain, the product of a relation with a mother she felt was not human, without reverie, cold and distant.

The next day the patient opened the session in an unusually lively voice, telling me about yet another dream:

> There are lots of little beads on a table, including some in a beautiful periwinkle color. They all belonged to my mother, but I was uneasy. I was worried that my mother might give fewer, plainer beads to me than to the other children, or that she might not give me all the beads I wanted.

No sooner had she described the dream than her voice became suddenly dark, complaining and monotonous. She started to talk in a resentful, hostile tone, accusing her family and her mother in particular of being mad. I linked the dream to the previous sessions and her resentment, conveyed in her usual monotonous, complaining tone of voice, to her dissatisfaction as a child for a mother – represented by the analyst – who has a breast/beads of value but keeps them for her brothers and sisters and is in any case not willing to give her as many as she wants, leaving her dissatisfied and frustrated.

I also asked her whether she had realized that she changed her tone of voice; from lively and bright it had become complaining and depressed. She said:

You are quite right in noting how I am communicating with you today. The fact is that I have only today become aware of using two languages: the older, more maternal one, which is lost in my memory. That is the one I use here, which you have picked up. You could call it my mother-tongue. Then I have another, very different language, that I use outside. But what a struggle it is to translate from one language to another!

A few days later a metaphor of the transformation in progress in our relation comes to light: Luisa dreams that *she is at table playing chess with a man. Both are meditating at length before making their moves. But the moves were intended to find the best way of giving nourishment.* The dream shows not only competitivity but also reflection and play, a metaphor of the lighter mood gradually replacing the previously leaden atmosphere, enabling her to accept my nourishment.

But after a few days the sad complaining little girl is back, in this dream: *There is a tree that looks like the face of a person complaining. She can't understand what is being said but the tone and the atmosphere that face creates suggest suffering.* Luisa complains about having to live with a depressed husband with no interests, so different from me who she sees as a person with plenty of interests. Then she says: "Before I met you I never realized what meaning could be put into the way I communicated."

She then told me of another dream: *she is picking pansies with one of her pupils. They scrabble around together in a child's play-chest and find a woman's trinkets – a necklace, a bracelet.* She says the pansies created an aura of nostalgia and remembers that at the weekend she had gone to the florist and admired a lovely bunch of forget-me-nots. She wanted to buy it but it was already sold!

These happy moments in our relation were interrupted by the sad news that her cancer had again progressed. In one of our last sessions before the summer holidays, Luisa comes to my consulting room with a funereal expression and says nothing. She feels desperate and then complains about her destiny, of the disease that can kill her, and lastly of the void she feels inside herself and of the uselessness of our work since her life is ending. I comment that not only the relapse of the illness, but also our approaching summer separation, make her feel like a poor little girl without a mother/analyst inside her to contain her despair and her fear of dying. The void inside her is for an absent internal mother/analyst who leaves her on her own with the illness that threatens her with death. She interrupts me saying:

It's true, you have described my mother. I can't actually remember, but your words have brought to mind the image of a woman who was never content with anything, always complaining, who had a hard life, just like my own mother, with lots of children . . .! But how can I transform this nucleus we are talking about now? It's so different from what animates my relations in real life outside!

In the following months, Luisa had sometimes to be absent for a couple of weeks during chemotherapy. In this period her elderly mother died, leaving a will in favor of her brother, to the disadvantage of both Luisa and her sister.

When she comes back, she starts off by saying she is pleased because she has tolerated the chemotherapy well, even though she could not attend our sessions. But then she complains about her unfair mother and also her doctor, who has not been up to her expectations. She then tells me this dream: *I am lying in a bed and it is as if I were double. I try to reconstruct myself but with some very primitive materials.* She says:

I am ashamed to say that I feel no grief about my mother's death – on the contrary, I am glad. There is a hatred inside me that I cannot control, a bad part that invades and neutralizes my good part which must still exist.

I hint at the possibility that the little girl who hates is a victim of a very early experience which has created this feeling and has fueled this bad part, perhaps as a response to her relation with a mother who could not contain her, who was inadequate and did not satisfy her needs. She says:

As far as I can remember, I found my mother's body repulsive. It was repellent. It made disgusting noises and I was ashamed for her. I hated touching her skin. I remember that my younger sister, as a newborn baby, had a serious genital rash. My mother often used to say that babies disgusted her. Perhaps she was tired of all these children.

I now link these fantasies with the experiences of herself as a tiny baby who does not feel contained by a mother whose skin produces feelings of disgust and repulses her – a baby who had to live with a maternal body full of vulgar noises which fed in her a resentful, bad part that felt hatred for her mother, is glad at her death and fears she cannot transform these feelings. However, I remind her that the dream speaks of a "reconstruction" that she, on the analyst's couch, wants to do, even though with "primitive materials". I point out that these materials might represent the earliest emotions linked to the sensory experiences of her contact with her mother's body. I also ask her to note the transformation implicit in the dream related to the possibility of reconstruction of an internal mother different from the real one who was the cause of such contempt, resentment and anger.

Carla

Carla is about 35 years old, very small and pretty, like a little girl who has never grown up. She came to my consulting room one day with a suffering, misgiving, complaining, discontented air, to tell me she does not need me, but she doesn't want to upset her sister who has advised her to "do an analysis". For a long time her four times a week sessions were dominated by silence, interrupted by intermittent complaints. At the end of the session, Carla would get up, without saying goodbye, run to the door and flee like a little defenseless, persecuted animal.

Carla had had a very painful childhood; her father had committed suicide, after disappearing one day from home and never coming back. Her mother could not bear up under this sudden painful bereavement and had very shortly married her husband's brother, the patient's uncle.

In the transference Carla feels terror at being alone, and cannot draw close to me or depend on me. She denies my presence and the meaning of our encounters. Accepting my presence and her dependence on me would mean recognizing affection and the pain of having to separate. As a result, Carla denies every affect, above in all our separations for the weekend.

Another dimension of Carla's transference already comes out when she runs over to the couch and huddles up in her fur coat, like a little fetus, disappearing from sight. Then she starts to talk in a complaining, monotonous, weak voice which gradually becomes weaker and weaker, less and less comprehensible, until I cannot even hear her. Nevertheless, I can still detect the two tones that convey her despair and fill the space between us with impotence and suffering. The transference then becomes a subtle provocation, a demand for all my attention. I have to really tune in my hearing to sharpen my perception.

In countertransference terms I "feel" Carla's lament and the qualities of her voice as the expression of her desire to get inside me so that I can contain her and take on her pain. But when my attention is at its peak, her voice starts to fade away, disappearing and leaving me on my own. The vanished voice does not return and Carla gets up from the couch. Without looking at me, she disappears from the room.

Several dreams have helped us reconstruct the painful story of her childhood and understand the forms of her transference. In one dream, *Carla is in a Naples slum with a person who is emotionally absent and taciturn, who offers her milk, but she doesn't like milk.* In reflecting on her dream, Carla speaks about how fed up she is at having to come to analysis, the humiliation she feels and the anxiety about her husband who loves her. "It would be better if he didn't love me," she says, "then I would suffer less if I left him". I point out that a part of her unconsciously appreciates the good milk I offer her, but the apprehensive, abandoned little girl inside her is afraid of depending on and being nourished by me. She makes me bored and taciturn, or emotionally absent, so as not to have to recognize my affection which might be a dangerous source of suffering for her when we separate. The patient greets my interpretation in complete silence.

After a summer separation, Carla brings the following dream:

> *I am holding a newborn baby in my arms, but she is made of wax and I am afraid she might melt. The mother wraps her in swaddling clothes, but I am afraid the little girl might disappear.*

The dream combined with the complaints in her transference enable me to offer her an idea for reconstruction in the image of a little fragile child, as soft as wax, who fears losing her own identity, melting and disappearing. Carla again greets my interpretation with silence.

The next day she comes into my room with a funereal expression as if she were accompanying a lifeless child-part, and reports a fresh dream: *There is a little newborn girl whose mother is giving her milk, but it is sour and she vomits it all.* Complaining becomes the dominant theme of the session and arouses in me the fantasy of going outside and leaving her alone, like her father who one day went away, leaving her alone for ever, and her mother who immediately devoted herself to another man.

I thus offered her an interpretation aimed at making her understand that her desperate child-part, not content with my milk, was frightened by the affection that could grow up between us and tried to transform me with her desperate laments into the absent, irresponsible father who abandons her and the mother who consoles herself with her uncle, leaving her alone and resentful.

In a complaining, barely perceptible voice, like a little girl about to vanish, Carla responded:

> When I am on my way here I look forward to seeing you, but as soon as I come in I have nothing to say; in fact, I cannot even understand why I come here. I become frozen, as if turned to stone: I have no words, I cannot talk because my words cannot express my thoughts. I have no feelings here, and anyway why should I, since you do not exist for me. I feel far away, like a dot in space. I am disturbed by my emotions as a child and the memory of when my mother remarried. I would like to get revenge on them all, and make my husband, my son, everyone, feel what I feel – to go away for ever.

Francesca

Francesca is a 20-year-old student who is in analysis with me, four times a week, on account of a state of anxiety and severe conflict with her parents. She is the youngest of three children, and her brothers are much older. As the "baby" of the family, she was very close to the middle brother.

Her transference immediately showed a vigorous ambivalence towards me, swinging between gratitude and affection, and resentment and anger. She immediately started describing numerous persecutory dreams. She erupted in frequent attacks of envy after my interpretations, with hostile silences and verbal aggression intended to humiliate me and make me powerless to satisfy her childish requirements.

After three years of analysis, with an intense negative transference, Francesca seemed to start accepting the idea of cutting down her arrogance, and showed willingness to work with me on her frustrated and angry little girl's parts, dissatisfied with her relationship with the mother, who she felt neglected her because she was too busy keeping her husband and the two big brothers happy.

Francesca's negative transference was insistent and sometimes exasperating, and reached a narcissistic peak with a dream in which *she had enormous breasts that sprayed out milk on all sides, soiling her clothes, enough to feed all the children in the world*. The dream coincided with a week's absence on my part, of which she, of course, had had ample notice. The week before I was due to leave, Francesca did not turn up for her four appointments, without letting me know. She did arrive, however, punctually on the Monday of the week when I was away.

When I got back, after a fortnight that we had not seen each other, Francesca walked in with a surly, angry frown on her face. She marched across the room, kicked the couch and tossed herself noisily onto it. She arched her back stiffly and started shouting insults at me like a resentful child. She was so angry that sometimes she lost her breath, like a little girl in a convulsive, desperate fit of inconsolable temper. Her accusation was that if I really felt anything for her I should not have stayed quiet all week, without phoning when she did not turn up. In her eyes this meant I was not capable of treating her, let alone understanding her feelings. Therefore she no longer had any interest in me since I had shown none in her, leaving her alone all week. As if in revenge, she threatens she will not come to analysis any longer.

At that precise moment of dissonance, the provocatory tone of her angry shrieks and her insults had set up a reaction of resentment in me, with evident emotional distress. But a moment later, as I sensed the despair in her complaints, a new image came to mind, which I communicated to her in as calm and affectionate a voice as possible: she was a little girl, angry and desperate at feeling abandoned, who had wanted to pay me back by leaving me alone the week before I was due to leave, and now she was trying to "intimidate" me affectively and make me feel like an inadequate, insensitive, bad parent who only deserved to be abandoned too. I pointed out that if I had phoned it would just have fired up her angry, intolerant and vindictive childish part rather than smoothing it out and transforming it. Francesca lay back on the couch and remained silent.

My comment had created an atmosphere of intimacy and intense affection. Her new awareness radically transformed her transference, and she now showed interest in working with me to tackle the early, unconscious origins of her swift, violent, disrupting tantrums, and the provocative attitude she still tended to take in our meetings. This enabled me to help her cut down to size this little girl's overbearing, omnipotent parts, envious of any interpretation I offered.

Our working through reached a milestone with a dream:

> *Francesca is with a baby only 8 or 9 months old, whose mother has died. To comfort the child, Francesca picks him up and holds him up high, as if he was flying. The little boy likes the game and spreads his arms out like wings.*

This dream gave me a lovely vision, which I offered her in warm tones, of her lifting up a little baby-angel into the air as consolation for the painful loss of its mother, identified with the analyst who she felt had abandoned her.

At the same time Francesca told me about a moving experience she had had the day before in the institute where she works occasionally as a volunteer, helping out with maltreated children. She had seen two small boys, Valerio and Cosimo, both entrusted to the care of a charming, affectionate, generous couple. But the two children were completely different. Both had a highly traumatic childhood history, beaten and abused by their parents. But Valerio was outgoing, attentive with his new "parents", adapting well and always ready to run to them. Cosimo, on the other hand, was closed in himself, still angry and nasty, with a decidedly naughty look, always on the lookout for opportunities to play nasty tricks on his loving foster-parents.

Francesca says she identified closely with the two lads. She felt sorry for them and wonders whether two such different little personalities will manage to live together in their new family. I remark that Valerio and Cosimo have made such an impact on her because they show different, split childish parts that live together in her own personality. The Valerio part, comfortable in its relationship with me, is capable of listening to me, letting itself be comforted by what I say, and contained by my affectionate availability as a foster/parent; the Cosimo part, on the other hand, angry and resentful at me, is unpleasant and inconsolable. This Cosimo had refused me for a long time, seeing me as a persecutor; it was intolerant of our separations, and stayed away for a week to make me pay for going away myself.

Francesca interrupted and said, in a tender, sharing voice: "It's true: the child in the dream is me and I probably suffered a lot when I was very small". I return to her own story of how difficult she had found it to put up with the pain of her mother's neglect, seeing her totally absorbed by her father's demands, as like a spoilt child he always wanted her nearby, at his beck and call. Francesca started talking again:

> My mother probably always neglected me, busy as she was with my father and brothers. When I was little I had an old nanny who I was very fond of, and who I felt loved me. This helped me suffer a bit less.

Then she goes back to the previous day's events:

> The foster-parents told me that Cosimo's mother had been offered the chance of following the child, moving in with him so as not to leave him alone, but had refused, saying she had to care for her husband even if he was a violent drunkard.

The metaphor is striking because we do not link it immediately with her own life, feeling more like the little boy whose mother had abandoned him for ever, because she was too busy with her husband.

After a short silence, she adds:

> That reminds me of a film I found very beautiful and moving. In Italian it was called *Se mi lasci ti cancello* (literally: If you leave me I shall erase you). [The original film is *Eternal Sunshine of the Spotless Mind*, 2004.] There are these two people who decide to separate rather than constantly fight. He meets up with a group that helps him relive his past experience, and erase it from his memory. But, once it has been cancelled, the couple meet again, and decide to join up once more, but this time they manage to live together harmoniously, not like before.

It was clear that the film metaphorically referred to our separations and suggested the idea of her negative transference which had caused us both such distress and suffering for so long. But work on the erased memory (was it implicit memory?) helped us establish a different relationship, affectively more in tune with each other despite the conflicts and dissonance of the earlier period.

The week after this session, Francesca came in looking happy, and announced she had had a *wonderful* dream.

She was with D. [her boyfriend, who often cropped up in her dreams, representing me], *her mother and other people in their house in the country, where she had spent a lot of her childhood. In the dream the house was beautiful, bigger than real – almost a castle with a little village within, where D. had been born. As they walk into the castle-house she sees that all her toys are there, including a Lego set she had loved as a child. A cousin was next to her, with her two sons, a 1 year old and the other 3. Francesca suddenly felt like the 1-year-old boy, as tiny as him, and a dog, like her old dog, came up to her and smothered her with little kisses.*

When she had described the dream, Francesca said that her dog, like the one in the dream, was already old when she was born, and she remembers the difference in size, the dog being much bigger than her. She loved him and they spent hours playing together. She recalls an episode in the house in the country when she found herself alone in the garden because her parents were out and the gardener, who was meant to be keeping an eye on her, was not in sight at that moment. She was suddenly afraid and started bawling desperately. The dog had come up and comforted her with little kisses until her parents got back. "Maybe," she says, "like in the dream, he wanted to console me". Then, in a different, more severe tone, she adds: "My cousin is a strange woman, always attached to her big son but neglecting the 1 year old who needs her so much."

The mood in our sessions had become very affectionate and the way Francesca had communicated her emotions aroused by the dream had conjured up the image for me – which I described to her in a warm and friendly manner – of a little girl who goes back to her childhood home in the country (which recalls the place where she is in analysis) and finds all her old toys, including the Lego set which meant so much to her, symbolically holding together (*lego* in Italian means to bind) the people closest to her affectively, who helped contain her. I also suggest that identifying with the 1-year-old baby in the dream had taken her back to when she was a little girl herself and though she cannot actually remember it, the dream had enabled her to relive emotionally the frightening experience of being put aside and neglected by her mother for her big brothers, like the baby left on its own while her cousin concentrates on helping the bigger brother. This loneliness put me, in the dream, in the role of the faithful old dog who stays close and tries to comfort her with his kisses/words.

I feel Francesca is attentive and affectively close when she replies:

That's exactly how it is . . . in the dream I felt like the little boy left on his own . . . you were in fact the dog who filled the gap left by my mother, always taken up with my father and brothers. This going back to my infancy has moved me enormously . . . it's incredible that in a dream we can relive such old emotions. But don't you think it's odd that I should have chosen my dog, who can't talk, to represent you?

I point out that the little boy in the dream, just like the dog, couldn't speak but that the dream has offered an opportunity to talk about her as a little girl many years before, alone and frightened, and for her to experience emotionally once again those painful moments of her childhood.

A dream a few months later seemed to set the early conflicts of her infantile part in Francesca's private mental theater, in the strongly traumatic atmosphere of her family, with the defenses the young girl had set up to cope with them. In the dream:

Francesca was holding a newborn baby; his eyes were vivacious, attentive and curious. As she held him in her arms she felt at one with him. Around them a conflict was raging. Bombs were falling on a village bursting with refugees – people were horribly burnt but they went on dancing as if to protect themselves from the horrors of war, or erase them. She and the baby watched the scene with detachment and indifference.

Francesca spoke somewhat resentfully about the conflicts in her own family. Her mother was so worried about her big brother whose girlfriend had left him that she had no time for her daughter. She even accused her of being selfish and thinking only about her problems of the moment. Francesca noted that

what happened before in my family is repeating itself. My mother's anguish at my brother's heartbreak distracts her from me and my needs. I'm furious at her but I admit I am fond of her even if our family is always at war! I have to be detached and unmoved in order to defend myself and the little baby in my arms while bombs are exploding all around us.

In response to these associations I merely comment that the metaphorical bridge that in analysis had enabled her to link past and present is now, in her dream, enabling her to rebuild the traumatic aspects of her family, particularly her mother with her preoccupation with her sons and inability to satisfy her daughter's needs. The baby in her dream is her own infantile part with which she has identified and which now has to set up indifference and detachment as defenses, so as not to be dragged into the family conflict. In the dream this conflict burns and destroys internal parts of the self, and to protect itself from the horrors of war it had to set up manic defenses like dancing in the midst of disaster.

Renata

"I'm glad I've been able to rewrite my personal history and tell myself the whole tale." This was Renata's opening remark one day in her fourth year of thrice-weekly analysis with me, which she had started after ten years in the hands of another analyst. Renata is a sophisticated 50-year-old lady from an upper-middle-class intellectual family. She came to me after her earlier analysis, dissatisfied at how that first approach had gone, and dominated by a profound anxiety that made her relational life particularly problematic. In addition to frequent bursts of anger at work, Renata said she had suffered from Crohn's disease for years, and was always afraid it would flare up. She complained that she was completely unable to set up a stable and sexually satisfying affective relationship and, in fact, in all the years since her divorce she had never had a new partner.

In analysis it immediately became clear that her family was an emotional breakdown; her mother was depressed, the paternal grandmother wanted to order everyone around, and her father was virtually absent, more interested in his own life than the family. The whole situation had caused her repeated trauma in childhood. Her mother was a cool, detached intellectual, whose husband repeatedly walked out on her. He was successful and wealthy, traveled frequently, and got tied up in numerous other relationships.

One particular feature of her mother, which became important in the transference, was her language. Though she was of German Jewish origin, she would speak only English at home, creating a sort of phony communication, that certainly did not correspond to her original culture. Then she had added another falsity: she had renounced her Jewish origins and been baptized.

Renata's father, constantly tied up with his frequent trips and life abroad, was authoritarian when at home and had little patience for his small daughter's insistent complaints, peevishness, arguments and provocations.

When she was 2, a baby sister was born, taking her mother's already cool, scant attention from her even more. This was an extremely important early infantile trauma that surfaced insistently in the transference in the shape of un-restrainable anger, resentment, dissatisfaction, often sadness, insomnia, and fierce anxiety that she would not cope with, originating from this old fear of being set aside and abandoned.

Another noteworthy point that came to light in the transference was that she could not stand any sort of argument or disagreement; she could not put up with being contradicted, or not being listened to and understood, or being pushed aside by some comment or gesture that she had not been able to foresee and control. Disagreement, arguments and conflicts with me also fanned the flames of her worry about being left aside and not being listened to. Like a reflex, this automatically fueled uncontrollable feelings of resentment and anger.

Renata was an intrusive patient, highly critical and provocative, insolent, complaining, and often argumentative. She kept a tight rein on her vocal expression and language, and the content of her associations, but tended to make ironic comments on my tone of voice and language, my movements, even how I dressed. She was envious of what I could find out about her, sarcastically belittling whatever I said. She often provoked me with some know-all comment or interpretation, or humiliated me for whole sessions, saying she found my interpretations a concentrate of banality, repetition, and boredom, that could never possibly have any effect. My efforts to convince her that the banality, repetitiousness and boredom that she felt came from me might well be the result of her own attempts to shake off these unpleasant feelings and emotions dating back to her infancy only evoked a sarcastic and sceptical response.

For the first two years of analysis I used all my patience to contain her provocations, careful not to be tempted into that argumentative atmosphere her behavior tended to attract. It took me some months to grasp the infantile nature of this negative modality of projectively identifying her own worst parts countertransferentially in me, particularly the boredom and obsessive repetitivity she brought to the session, whining, however, as if it came from me, not her.

For many months she did not dream, indicating that she was not willing to engage herself emotionally with me nor even to try to commit to mind what she could learn from the sessions. She practically boasted that she had obliged her previous therapist to work without dreams, and she could not understand why I should be interested in them, as she was not. At the end of this first period of analysis, however, despite her angry provocations and her apparent lack of interest in or even refusal of my interpretations, Renata started to dream, and was astounded at the work this opened up. To begin with her dreams were strongly persecutory: terrorists were stopping her traveling; or she identified with the pupils at a local high school who had flooded it. However, she seemed to show some awareness in these dreams that the violent, persecutory presences might make things difficult for me and jeopardize our travel together.

By working on her dreams, we managed to get deeper into her psychic reality, and started to understand the origins of her violent intolerance of what she felt was my lack of attention and interest, my distance, or my poor memory for whatever she told me. We started to understand that this intolerance, that fueled her anger, resentment and persecutory tendencies, was linked to early childhood emotions. Many could be traced to when her sister was born, when no one in the family – particularly her mother – seemed to take any notice of her, and what she wanted, any more. She had felt put aside, painfully powerless, and totally forgotten by the whole family. This built up intense anger, that made her spiteful, provocative, willful, whining – unbearable! The anger and tantrums were one way of attracting attention, so she no longer felt like a pathetic, worthless, forgotten child,

As a reaction to her "spiteful outbursts" her father also became intolerant and more authoritative, sometimes shutting her up in the dark cellar for a whole day. This "black hole" not only terrified her, but also stood for an unbearable affront to her narcissism, for her frustration and violent separation from her parents, besides the anguished loneliness of the dark.

This old process from her distant past was exactly what marked her transference, which was often dominated by a persecutory feeling about any disagreement or argument; she felt this as a conflict that could create a gap between us, when she went back to being the small child left on her own, considered the dunce of the family.

Her fear of argument led Renata to become critical of whatever I said, her sarcasm being unconsciously intended to stop me talking, especially to stop my interpretations which she felt were distant and different from what she expected. Added to this was her envy, which made her criticize me. She would interrupt me while I was speaking, and take a very stiff pose, gesticulating with her hands like an obstinate teacher. She would tell me arrogantly that what she needed was an "individual consultant" more than an analyst, highlighting her intolerance of the asymmetry in our relationship, and the fact that I was available to other patients as well.

As I said before, whereas in her earlier analysis Renata had never dreamed, after an initial dreamless period with me she started to dream quite often. This brought up evidence of her rigid, intolerant internal mother, abandoned and depressed, with the falsity of her dual linguistic and religious identity, her inability to contain her daughter, and her alarm at the child's sensory awareness and sexuality. The evidence showed an absent internal father who flashed his money around but could not understand his little daughter's wishes and feelings; this father could not put up with her provocations and naughtiness, and was ever ready to shut her for hours in the black hole of the dark cellar.

Her own part as a small child, on her own, not contained in any way, never affectionately cuddled against a warm body, left to her own devices once her little sister arrived, had no choice but to develop a sort of motor stiffness – evident in her behavior and posture even now in the sessions. She had been able to express her anger and resentment only by shouting, acting grumpily and being naughty, provoking her parents to get their interest, while at the same time testing how far they would put up with her insistent, exasperating demands. These outbursts sometimes became real tantrums, threatening the stability of the whole family; she could not control her rage, which just grew steadily while her thought processes remained paralyzed, leaving her totally unable to manage it.

At work she also had frequent outbursts of temper when she shouted angrily for several minutes before suddenly cooling down. These tantrums arose when an employee did not listen to her closely, or did not remember what she had ordered; sometimes they were triggered by her own disappointment when something she had expected did not materialize, or someone contradicted her on questions related to her work.

* * *

Renata's analysis finally turned the corner towards the end of a long period when she had been particularly provocative, looking for arguments all the time by belittling whatever I said. She humiliated me by reducing to banalities all my attempts to understand the reasons for this annoying negative transference.

One day, Renata walked into my office with a tense frown and worried expression, definitely distressed about something, but also aggressive. The lines on her face seemed particularly heavy and she held her whole body stiffly, like in armor, ready for battle. As soon as she was on the couch she told me that analysis was not doing any good; she had been worried about her intestine – on account of an attack of Crohn's disease – and her gums were very painful. Then, with a sly knowing look, she suggested that her gum problems might be psychosomatic.

I was surprised by her self-diagnosis, though it did sound very much like just another trick to test me once more and see if I would come out with some banal remark that she could criticize, to slight me. I replied that I did not agree, and that the sore gums might be due to something else – like not really wanting treat-ment (metaphorically using her unwillingness to go to the dentist to represent her unwillingness to accept therapy from me). Renata only grasped my actual words, which she interpreted as insulting and out of keeping, but which automatically made her feel like the little girl of her youth, ignored, contradicted and not listened to.

Her reaction was unexpected: she arched up stiffly on the couch, clenching her fists like a baby in a fit of rage, and, waving her arms around, she set into me, shouting and insulting. Her attack was extremely violent: I didn't understand any-thing about her; I was exploiting her financially without giving her anything in return; the money she gave me was not worth what she was getting, and so forth. But what struck me most was the tone, pitch and volume of her voice. Renata was screeching so loudly that the sound carried well beyond the door of my office, right through the whole building, even down into the courtyard! Her shrieks were so shrill that they penetrated my ears with the force of a projective identification that enabled her to evacuate her anger and made me feel invaded and paralyzed by her violence. At the height of her angry display, waving her hands around furiously, she screamed: "You must be out of your mind!"

Despite the difficulty of the situation I was not unable to think! I took advantage of what seemed to be a brief pause in Renata's tantrum to tell her, in as calm a voice as I could muster, that her temper and her shrieking made me think of an angry little girl who was so furious that she could not think straight, and this in fact sent her "out of her mind". This might have happened to her when she was little and no one listened to her or understood her; her mother constantly contradicted or ignored her, all taken up with the baby sister; it could have happened when she was sent out because of her angry demands, or no one took any notice of her, or perhaps she was even closed up in that black hole in the cellar.

Renata's response was to relax unexpectedly on the couch, her arms alongside her body, her hands loose; after a few seconds of silence she asked me, in quite a different voice from before – no longer argumentative, but almost ironically affectionate – "Are you perhaps telling me off?" I replied that I was not telling her off at all but was trying to contain her anxiety and anger, to restrict this attack of uncontrolled emotions, to help her understand them by calling up the image of the little girl who had relived here with me, because I had contradicted her, the anger that so many years ago used to send her "out of her mind".

The session ended here. From this time on, however, Renata's transference changed dramatically, to the point of convincing me that my basically reconstructive intervention had served her as a source of worthwhile insight and certainly brought about a change. Her anger at work and with me in the transference certainly did not go away overnight, but she could now link it, as if by a bridge, to her childish part, so intolerant of not being listened to, of not having her parents' or my full attention, of being contradicted, and so willing to throw a tantrum at the first sign of any discord that made her feel like a silly child, to be left aside.

Renata behaves less arrogantly in our sessions now, with less control and less need to "rationalize" things. When we work on her dreams she agrees now to identify herself with that child who suffered because of the distractions, inadequacy, absences and forgetfulness of her mother, identified with me in the transference.

One weekend she dreams that *she is at home with her mother and realizes there are no more family portraits on the walls. There are only the patches left where a robber has stolen them.* When she has finished describing this dream Renata says nothing for a while. I propose the image of a young girl for whom the separation from the mother/analyst is the equivalent of a thief removing the affective traces of familiar presences , leaving empty spaces on the walls of her inner house. Renata replies emotionally, with the voice of a little girl: "When my sister was born she stole all my mother's affection, all her attention. In that dream I am together with my mother – maybe her? – looking through all the painful voids left inside me."

I tell her that her mother's neglect and the affective void she feels once more in our separations have left the young girl with no containment and no stimuli linked to her sensory awareness. This helps explain her difficulties in managing her body serenely and living comfortably with her sexuality. She agrees.

The next day Renata describes another dream, in which *I come into her bedroom and sit at the foot of her bed, and we start to talk about sensory feelings. Then I ask some questions and she realizes that this meeting is unscheduled.* When she has finished telling me about the dream, Renata says: "My mother was very fussy about timetables. At seven each evening I had to go to bed, with no questions asked."

I pick up the thread of our session the previous day, when we had talked about a young girl who had never been held and cuddled, and never been properly contained and lovingly stimulated by her mother, who was cold, depressed and distant, and fussy about keeping to times. Now, finally, in her dream the analyst had become a tender and affectionate mother, who "outside the scheduled times" allowed her to talk about her sensory feelings and possibly even her sexuality. After a short silence, Renata replied, in a warm voice with a hint of irony: "But in the dream I only let you come into my bedroom, certainly not into my bed!"

In the next months we still had a few tantrums, when Renata shrieked uncontrollably at an employee who had disappointed her, who had not paid enough attention, had not remembered exactly what she had been told, or had let her down somehow. I could link these attacks to her early unconscious when as a child she was distressed because she felt her mother did not pay her enough attention, and betrayed her confidence, disappointing her expectations.

Unexpectedly Renata remembers a fragment of a dream: *she was in her house in Italy with her mother and her sister . . . a house where there was only suffering.* Then she adds: "But my father let me down too when he made me come and live in Italy, taking me away from the town where I was born."

In addition to the lack of attention and let-downs, and the scant containment by her mother, it became evident during analysis that her mother had been highly anxious and depressed on account of her husband's lack of understanding and frequent absences. Sometimes this had the effect of shifting onto her infant girl her own depressive anxieties and unhappiness; it was as if the conditions had been created in the patient's infancy for an inversion of the process of projective identification which, instead of going from the child to the mother – as would be natural – went the other way, from the mother to the child. The child, whose thought processes were not up to the task of managing these emotions, found herself obliged to deploy extreme defenses like anger, resentment, tantrums and shrieking, so as to lob back to her mother the anxieties that the child herself was not equipped to work through. The same happened with her father, who responded to her provocations by closing her away in the "black hole".

This was in fact confirmed in a session at about that time. Renata admitted that her childish provocations must have been very stormy, but all the same they needed to be contained and worked through, and certainly not acted out by her parents – particularly her father – by closing her up in the cellar. This led her to recall a painful session with her previous analyst who had threatened to stop analysis on account of her continued provocation. She acknowledges that with me she had never felt threatened with the "black hole" and in fact felt I had set a limit to her anger, so she felt contained and had been able to work through it without being intimidated.

During the session Renata recalls two short fragments of dreams. *In one there was her Aunt B., who was adopting a small girl. In another there were guests at her house, but far more than she had expected.* Aunt B. was the person who had introduced her mother and father. I suggest that this aunt seemed somehow to represent those two parents, and in the dream she also represented me, in the role of a good relative who takes care of the child-part. Her immediate reply was: "But the little girl was happy to be adopted . . . I really don't understand this second dream".

I then suggest that all the things we have discovered in the last few sessions – the personages, emotions, affects, anger, and understanding that have passed through our "analytical home" – are in fact a bit more than she had bargained for at the start of this experience with me. Renata finds this idea interesting. She admits that she has now understood many things, despite her problems accepting my method of analysis, and despite her arguments because I contradicted her, and the anger she had felt in analysis.

We therefore come to the end of this *tranche*, which coincides with some of the patient's fantasies of terminating her analysis with me at some not too distant time in the future. The sentence I quoted at the very beginning: "I'm glad I've been able to rewrite my personal history and tell myself the whole tale" came up in a recent session, when Renata described this dream: *I am with Tino, a friend of mine, who asks me if I'd go with him to take some old papers to the land registry. I hesitate a moment, then decide I'll go.* We ask ourselves: "Are these perhaps the official papers of an old house that has been restored by analysis?"

9

Reality and metaphor in the analytical relation: transference love

Material reality and psychic reality

Freud grasped the difficulty of weighing material and psychic reality against each other. At the start of his psychoanalytical reflections he considered the work of analysis as *reconstructive*: it could bring what was repressed to the surface and was therefore based on a material reality, meaning traumatic events that had actually taken place but then with time had gradually been deformed and transformed. In those early years Freud was diffident about *construction*, which seemed arbitrary, as it was not based on historically proven facts (historical truth or material reality), which was the scientific approach Freud wanted his investigational method to resemble.

Closer to the end of his life, in *Constructions in Analysis*, Freud (1937b) uses the terms *construction* and *reconstruction* interchangeably to describe a certain focus on the recollection of a repressed (or deformed) trauma, reactivated *by* the transference and relived *in* it. Evidently Freud had elaborated on this concept in those years, and starting from his widely known letter to Fliess on 21 September 1897, he had contemplated the distance between material and psychic reality, noting that the latter was more important than the former in analysis.

Analysis had thus to be able to reactivate a recollection linked not so much to material reality as to psychic reality and the patient's ability to relive experiences from his past, in the present of the relation, through *retranscription of the memory*. This is a fundamental concept of psychoanalysis, that Freud called *Nachträglichkeit*, and which is the basis for reconstruction work on dreams and the association that links the present, in the analytical relation, with the patient's autobiographic past, and current experiences to those of infancy.

★ ★ ★

Psychoanalysis is continuously assessing and trying to understand the different levels of reality. External and psychic reality, material reality and fantasies, conscious or unconscious, all enmesh continually during analysis and can be very hard to untangle. The analyst's work consists of trying to separate these realities and translate one type into another – the real one into the metaphorical. An analyst would be wrong to allow too much time for the enticements of outside reality while overlooking patients' internal or psychic reality, but equally wrong to concentrate excessively on patients' psychic reality without due attention to their external reality and how they "use" it to try to control their anxieties and defend themselves against the painful feelings of the relation.

★ ★ ★

The question of material or external reality, as opposed to internal or psychic reality, is particularly important in relation to the "truth" psycho-analysis sets out to discover in its patients. Freud was well aware that the truth of a narration – deduced from associations and dreams – could get mixed up with the patient's emotional truth, which had to be kept strictly separate from material or actual reality. But it is current psychoanalytical thought that has led us to consider truth in analysis not in absolute terms, but in terms of how close it comes to the patient's emotional reality, which is what gives this psychic reality specific, profound meaning in the trans-ference. Thus, the accuracy of an analytical construction, meaning how the material provided by the patient is selected, how it is communicated, worked through, decoded and transformed metaphorically, and the interpretation this construction discloses, never lies in its true historical precision – which is the realm of material reality – but in the extent to which it grasps the metaphorical aspects of the transference at that precise fleeting moment of the relation.

This is the only approach that gives *meaning* to an experience. Consequently, truth lies in this meaning, as that is where patients find them-selves. In any event, attribution of a meaning – unmasked by psychoanalysis – is intrinsic to being, and confirms Merleau-Ponty's statement that human beings are condemned to find a meaning to their existence. But this meaning also depends on the person's relations with the world, hence assuming a *relation* with the other party, in this case. It is this relation that gives rise to a reality that is neither material nor external, but is the patient's psychic or internal reality.

★ ★ ★

When we analysts listen to patients telling us about an episode that really happened, we realize that they present it on various levels of reality: there is the "real" person who was involved in the event outside analysis; and there is the "patient" who is trying to tell the analyst something that goes beyond actual reality and takes on a specific metaphorical dimension. But there are three factors that oblige us to consider this a dimension of the transference: first, the *projection* into the present of an internal object dimension regarding the patient's feelings towards the analyst in the here and now of the session; second, the *repetition* of repressed affective experiences from the past, made possible by retranscription of the *autobiographic memory*; third, the *repetition* of affective and emotional experiences dating from the earliest significant relations (particularly traumatic ones), stored in the *implicit memory* where they form part of an unrepressed unconscious. These manifest themselves in the form communication takes during the encounter, making up the "musical dimension" of that patient's transference. Thus various complex levels of reality mingle and blend: the actual reality and the metaphorical reality, or that of the transference with its range of content and formal aspects.

So how is an analyst to tackle this tangle of realities? First of all, the analyst must grasp the metaphorical meaning of the "real" communication, decoding the message by shifting from one reality to the next; this is the most complex but most creative of the analyst's tasks. Then, from the meta-phorical reality, the analyst has to pick out the most significant components emerging in the transference, paying particularly close attention to their formal aspects and the *musical dimension*. By this I mean the tone, timbre and volume of the voice, the rhythm, grammar and timing of the language. The assumption is that language contains a dual semantic sense, and that music is a language *sui generis* whose symbolic structure parallels that of our emotional and affective world (Langer, 1942). This structure is rooted in the unrepressed unconscious, which contains fantasies and defenses connected to the patient's very earliest childhood relationships.

On these complex elements of significance and signifying, analysts have to base their construction, like a mosaic whose pieces are the various trans-formations of one reality to another and the narrative, communicative and musical components of the transference. Analysts may then decide whether or not to tell their patient about this construction, in the form of an interpretation. But if they do, how they explain what they have constructed to the patient will also influence the interpretation: their voice, its timbre and volume, the rhythm of speech and the language structure they use all become factors that reveal their own transference and the counter-transferential emotions induced by the patient's transference.

The interpretation, however, has one aim: to disentangle the different levels of reality and assign each to its rightful place, so that patients can identify, in what they have communicated, and how, the work of the different parts of their self and of the different affects, fantasies and defenses, recognizing them as aspects of their "true" reality in the transference.

All this is possible in the "setting", which is simultaneously a container to hold one reality (in the transference) separately from the other, the "actual" reality, and a "shared construction" that highlights the difference between the two realities. Seen like this, what happens in analysis is very like a "fiction" or a "stage set" that has its own reality (in the transference) which is not the same as the reality outside the setting. It is a bit like being at the theater. In fact, a dream is in a way a private theater (Mancia, 1996b; Resnik, 2002) where objects from outside, or real reality, are used to stage a performance about the person's internal objects, hence the transferential (metaphorical) reality. But some patients cannot accept the fiction of the transference and refuse all the metaphorical aspects of their communication, remaining fixated on the solid, material "reality" of what they have lived.

Clearly, analysts too have a part in this "fiction". They do not behave like a person from the outside, "true" reality: they are not vengeful, have no wishes of their own, do not interrupt, and are impartial − or at least should be all these things. However, we must take a closer look at the role of the analyst and his or her unconscious in the relation. Despite its asymmetry, the work of the analytical couple is based on the encounter of two types of unconscious − repressed and unrepressed. This can lead to collusion by unconscious, unanalyzed parts of the therapist, especially in the unrepressed unconscious connected to very early (traumatic) experiences from his or her own childhood, with their equivalents in the patient's unconscious.

★ ★ ★

Looking at the analytical encounter as a tangle of different levels of reality, we can view the patient's acting out as attempts to bring the reality of the transference into the sphere of true reality, i.e. to mix up the two. This might happen, for example, as defense against the pain induced by the transference, its frustrations and disappointments. But the analyst is acting too, in response to the patient's unconscious desire to get rid of the analyst from the setting. For example, a *projective counter-identification* (Grinberg, 1962) can be considered a defense put up against the difficulties of understanding the patient's need – hence also helping – to keep the different levels of reality separate. In this sense the analyst ends up colluding with the patient's unconscious wish (to keep them mixed up).

★ ★ ★

We must now look more closely at the part played by *projective identification* in this discussion of the levels of reality in analysis. Melanie Klein (1946) described projective identification as a defensive mechanism used by the patient who repeats childhood experiences (going back to the paranoid-schizoid position): it involves splitting off parts of the self and projecting them onto the analyst, who is then identified with these parts and their related affects. Herbert Rosenfeld (1987) subsequently produced a brilliant description of these methods and how patients use projective identification to evacuate sadistic or painful parts of the self, as a defense against separation, to control an object, provoke countertransferential feelings, and so on.

I think it is particularly interesting to view projective identification as a defense mechanism that tends to confuse the patient's different levels of reality. Projective identification of parts of oneself into the analyst means entering with one's own psychic reality into the other person's reality, trying to demolish the analyst's separate identity. In this attempt to confuse the levels of reality, therefore, patients build a defense not only against having to acknowledge that their own psychic reality is distinct from true reality, but also against separation from the object, this being indispensable if they are to acquire an identity of their own. At the same time the analyst is made to feel impotent on account of his or her failure to help patients distinguish the two levels of reality.

The question of levels of reality is particularly interesting in relation to the affects that develop during analysis. From many points of view these are similar to the affects blossoming in everyday life, which always contain elements that can be found in the transference; at the same time, however, they differ because they develop on a different level of reality – marked by the fact that material reality masks the reality of the transference.

Transference love

A fine example of this sort of confusion between levels of reality is transference love. The emotions surfacing in this analytical situation are all "real" but their level of reality is different from falling in love outside this setting, where elements of the transference are present, but are masked by material ones. In analysis these affects are uncloaked and recognized as part of the transference, which means they are unattainable. The analyst has therefore to manage them as "unreal" or – to put it better – as part of a metaphorical reality different from "true" reality, trying to transform them through interpretation.

Freud (1914c) holds that transference love is impersonal, a sort of inevitable fate induced obligatorily by the analytical situation, which has nothing to do with the analyst's personal qualities! Here we have a first contrast between levels of reality: the patient considers the love *personal* and aimed at the analyst, but for the analyst it is *impersonal*, a feature of the transference. The analyst has therefore to analyze the inevitable fate awaiting the patient, with great care to leave intact the patient's need and longing as forces driving work and change (Freud, 1914c, in Spector Person et al., 1993). If the patient's wish were fulfilled, the analyst, according to Freud, would end up like the priest who went to convert an insurance salesman and came out without having converted him, but with a signed policy! That would be a fine example of confusion and exchange of levels of reality, which would be a triumph for the patient but a failure for the treatment.

Freud's analytical approach to transference love is to treat it as if it were "unreal", bearing in mind its unconscious origin. He really means that though it is real, transference love belongs on a different level of reality from what happens outside the analytical relation. Even so, Freud considers that the love arising in analysis has all the features of "true" love, but also some distinguishing features of its own: first, it is brought on by the analytical situation; second, it takes no account of outside reality (since it is part of the transference); third, it idealizes the subject; fourth, it can serve as a *resistance* against painful activation of a repressed recollection.

This last point raises a question also put by Betty Joseph (1993): transference love is not necessarily a resistance, since it may be the only way patients have to live the relation with the analyst, as they are governed by object dynamics linked to their affective-emotional history. In the transference, as we have seen, the patient's memory is retranscribed so as to let him or her relive and give fresh meaning to a past love that has been repressed, through the process of *Nachträglichkeit*. But at the same time the enamorment and sexual desire in analysis may be linked through the transference to very early childhood sexual experiences, possibly traumatic, that are filed away in implicit memory as part of an unrepressed unconscious core of the self, that cannot be represented either symbolically or verbally.

These situations have some points in common with the arts, for instance, the theater, where the illusion can be enjoyed simultaneously as reality and fiction (Eickhoff, 1993). In some ways, transference love also reminds us of a tale by Borges (1949) in which the tone of emotion, the respect and the sensitivity of the story were all true, but the circumstances, time and one of the two names were imagined. Similarly, in the transference, the emotions, events, sensitivity and affects in play are all true, but the circumstances are false – the setting – and one of the two names – the analyst's.

Projective identification in the here and now of the session plays an important part in transference love, as the patient projects his or her intrapsychic relations and the affects dominating them onto the analyst. The projective identification of the patient's wish convinces him or her that the analyst is also emotionally or erotically involved. This is an example of confusion of levels of reality responding to the patient's attempts to turn the analyst into a lover, as part of an unconscious, narcissistic defensive plot to cancel out differences from the analyst, the separation, and the asymmetry between them.

Not only analysts' abstinence, but also their work of containment, elaboration and interpretation, must be aimed at converting their patients' desire and longing into energy, to fuel work and change. Analysis must in fact walk a tightrope between the virtual, symbolic, metaphorical reality of the transference, and the real, material reality of acting out. Analysts must keep their balance without falling into the trap of acting out reality, while nevertheless allowing their patients to use the metaphorical reality of the transference so as to find their own true reality outside analysis.

Thus, the appropriate setting – in which abstinence is obviously essential – is the one way of keeping the two levels of reality separate, and transference love can be considered the only way a patient has of loving as it depends on the internal representation of his or her objects, fantasies and unconscious defenses, which add up to the theater of the mind (Oedipal and pre-Oedipal); at the same time the patient can acknowledge the metaphorical level of reality, while keeping it distinct from true reality.

This love is in any event connected to a *Nachträglichkeit* that is lived, in the transference, by retranscription of repressed recollections, with the related fantasies and defenses. In real life, however, this is acted out. Then we can add those childhood experiences – especially traumatic ones involving sexuality – with fantasies and defenses that are stored in the *unrepressed unconscious*, from which they influence a person's experience of love in real life, besides the quality, intensity and, if possible, working through of love in the transference. Retranscription of the memory of events during life connected to repression, and influenced by early implicit retrieval, can affect a person's fantasies and their experience of love and sex in actual reality and in the transference.

A critical look at recent literature and the "state of the art"

This fascinating question has been tackled by various authors. We shall take a quick look at some of them here.

Friedrich-Wilhelm Eickhoff (1993) goes back to a definition of the transference offered by Sandler et al. (1973), more or less in these terms: *A particular illusion regarding the other person which in some ways repeats the relation with an important figure from that person's past.* The idea of an illusion harks back to Winnicott's (1967) play and transitional object and also to works of art: "a province midway between truth and deception . . . where we abandon ourselves consciously and freely to the illusion" (Gombrich, 1959). This is a process of illusion and symbolism at the same time, since it anyway stands for something else. Eickhoff (1993) makes reference to Kohut (1971) when he says that in its central aspects the analytical situation is not real, in the usual sense of the word. It has its own reality that resembles, in some ways, the "reality" of art, for instance that of the theater.

I think the analytical situation is real enough but the intrinsic features of the relation established by the "analytical contract" mean that it belongs – as I have already suggested – to a reality *sui generis*, which is different from what you might encounter outside analysis, i.e. outside any analytical contract. The analogy with the theater is very convincing, with the metaphor of a stage where the dynamics are represented between internal objects (the intrapsychic dimension) and between these objects and the self and the other party (the intersubjective dimension). This metaphor also connects the reality of the transference (therefore also the reality of transference love) with the reality of dreams, that represent the transference as a whole.

Eickhoff looks back to Freud (1914b) in *Remembering, Repeating, and Working-Through* where he calls transference neurosis a "province midway between disease and life", since it is comparable to an *illusion* (or play) viewed simultaneously as reality and as fiction. Transference love must thus be treated as "unreal" (in the sense that it is just metaphorical and therefore different from real love).

Roy Schafer (1993) maintained that Freud had abolished the frontier between transference love and real love, meaning the limit between the analytical relation and real-life relation. In actual fact, both normal and transference love have infantile prototypes: repetitive, idealizing, conflictual. Freud is to be credited with having perceived the resemblance, even though later he defined transference love as unreal and less "true", treating it technically as unreal despite the fact that he could not deny its authenticity.

My own feeling is that transference love is *real*, but not *authentic*, in the sense that it is *impersonal*, its target being what the analyst represents, not what the analyst really is. This was one of the rare occasions when Freud specifically mentioned the countertransference, even though he did not apparently consider it cast much useful light on the patient's transference.

Schafer (1993) notes that the patient's attempts at seduction may express the hostility of a *negative transference*; he calls it hostility masked as love and intractable desire and suggests that transference love can be exploited to undermine the analyst's professional authority. This leads to the idea of transference love as resistance. Schafer, however, proposes that transference love may be sent out ahead to prevent access to the negative transference. A woman's offering of romantic or sexual feelings to the analyst might also express a desire for consolation. But I think it is also a defense against the fear of being left alone.

Schafer criticizes Freud's attitude to women, which he maintains is patriarchal, sexist and phallo-centric – what today might be called *machist*. The very fact that he considers transference love "intractable" reveals his defensive position towards women as a man more than an analyst. Freud does not discuss the possibility of transference love by a male patient for a male analyst. The question comes to mind: what difference can there be between male and female transference love?

Max Hernandez (1993) considers love a compulsively repetitive event, hence a "reprint" of something written in the unconscious *illo tempore*. This awareness protects the analyst well in the countertransference. Hernandez finds that transference love disrupts analysis, particularly the form of knowledge referred to as *insight*. Therefore the appearance of "passion" in the transference expresses a resistance that jeopardizes the continuation of therapy.

Here we come to one of the paradoxes of analysis: love is indispensable to keep the relation going, and for cure, but at the same time it is its main obstacle. I am of the idea that much depends on how one manages transference love. I believe it is the only way for the patient's internal objects to manifest themselves in the analytical relation, and for the traumatic experiences, fantasies and defenses related to sexuality to be represented in the transference and in dreams. Analytical work on these manifestations, without acting out, is therefore the only way to gain insight and set in motion the process of reconstruction that is essential to achieve lasting transformation in a patient – male or female.

Hernandez says that the patient's object of desire is not the analyst: it is the wish to erase the differences of sex and generation based on a successful Oedipal solution. His idea is that if transference love aims to eliminate the differences through erotization, negative transference aims to eliminate the diversities by destroying them. The patient sees the difference and the asymmetry as threats to his own narcissism.

Betty Joseph's (1993) clear ideas had great significance for the transference. She pointed out that Freud had already stressed how a woman inevitably put into her relation with the analyst her habitual type of object relations, especially those with internal objects: love, hate, ambivalence, defenses against love and dependence – the whole range. This is what we analysts mean by "falling in love". With such patients it is important to dig back to the childhood roots of the love. This is the main point of work on the transference. These patients (who may be male or female) are convinced the analyst is also emotionally involved. This is the result of projective identification of the patient's wish onto the analyst. The patient's attempt to turn the analyst into a lover is anyway part of a narcissistic defensive project designed to deny the difference from the analyst and the *separation* from him or her.

The woman described by Betty Joseph induced a subtly erotic atmosphere in the transference which tended to narrow or eliminate the gap between the two. Both had to get involved in this acting, which was a sort of perversion of the transference, through which the patient tried to cancel out not only the difference and the asymmetry of the relation, but also the analyst's work, her separation and her ability to help her patient.

Grasping these aspects of the transference, acted in the session or outside it, is itself an important technical advance. Transference love, according to Joseph, can manifest itself with demands for availability and love, like Freud said, but it may sometimes take an attitude of silent scorn or disdain, or even a more shifty and perverse form.

Instead of talking about "falling in love", Joseph (1993) suggests simply describing the nature of the object relations the patient brings up in the transference. I think that these may take the form of either love or hate. This makes a difference even if the aim is the same. I therefore think it is useful to make the distinction between transference love and hate or negative transference. Our attention should be focused on the idea of projective identification which Joseph notes the patient uses, unconsciously in fantasy, to project parts of the self or impulses onto the analyst. Sometimes we fail to notice this subtle strategy until we find ourselves obliged to behave in a certain way, or to take a clear position instead of remaining impartial.

Joseph (1993) points out that the question naturally extends to the cases of transference where not only figures from the past – from the patient's real life – are introduced into the analytical relation, but also complex interior figures of fantasy created in early childhood, formed in the interactions between real events and the child's fantasies and impulses towards them.

This elegant suggestion leads us today to contemplate the possibility that the interactions between real events on the one hand and a child's fantasies and wishes on the other are stored in the early implicit memory, forming an unrepressed nucleus of the self that can affect the patient's sexual life as an adult, besides appearing in the transference.

Merton Gill (1993) questioned whether the transference happens only in analysis, or also outside this setting. He wondered whether enamorment in analysis is similar to love in "real life". He noted, however, that the transference is always at the service of resistance. I find this generalization hard to accept because the transference also contains defenses and relational modalities representing the projections of intrapsychic and intersubjective object dynamics. The transference represents the patient's affective/emotional life story from infancy; with the patient's fantasies and wishes they form part of the unrepressed unconscious which, as we said before, must inevitably come to light in the transference. Love in analysis cannot therefore simply be considered a resistance to therapy.

Fidias R. Cesio (1993) recalls that Freud (1901) was the first to experience transference love, with his patient Dora. It was already late when he realized that the love Dora had developed during analysis was a repetition of her love for Herr K. Cesio's description of what happens in certain specific transference situations is poetic: the spirits of the dead invoked by the psychoanalyst manifest themselves in transference love, which is tragic, epic and incestuous and, if they are not heard and adequately interpreted, they end up destroying the treatment. It is hard to disagree – also as regards the possible ways out. Freud suggests three, but Cesio says there is also a fourth: identifying and interpreting the words and deeds as part of the transference, and their metabolic and symbolic value, to re-establish the analytical setting.

All this takes place in a setting of total abstinence, obviously the analyst's sole basis for making the patient understand, through interpretation, the imaginary, illusory, unachievable and incestuous nature of these wishes in the transference; this will help solve the patient's Oedipal drama, transforming the erotic transference to a state of affection or tenderness. A dangerous sentiment for analysis, resulting from transference love, is jealousy, which is part of the primitive, narcissistic, incestuous expression of the Ego.

Cesio (1993) suggests there are various levels of reality, with a difference between *virtual* reality – in which the transference arises within a session and a setting – and the *real* reality transference love acquires when it invades the setting and turns into acting. Virtual reality appears in the setting, while real reality leaves the setting and becomes acting. Even against this backdrop, though, Cesio too still considers transference love a resistance. If the analysis is conducted properly, in abstinence and with interpretations, the transference love never becomes real, it is never acted out. Should this happen, though, part of the fault lies with the analyst, who is turning every construction and interpretation to serve his or her own passion.

Transference love can show itself through jealousy, or such immediate and violent demands for love as to threaten the analytical relation. In this love things that have been repressed, and buried in the unconscious, are revealed. But, I would add that early passions, those that make up pre-Oedipal identificatory love (Benjamin, 1995), deposited in the implicit memory, where they are buried in an unrepressed unconscious, can also be so violent and pressing, or so underhand, sticky and repetitive that they too jeopardize the analytical relation; this can happen if they are not interpreted properly or if the partners are not able – sometimes through dreams – to formulate a reconstruction that takes patients back emotionally to the old, unrepressed fantasies and defenses that have influenced their sexuality and the main features of their personality.

Cesio (1993) says that the "love that kills" is the passion that ends up destroying whatever it most wants. This love wants total possession of the object, to the extent of demolishing it and causing its own destruction in the process. Transference love can therefore be considered a narcissistic-incestuous manifestation expressed in a tragic form. Clearly, the abstinence in the setting merely enhances the frustration, disappointment and original suffering, through exclusion and jealousy.

The analyst too, however, can suffer frustration as his or her wishes are not met, just like a patient, though the form and intensity are different and there is always the control of the setting. Abstinence, therefore, with the analyst's interpretation, containment and working through, is what converts the patient's need, wish and longing into "energy" that pushes him or her to work and change.

Cesio (1993) confirms what we have already said in this chapter. Analysis treads a very fine line between reality in its various forms: virtual, imaginary, symbolic, and metaphoric in the transference, and "real" and material in acting out. The analyst must keep the balance on this line without slipping off into the reality of acting, while still giving the patient the chance to use virtual and metaphorical reality in the transference to interpret reality outside analysis too. Cesio maintains that with interpretation and construction we introduce the patient to a diachronic temporal dimension, so we see there the repetition of an infantile love. Cesio's opinion is in line with what we have already insisted – our analytical task is to make history out of the transference love by linking it to infancy and early relations based on identificatory and object love, which have helped form the affective and erotic representations that inevitably come to light in the transference.

175

Jorge Canestri (1993) picks up one of Freud's formulations when he says there is a "scene change" a bit like a fire alarm going off during the performance at the theater. Freud had no doubts that transference love was at the service of resistance. It should be neither satisfied nor repressed but must be left alive so as to disclose the patient's fantasies and defenses, details of sexual desire, and infantile object choices. This will make it possible gradually to attenuate and transform the amorous passion.

Thus transference love can be seen as one way in which the transference manifests itself. Canestri (1993) asks whether transference love is in fact an effect of the analytical situation itself, or whether it comes from the patient's world of internal objects. I have no doubt that the analytical situation activates and highlights the world of internal objects, which are projected into the here and now of the session. Therefore, the transference itself cannot create anything that is not already inside the patient's psychic world.

Besides Freud's comparison of the analytical situation with play-acting – which in itself suggests an "as if" situation – Canestri looks at various other authors' comments on transference love.

Greenson (1965) suggests getting the patient's reasonable Ego to understand that its transference feelings are not realistic (meaning they cannot be achieved?), that they are based on fantasy and originate from early in life. Gaddini (1977) maintains that eroticizing is always a defense, while Green (1990) believes the transference includes passion and folly. Bion (1970) connected the psychotic part of the patient's personality to eroticization of the transference, which becomes the way this part operates in the relation. Canestri says it is clear – as it was for Freud and is for all of us – that sexual acting out implies getting burned even before the fire bell rings!

Daniel Stern (1993), in line with his research, poses the question for transference love of isomorphism between past (infantile) and present love (in the transference). He acknowledges that Freud considered present love a transformation of the original events during a person's development, so that, as he puts it, the recollections have made a long trip from past to present. However, he also points out that the basic physical language of affectionate love is already learned and practiced in the fourth and fifth months of life. He notes the many similarities between childhood love and adult enamorment: looking into each other's eyes without speaking, staying close together with bodies touching, moving in time with each other, kissing and cuddling; the "code language" of closeness is different from people who are not in love. Stern is convinced that from the end of the first year a child becomes capable of intersubject relations. This intimacy is reflected in transference love, which thus shows its roots in preverbal, pre-Oedipal life.

176

Stefano Bolognini (1994) distinguishes various categories of transference love, with specific clinical features. He maintains, however, that erotic transference and the countertransference it induces form an area of the analytical experience that has enormous potential for transformation and maturation, though of course it can also cause distress and disaster. He therefore sites the scenario in the *Oedipal area*, since that is where it manifests itself, taking on its most typical features.

My own theory, however, is that we must go back to the deepest early preverbal, presymbolic, pre-Oedipal area whose events are recorded in the implicit memory. These give rise to the fantasies and defenses forming an unrepressed unconscious core that may well have influenced the Oedipal area, affecting the development of sexuality and therefore also the erotic dimension of the transference.

It is worth looking at some of Bolognini's various categories:

- *Eroticized transference:* this is a psychotic type, or perhaps we should say connected to the psychotic parts of the personality. Rapaport notes that whereas in a neurotic transference the analyst is seen as if he were the father, in an eroticized transference the analyst *is* the father, or mother.

  This concept seems to come very close to Segal's (1957) symbolic equivalence. A characteristic of this type of transference is the archaic nature of the levels of mental functioning. The object is idealized. Eroticization is therefore seen as a defense against separation from the pre-Oedipal transferential object. The underlying fantasy that gives rise to defensive eroticization is separation and abandon. Eroticization is therefore an attempt at psychotic restoration of a narcissistic state of union with the pre-Oedipal object.

  This type of transference does not induce countertransferential responses that lead the analyst to act in the session. The reaction is more likely to be boredom, or other feelings like impotence, irritation and similar, that certainly does not encourage the analyst to act sexually, though they do not protect against other forms of acting.

- *Erotic transference:* this is a neurotic repetition of erotic fixations on an "impossible" object (which can therefore never be part of a real relation because it is unachievable): the generation gap cannot be bridged, and it is absent. In these conditions of transference the analyst stands for the Oedipal couple. For a neurotic patient, unlike a psychotic one, the analyst represents the object rather than actually *being* it. *Repetition* is the basic feature of this transference, just like in life outside analysis. Bolognini sustains that erotic transference serves as: a perverse defense, linked to libidinization of the past which had caused suffering; unconscious aggression towards the parent of the same sex; the expression of a parental Oedipal situation, their behavior being seductive and collusive towards the child; the child's internal Oedipal despair.

This kind of transference gives rise to a compulsive, maniacal seductiveness that tends to deny inferiority, exclusion and narcissistic hurt. The transferential object is in any case perceived as "exciting". The same feeling is induced in the analyst (through projective identification of excited parts of the self), who is led to share the illusion of love with the patient. In this situation of Ulysses and the siren, Ulysses the analyst must stay firmly seated so as to resist the fascinating illusion of their song. More than one author sustains that if an erotic transference lasts long it is because of the analyst's unconscious collusion.

The unconscious feelings of this sort of transference are *exclusion*, *inferiority* and *envy*, and these justify the attack on the parents (represented by the analyst). The attack itself causes excitement. Bolognini specifies that behind the erotic transference there may lie a "polemical", disturbed and conflictual relation with the primary object. On the level of the object relation this type of patient is looking for a "forbidden" alternative object, or one that is "impossible" in Oedipal terms.

- *Amorous transference:* this is the most conflictual sort of transference. The patient's feelings and fantasies of love encounter a series of complementary sentiments, of danger, destructive fantasies, communicability and symbolic experience in analysis. Faced with this transference the analyst must treat the patient sincerely though obviously the approach must be rigorously symbolic (i.e. without acting). The analyst's awareness and his or her *guarantees* (not to act) permit contact with the patient and his or her intense experience.

  Bolognini (1994) mentions R. Horacio Etchegoyen's belief that each analyst must experience a moment of love, of enamorment, since the analytical relation reproduces the object relation of the Oedipal trio. One wonders, in the light of recent findings, whether the analytical relation is not more likely to reproduce the pre-Oedipal dyad (rather than the Oedipal grouping), where the dependence on the mother and the symbolic presence of the father cast the foundations of identificatory processes that influence the development of sexuality.

- *Affectionate transference:* this happens only rarely. It can be defined as the transposition onto the analyst of a better relation between internal objects, involving sexual specificity and gratitude, with free appreciation of the object and of the subject's relational potential. This sort of approach, or internal attitude, is based on a *depressive position* the patient has managed to reach through a process of separation. The affectionate transference has none of the excitement of the previous types, and shows emotional fertility, an incipient but genuine parental attitude. It is a stage of growth, expressing the introjection of a good parental couple, admired affectionately, that has come unharmed through the Oedipal conflict and worked in analysis to improve and reconstruct the relations between internal objects. In the final phases of analysis, this new situation makes the analyst feel pleased about meeting the patient, with pride in the success, and pain at the inevitable separation.

The analyst must not deal defensively with the amorous – or erotic – transference but must use it to interpret the patient's feelings and his or her desire to act out and get the analyst to do the same. Here the analyst's "guarantees" are extremely important and are based on an awareness of the illusory nature of the transference, morality and professional ethics, and technical skills. The analyst has to rein in the highly explosive forces of an erotic transference by, first, a good analytical Super-Ego established with his or her own analyst or supervisor; second, a private life that gives physical and affective satisfaction; third, attaining, through analysis and his or her own life experience, what Erikson (1974) called the stage of generativity, when a person becomes interested in guiding the next generation; fourth, the analyst's own internal situation reached by work on him- or herself and confidence and love for the beauty of the analytical method.

In summary then, the broad literature on transference love tells us, first of all, that this affective and emotional state arises fairly frequently in an analyst's encounters with the patients. It is not necessarily a defense, but one of the various forms the transference may take. It is absolutely real, but its reality is not material. As part of the transference it must be tackled analytically with a view to bringing the patient – man or woman – back to the elements of *construction* that made it possible for these sentiments to become manifest in the relation, and to the items of *reconstruction*, rooted in the implicit memory, that are the "reasons" for these unconscious feelings and emotions in the transference. Analytical work on them should enable the patient to discharge verbally and think symbolically about sexual emotions and fantasies, together with defenses that were originally pre-symbolic and preverbal.

The case of Z.

I met Z. at a meeting about music. A colleague introduced us and Z., after saying how much she liked my presentation, asked for an appointment to talk about some problems and anxieties that had arisen since the recent death of her mother.

At our first encounter, she started talking almost exclusively about how depressed she had been since her mother's death, but then she proceeded to express admiration for me, and said she would be enthusiastic to start analysis. We started shortly thereafter, in October 1990, initially with three sessions a week, and after a few months increasing this to four.

Z. is in her fifties, a good-looking professional woman, married, with children. She herself was an only child and lived with her mother; she hardly knew her father, who had left town once she was born and set up another family elsewhere. He turned up only rarely, but wrote to her often to start with, then increasingly rarely, and finally his letters stopped. He always promised his little girl he would come and see her soon, leaving her painfully waiting, but always letting her down. She was an adult when she re-established contact with her father, who came to her wedding.

She described her mother as suffering frequent attacks of depression; she was lonely but liked meeting people and had a promiscuous sex life. The mother was very close to her sister, who lived with their father – the patient's grandfather – who Z. saw as an ideal figure who greatly influenced her own career choices. Z. lived with her mother, as I said, but she could not help her daughter with her studies and sent her to boarding school for several years.

Z. told me about some traumatic childhood events. When she was 4 or 5 years old a man came up to her in church and said he wanted to show her the church organ; he sat her on his knee and masturbated her. She vividly remembers her despair. As an adolescent she felt an intense, irresistible need to masturbate. She told me that she had started to masturbate by chance when she had crossed her legs one time and felt a strange but pleasant sensation, like an orgasm. After that, for a long time she felt intense erotic sensitivity, which met with her mother's rigid prohibition. Her mother wanted to know about everything she did and obliged her to promise she would not masturbate. But then another trauma happened in adolescence: walking into the bathroom one day she found her mother toweling one of her young lovers, with his penis erect. Her resentment at her mother, who forbade her the pleasure she so freely allowed herself, and her jealousy at her mother who gave herself to others, remained central elements in a constellation of emotions that came to light in the transference.

The first weekend separations brought to the surface the main problem of her analysis: the absent parent (father and mother) and the anxiety this produced. She defended herself by *denying* any feelings for me, and by intense sexual activity with some compulsive elements. She recalled in the sessions her erotic excitement when she was left alone as a child and placated her anxiety with compulsive masturbation.

The transference showed intense amorous and erotic interest, accompanied by idealization, and passion made up largely of fantasies. She found my voice elicited feelings of sweetness, love, eroticism – a form of seduction, a mother's voice that she allowed to caress her childish part. But at the same time she was afraid of creating any bond with me and suffering when I was absent. She defended herself by rationalizing the risk of analysis suffocating her creativity, making her banal and flat, and depriving her of her ability to marvel at things like a little girl.

In one of her very early dreams:

She is at home after a robbery. The drawers in the room have been turned inside out and she is worried about three jewels that belonged to her mother [at that time she was coming for analysis three times a week] *that she had hidden among her hats. She looked for them but realized they had gone. The thieves had come in through the ceiling, making a hole in a corner of the room.* [Here she points to a corner of my consulting room.]

She associates with the dream her feelings about the loss of her mother, who was always worried about being robbed. She was afraid of falling in love and suffering from jealousy. My comment was that her thieving childish parts had crept furtively into our room to steal the valuable things I/the mother kept aside in my head rather than asking for them. Perhaps she was afraid she could not have them all for herself.

Z.'s transference was initially mostly maternal. I was the mother who betrayed her, who was not available totally for her, and who did not give her the guarantees she wanted to be protected from jealousy. In another dream:

I was arranging the session with a break half-way through but after the first half I could not come for the second because I was busy with a French philosopher. [Before this patient started analysis with me she had had an unsatisfactory experience with a Lacanian analyst.] *In the dream she is angry about what is going on and on leaving the room she meets a little boy with a man, possibly her father.*

In association this dream reminded her of her feelings of exclusion when her mother was tied up with her women friends and paid no attention to her daughter who, as revenge, provoked her.

During the first winter holidays she said she had been well but at the New Year's Eve party her legs had been very painful. She was not happy, and was worried that her daughter would soon marry and leave home. That night she had had the following dream:

> I am here on your couch but you are behind me, with a nurse. You are talking together and I am worried because I am afraid you are planning electroshock treatment.

She associates the dream with her recollection of her mother having electroshock therapy for her depression. I comment that the couple she sees behind her might make her jealous and take advantage of her, as a little girl, exciting her with electroshock therapy and making her lose control.

This set in motion a long string of detailed narrations of erotic experiences, told in an excited girlish voice. She created an atmosphere of erotic "passion" in the session, which got me involved. Her session was drawing fast to a close and I felt I had to stand back at the right distance so as to understand the significance of these operations by the infantile parts of her self that were so passionately and erotically engaged in the relation with me/mother, and the projective identification of these feelings.

In the same period she dreams *she meets a little boy who follows her along the street, and then spies on her in the bath through a chink in the door.* Presumably the peeping-tom was me, and this corresponded to the countertransference I felt had been set up at that time. But the little boy might also have been the projection of that part of her own little-girl self who had watched her mother's erotic play with her young lover in the bathroom.

Z. relived with me her adolescent erotic experiences, when her mother had sent her away to school, and she masturbated, with distressing guilt feelings. In one dream, she sees *a bitch on heat which was dangerous because it had wounded her on the palm of her hand. To treat the wound she had taken a little bottle of vinegar, which she held close to her chest.*

She recalled, in her association, that her grandfather had loved balsamic vinegar and used to pick up his little granddaughter and hold her on his lap. Z. remembered these moments with much affection and tenderness. She also remembered a long period of frequent masturbation when she was engaged; the two of them went in for heavy petting, but never had full intercourse. Her mother kept an eye on all their meetings and accused her – with no proof – of having sexual relations. What a cheek, says the patient, when she had so many men herself and had no hesitation about being seen in the bathroom drying her lover's penis! Fear of her mother's anger stopped her masturbating. Z. would have felt too guilty and anxious because she would have had to tell her mother – they had agreed on this "perverse pact".

For a long time Z.'s transference was dominated by erotic fantasies. She remembered as a child having had a tape worm, and associates a dream in

which *she is sucking a penis but it becomes flaccid and turns into a tape [worm],
that ejaculates sperm mixed with urine.* In another dream *there is a man with a
pointed nose that gets longer or shorter. She blows on him to make sure he stands
up straight, and he sprays out pee.*

She associates the dream with a dog show, where she was holding up her own
dog's head (a bitch) to show her to the judge, who had a beaky nose like the man
in her dream.

I interpreted these metaphors as expressing the intimate side of her relation with
me/judge and her wishes and torments in the transference, where she showed
her excited part/dog (the bitch on heat in the earlier dream) and sucks at my
penis/nipple, but no milk comes out, so it turns into an object – the tape worm –
that takes her back to her anal stage as a child.

She recalls a period when she agreed to go out with a perverse and psycho-
pathic admirer, because she hoped to gain something in her work. He took her
to luxury restaurants and receptions in fashionable venues, but insisted that she
– who was blonde – wear a black patch on one eye, like Moshe Dayan. This
highly exhibitionistic, perverse game went on for a long time and she broke off
finally because this man's obsessions and violence frightened her.

Naturally, on occasion she made an exhibition of herself with me in the session,
arriving dressed eccentrically; there was the erotic "black widow" outfit, wide
"femme fatale" hats, or the living statue, with careful attention to every detail. She
told me all about her erotic fantasies which directly involved me; her intention was
to get me emotionally involved and excited by her tales of our sexual encounters.
These descriptions were obviously arousing, and suggested I interpret her
fantasies at that time as indicating she wanted to get me outside the setting and
"mix up" the two realities – the real and the transferential – as a defense against
her fear of being abandoned; however, she also aimed to relive emotionally with
me unconscious erotic experiences linked to her earliest relations, stored in her
implicit memory.

I reminded her of a dream in which *she was a little girl, in intimate relations
with a man.* This might have been a metaphor for an unconscious episode of
seduction – real or imagined – that had happened when she was very small.

In another dream about that time:

> *There were two wounded baby birds on a rug in her bedroom* [associated
> with a bird that had fallen out of its nest and she had really saved it]. *Her maid
> wanted to sweep them out, but her daughter put a fake fly in her mouth
> to induce them to eat. Then Z. found a real fly buzzing around her, and she
> couldn't catch it.*

She associates the emotions of the previous session. She had thought about the
irreparable loss of her mother, and her feelings with me in the session (love and

excitement, accompanied by a feeling of emotional void that somatized to the vagina). I comment that the little birds seem like parts of her as a girl (frustrated and humiliated but still endearing), separated from her mother/analyst. Her "maid part" that was very active at weekends wanted to sweep them away (consoling herself with sexual activity) but the baby birds seemed to need a fly/nipple, though in the dream this bait was fake and the real one was unattainable – always somewhere else.

Almost the whole of Z.'s analysis was involved an area of the transference marked by passion mixed with tenderness and seduction, which I interpreted from the outset as a defense against the fear of being abandoned and left alone. But this acting was also a repetition of the seduction from her early infancy. She projectively identified this seduction and excitation in me. So she felt I was highly seductive and excited. She did not hear my voice in the session solely for what I was saying, but also for its "musical" qualities. Z. repeatedly told me in our sessions that my voice gave her great pleasure, as she heard in it the sweet voice of her own mother. She then abandoned herself to fantasies of "union", telling me she wanted to be with me, to live with me, to come to La Scala theater with me to listen to music together.

These messages bore the sentiments of a person "authentically" and "really" in love, and often finished with her admitting that she desired me and wanted to blend in one with me. In this period she had a dream in which *a viola and a violin were being played in perfect harmony* and associated this with our dialogue/duet in analysis, as a metaphor of a state of union. My viola-voice then became the soundtrack of the film *Tous les matins du mond* which she had seen several times, letting herself go in amorous fantasies.

During this period she started asking me insistently to take her to La Scala, which she felt as a maternal container, though at the same time taking her to the theater would make me the father/analyst who recognized her and made our relation "official". La Scala theater reappeared in various dreams, and marked out one of her analytical paths. In a dream from the early period of analysis (when she was strongly idealizing), *I was represented by a little man up on a platform, and she made him come down on a ladder.* The man was definitely me/father/analyst, who Z., in her resentment, saw as a little man, and made him come down from his platform.

Later on in analysis, when the La Scala question had been worked through at length, Z. dreamt over the weekend that *she was high up on the cornice of her house, and felt dizzy. An untrustworthy man sets up what he says is a safe stepladder, but she sees a crack halfway down that makes it risky.* Evidently she is once again seeing me as unreliable, putting up unsafe steps (*scala* means stairway, or steps, in Italian). Then in a later dream Z. seems finally to have grasped that if I had given in to her demands to go to La Scala our analysis would have failed. In this dream *there was a stepladder* [the *scala*] *leaning against a wall, and ending up merging into the wall itself. It didn't lead anywhere.* (It was part of the wall, i.e. part of her defenses.)

At that stage of analysis, Z.'s transference had become basically paternal. My countertransferential feeling had also changed. Now I was worried mainly by her distress and the unrealistic sides of this love. I tried to explain to her the various levels of reality on which she was living these feelings for me: they were not for me as a person (or not just for that at any rate) but for what I represented symbolically – the unreliable, insensitive, absent father, who never kept his promises, for whom she could feel only despair and frustrating love. She had no way of filling this affective void, which she was obliged to somatize to her vagina, where it became an empty container that she filled during our separations.

Z. often denied the level of reality in the transference and the metaphorical aspect of her love for me; she insisted that I interested her for what I was, for how I spoke, for what I said, for my tastes and interests, so close to her own (we had met at a conference on music and our paths did in fact cross quite often at performances at La Scala). At that point I had to be very careful about how I spoke to her, and to the timbre and "musicality" of my voice; sometimes when I felt that the temperature in the transference was hot and the atmosphere highly charged with eroticism, I preferred not to say anything, but just waited until things quietened down to a state of affection, with no excessive erotic overtones.

Obviously Z. described many erotic dreams involving me directly. In one of these

> We are in my study, and I sit down in front of her, and strip off my clothes, down to a pair of black underpants. In the meantime she has drawn on her stockings. The atmosphere had become very erotically charged. She then started to encourage me, telling me it was necessary to make love and it was the right thing to do – after all Freud did it. In the dream, she invited me to read Freud's book!

She said she was afraid her own erotic desire would weaken with time, and if that happened she was worried no one would love her, and she would no longer be able to seduce anyone.

* * *

At this point a highly significant thing happened in the transference because she talked about an event dating back a long way, to a trauma with her father, that she had never got over. She was organizing a party in the country, and invited me, asking me insistently to come. I interpreted this by linking it to her difficulty accepting "reality" and the limits of our relation, and her desire to take me, defensively, outside the analytical relation so as to overcome the feelings of frustration and dissatisfaction she felt with me in analysis. I pointed out to her the similarities between this request and her wanting me to take her to La Scala.

Clearly I did not go to her party and afterwards she told me, angrily and despairingly, that she had waited all the time for me to arrive. Her resentment was tangible in the session. She was convinced that I had promised to go and insisted that my absence was a sign of my selfishness and lack of sensibility. She remembers her wedding day, when she did not want her father to take her up to the altar. Her father, nagged by her mother, had come, without telling his daughter, and had given her a family jewel as a present. But afterwards he got lost in the crowd of guests and did not come to the reception.

This is a clear case of *Nachträglichkeit*, with a situation in the transference that takes us back to the earliest experiences. I connect her despair and resentment towards me with that of her youth: the promise she said I had made but not kept was her father's broken promise; my selfishness, distance and lack of sensitivity were those of her father. Later, when Z. returned to this episode, but in a different affective mood altogether, I was able to make her understand how important it was for our analytical relationship that I did not agree to "act out" with her by going to the party, as this would have meant moving out of our analytical relation and shifting with her into another "reality". I explained that this "failure to act" on my part may have caused her pain and disappointment, but at the same time had enabled her to live an event where her feelings for me were comparable to those she had felt years before when her absent father turned up at her wedding.

She now saw it was more logical that I should symbolize her thoughtless, selfish father, but she also found it easier to understand that the "reality" of our analytical relation could not be confused with "reality" outside analysis, unless we wanted to jeopardize our professional relationship.

I think this episode also greatly helped Z. understand why I could not agree to accompany her to La Scala or meet her anywhere other than in the analytical setting, despite her frequent requests.

This brings up the question of the *truth* or *falsity* of the relation and the feelings in play between the two partners. Z. told me one day, in despairing tones, that she had heard an analyst on the radio saying that the transference was "fiction" and feelings in analysis were not real (or was fictitious). This had thrown her into confusion and created profound anxiety. "Is what we feel here true or false?" she asked. My comment was to ask her rhetorically:

> How could you trust me if I refuse to come to your party, will not take you to La Scala, and will not go out with you, "truly" committing myself amorously

and sexually. How can you believe in me if you know nothing about me, as I keep my private life to myself?

She knows from a friend, a colleague of mine, that I am divorced, but nothing more, so the asymmetry of our relation persists in analysis. And, I insist, "How can you trust me if I represent, for you, the absent, irresponsible, unreliable and disappointing father you have waited for all your life?"

These feelings set up strong ambivalence in the transference that became increasingly evident during analysis and surfaced in dreams. In one of these, that Z. announced as highly erotic:

She is in a wheelchair, as if she was handicapped, in the analysis room. I am sitting on the couch and she comes up to me, trying to take my clothes off. But she is dressed like a handicapped person – not very sexily – and certainly hasn't got on the shoes the actresses wear in Buñuel's films. . . . Then I take off my trousers and she sees my penis erect inside my underwear . . . but she doesn't want to be with me, and says no.

The handicapped woman is her, feeling unattractive and unable to seduce me, but by denying herself she projects her frustrations and scant sex appeal onto me.

Feelings of denial and reversal of desire also dominated another dream that same week:

A man returning by train from Switzerland finds an unknown woman in his bunk. He fondles her during the night, but only out of a sense of duty, because she doesn't really interest him.

The associations and sentiments in the transference in that period suggested she identified with the unknown woman that the traveler/analyst was caressing only because he felt it was expected of him, with no real interest or feeling.

The ambivalence, jealousy, resentment for being abandoned, and anger mixed with eroticization of the transference had created an affective situation in which, in all the erotic dreams she narrated, there was never any actual penetration or complete and satisfactory intercourse. There was always some part of her, disguised as a spiteful little girl or a severe aunt, that prevented the conclusion of a relationship prepared with erotic games that enriched our routine "*jardin d'acclimatation*". It seemed to me that this figure that disturbed our intimacy was part of her that set up resistance to her wishes, and was highly ambivalent towards me/father, for whom she felt love but who she felt she could not trust because of his distance, unreliability, irresponsibility, and failure to live up to what was expected of a father/analyst/lover.

This transference situation was depicted well in this dream:

I am in a house like yours, in bed with a man. He lies on top of me and we are both highly excited. Our genitals touch but we cannot make love – there is no penetration because some unknown force is stopping us.

She comments on this dream by reminding me that the day before,

when we were saying goodbye, I looked you in the face, and you were very excited, like me! But this dream tells me we cannot stay together; anyway I cannot give myself to someone who gives me no guarantee.

This dream links up with another she had narrated much earlier, at the start of analysis. This was a sweet dream and we had done a lot of work on it:

We were together in a Volkswagen car, driving below a reservoir [bacino], and she was worried that the dam might burst and the water might flood out and drown us. ["Bacino" in Italian has another meaning too – a little kiss!]

I returned to the old interpretation about her fear of letting herself go in the intimacy of our travels as a *duo* (the *bacino*), as the passion might have broken down her defenses and drowned us.

During analysis she continued to display a high level of excitation inside and outside the sessions, which she often somatized to the vagina. She complained of a void that nothing seemed to fill, and which felt worse when we were separated at weekends. One Monday she told me she had had a very creative dream, but first she had to tell me about a painting she remembered by V., an artist friend, done just after his father died. It showed a man standing on his head, and was a simple picture, but very moving. Then she told me about the dream: *I took a sheet of paper, like V.'s painting, but instead of the drawing of the man it was blank. The empty page was surrounded by the frame, through which you could see what was behind.* Then she remembered another dream in which *there was a woman on her own, surrounded by void*, whereas in this dream the picture was the void.

I note that in both dreams she seems to have been able to represent the void, instead of somatizing it in her vagina. She responds that this is true but "I am very angry at you because I have to drop the fantasy of being the only one here with you, having you for myself. I am jealous that you have other women patients." I reply that her jealousy reminds me of her envy of her mother, who had different lovers on whom she could lavish attention. Z.'s comment is that the feeling of emptiness in the picture in the dream is linked to her immense, infinite childhood void.

Then we are back again, like a leitmotiv, to her love and anger at me because I am insensitive, I have made her suffer, and will surely do so again. She decides to "blackmail" me: she will no longer tell me about her intimate fantasies in the session, but will keep them hidden away in her office. Thus we started an ice-age of analysis, arid and cold, while she withheld her emotions from our encounters and kept them at work.

At that time she went to see the opera *Salomé* at La Scala and talked to me about her identification with Salomé and her delusional love. I tell her that Salomé is that part of her that does not admit freedom in love, and that this wish to unite with the other person makes it deadly. She responds that it is John's fear of union that is the cause of his death. I suggest that she is perhaps overturning things in her interpretation of the opera and identification with Salomé, casting me in the role of John, a father/analyst with whom she has always wanted to unite, and who deserves to lose his head for refusing to "act out" this love with her. This little girl is seeking, in her unconscious fantasy of con-fused love, a defense from the separation and the terrifying fear of depressive loss of self.

10

Sexuality, such sweet folly

What's sweet folly got to do with it? It is difficult to say what is normal, as sexuality is in fact a function that covers numerous others, passing through the complex processes of evolution and identification that make up our personal identity and the structure of our personality. This explains why personality disorders inevitably have an effect on sexuality, so the definition "sweet folly" fits sexuality perfectly.

Freud (1905) mapped out a child's sexual development in several stages: oral, anal and genital; sexuality as a whole developed in two stages, with a latency period in between. The first was between 2 and 5 years (the true Oedipus stage), and the second started at puberty and governed the final structure of the person's sexual life. Freud's classification criteria were the object relation and auto-erotism in the Oedipal phase, and the genital organs' subsequent effects on sexual life. When he speaks of genitality and pre-genitality Freud is referring to the effect of the genital organs: the pre-genitality period is during the pre-Oedipal phases, and genitality starts with Oedipus.

Later, however, Freud (1923a) seems to contradict himself, saying that it may well be that the genitals are in fact also dominant in the infantile phase. He feels that an infant's interest in genital activity is only slightly inferior to its interest later in life, although the difference is that for both sexes only one genital is in play – the phallus. Freud still maintains that the Oedipus complex is central to the development of a child's sexuality. It starts to decline as it is intrinsically impossible to fulfill the child's wish, but also because it is faced with the threat of castration .

A baby girl develops an Oedipus complex too, and has her own phallic organization and castration complex (Freud, 1924b), but the anatomical difference results in a different mental development. The girl accepts castration as something that has already happened, while the boy is afraid it is still to come. The girl's Oedipus complex is more univocal, in Freud's (1931) eyes, than the boy's because the girl shifts her wish onto the father's penis following a symbolic equation of penis = child. Her Oedipus complex peaks when her desire to have a child as a gift from her father can no longer be satisfied.

The girl child's Oedipus complex therefore poses one more problem than the boy's. Freud believed that seeing the penis and comparing it with her own tiny clitoris was the origin of penis envy. Thus, while the boy's Oedipus complex declined with the threat of castration, the girl's is possible *because of* castration.

Freud's interest in bisexuality led him to believe it was more marked in women than men, as women had two erotogenic zones, the clitoris and the vagina, which meant that women developed their sexuality in two phases, one zone after the other.[1]

The Oedipal object investment is also different for a boy and a girl. The boy's investment in the object (his mother) is the same before and after the Oedipal phase. But the girl, to some extent, also invests her father, on account of her potential bisexuality. The girl has to make various changes in her investment to reach maturity: first, *shifting the object* from mother to father; second, *shifting the organ* from clitoris to vagina, although this is discovered only in puberty; third, *shifting her attitude* from active in the clitoral phase to passive in the vaginal phase.

In *Female Sexuality*, Freud (1931) takes another look at the early stage of female sexuality, and finds that the child's primary pre-Oedipal bond with her mother is very old and important, intense and prolonged, and is deeply repressed. We now know, however, that the emotions and affects involved in this early relation cannot be repressed, as explicit memory, which is essential for repression, is not yet mature. These feelings are therefore stored away in implicit memory, as part of an unrepressed unconscious nucleus of the personality that will influence not only a person's relational life, but also his or her sexual life as an adult (Mancia, 2003a, 2006a).

Ernest Jones (1927) brought about an abrupt change from Freud's ideas on sexuality. He was the first to underline the part played in the development of sexuality by *envy* of the mother, who possesses the object of the baby girl's desires, her father's penis. This primary envy sets up in the little girl sadistic, aggressive fantasies against her mother's body and fantasies of taking over the objects she so desires, which are in her mother's body. But these very fantasies also cause fear of retaliation and revenge which can cause personality disorders and sexuality problems in the adult woman.

Ernest Jones suggests that in the very early stages the little girl's mind considers the mouth and vagina as one – recognizing the existence of the latter, although Freud maintains she does not. Also her desires to "incorporate" the father's penis and have a baby from it is also *primary*, not secondary to penis envy, as Freud sustained.

In the light of recent knowledge on children's development, the question comes to mind whether these sadistic and aggressive fantasies against the mother's body are perhaps reactions to the daughter's early experiences – possibly traumatic – with her mother, stored in her implicit memory where they form part of the unrepressed unconscious that will more specifically affect her sexuality as an adult.

The ideas of Ernest Jones that I have covered very briefly here are very important as they open the route to Klein's opinions and work. She was the one who truly revolutionized the concept of the development of female sexuality. She was convinced that the baby girl was aware – possibly unconsciously – of her vagina at a very early age. She also believed the Oedipus phase came early (Klein, 1928). In her first months of life the baby girl suffers persecutory anxiety about her mother's breast, linked to sadistic fantasies and ideas of revenge against what she sees as "bad", because it stimulates her envy but frustrates her wishes. To overcome the inevitable frustrations caused by her mother's breast-nipple, and to renew and confirm her experience with a "good" breast, the little girl looks for a new object: she finds it in the father's penis, making it the symbolic equivalent of the nipple.

Klein sees this shift from the breast-nipple to the penis as the core of the early Oedipus conflict and believes it is rich in genital instincts. The child will want to incorporate her father's penis through all her orifices: mouth, vagina and anus. As a consequence, her mainly negative feelings towards the breast, dominated by envy, will facilitate a *bad* relation with the penis, which will maintain sadistic, persecutory features. The interest of Klein's views on this question is boosted by the possibility that the baby girl's feelings get tucked away in her unrepressed unconscious as they are linked to such early experiences, so these too will carry on influencing her affective and sexual life even as an adult.

For Melanie Klein, the breast and penis are the little girl's first internal objects. If at this stage of her development the interiorized father's penis is *good*, and capable of placating her anxiety, as an adult she will be able to achieve satisfactory and lasting relations with men. If the interiorized penis is felt to be *bad*, her anxiety will persist and her sadistic instincts will be directed against her internal objects – the breast and penis – which she feels are bad and persecutory.

But the attack on her internal objects is a way of turning her aggressivity inwards as a cause of masochism. The sadistic attack on the interiorized paternal penis lays the foundations for *frigidity*, or for a tendency to indiscriminate, compulsive sexual activity to provide the woman with reassurance against her destructive and persecutory anxiety about the penis.

The concept of envy is basic to Klein's theory. It is *primary* and arises when the little girl realizes her mother has everything: milk, the father's penis, and babies in her body. She, on the other hand, has nothing, and depends totally on her mother, and her vagina is not able to really receive a penis. Splitting and projective identification of the envy are the defensive weapons that will mark the development of the child's personality and sexuality. Penis envy – and the desire for one – is therefore not primary, as Freud maintained, but secondary: first, to envy of the mother's breast and body which has the penis and babies; second, to frustration of the girl's Oedipal fantasies; and third, to the desire to repair the mother's body, which has been attacked in fantasy.

This last point is pivotal in the development of sexuality. If the little girl can integrate her sadistic fantasies towards the nipple-penis with fantasies of love and gratitude, she will accept the penis as an object that can repair and gratify her mother's body and later her own; her sexuality will thus develop "normally", to a certain extent, and her relations with men will be satisfactory. If, however, she does not manage to integrate and neutralize these destructive instincts and her mother is not able to help her transform them, projective identification will prevail over introjection.

The lack of introjection of a good breast-penis, able to repair, will make the penis seem aggressive and dangerous. The woman will respond to this danger with frigidity and vaginismus, to build a barrier she can control herself, for this cavity that by biological and psychological definition has no such diaphragm. Clitoral masturbation as the sole sexual outlet will be another form of defense against the danger of penetration by a penis she sees as bad, sadistic and threatening.

★ ★ ★

The development of sexuality has attracted the attention of many authors since Freud and Klein. Chasseguet-Smirgel (1964) noted that frustration caused by the mother's breast being seen as "bad" led to idealization of the father and his penis. This process, resulting in a change of the object, has a tremendous impact on a woman's psychosexual fate. Chasseguet-Smirgel offers an interesting idea to correlate clitoral sexuality with guilt feelings about incorporating the father's penis; this guilt prevents the woman investing the vagina erotically, shifting the investment to the clitoris which is external, therefore easier to control. This analyst sees penis envy as a protest against an omnipotent mother who has wounded the girl's narcissism by leaving her without a penis, causing "castration".

Clearly, penis envy and erotic desire for the penis are not conflicting but complementary, and penis envy is simply the symbolic expression of another wish: to separate from the mother and become an independent, active woman. Chasseguet-Smirgel (1964) therefore criticizes Freud's ideas of penis envy and female passivity, offering in their place independence, activity and desire, which can be linked more directly to current tendencies to give more priority to the female baby's primary identificatory love for her father.

★ ★ ★

Since the mid-1980s analytical thinking on the question of sexuality has shifted considerably. First of all, classical theories on the development of sexuality, dominated by the Oedipus complex, have come under fire for not taking full account of the complex early processes of identification and dis-identification of both girl and boy babies with the primary object, their mother. But identification with the father has also been underestimated, including his role in the pre-Oedipal phases of children of both sexes. The interest in the mother–child relation (boy or girl) shown by important post-Freudian analysts such as Klein (1932) and Winnicott (1965) seems to have eclipsed the father's role, whereas there is no question that he is present both before and during the Oedipal phase.

Current research has shown the complex role of identifications in the pre-Oedipal phases as regards gender identity. There seems now to be agreement (Benjamin, 1995) that both parents are objects of identification in a child's early stages of development. These *hyperinclusive* modalities (Benjamin, 1988, 1995; see also Fast, 1984) permit the boy or girl to identify with both parents. This "crossed" sexual identification enables the child to build up important parts of its self-representation and to elaborate fantasies about the erotic relations between the sexes. This is what has given rise to the idea of children, from a very early age, being *bisexual* – not in the biological sense of the term, which Freud had understood on the basis of organic considerations and in the wake of Fliess, but as a result of their identification with both parents (Fast, 1984).

From this new viewpoint the father has a vital role in the child's defi-nitely pre-Oedipal early development. The father is there as an internal representation of the mother, thus becoming an indirect component of the infant's dyadic relation with its mother, through her psychic reality. The mother's capacity for *rêverie* and for dealing with the infant's anxieties also largely depend on the father, on whether he is present or absent, loving or sadistic, concerned or indifferent.

But the father's role goes beyond being merely an invisible element in the mother–child dyad – referring always to either a boy or a girl. He is also an object embodying desire and independence, and representing the outside world. It is the father, with whom a child of either sex identifies, who is an object of dyadic love and becomes a symbol of release from the omnipotent mother's all-enveloping power, helping the child through the delicate process of separation and dis-identification from her (Greenson, 1968).

It is through identification with the father that children of either sex become aware of their wishes and of being subjects (Benjamin, 1988). But this identification is not merely the *deus ex machina* who fosters, justifies and makes possible separation from the mother, resolving the infantile dilemma between the desire to remain bonded to the mother but also to become independent. This identification is not just a defense against an omnipotent mother: it is a new prototype of love – *identificatory love* (Benjamin, 1988, 1995). Identification involves not only *being similar to* but also *being in relation to* so it is a key player in love and desire. This identificatory love develops while the infant is still in the pre-Oedipal phase; it does not arouse Oedipal rivalry, even though it is antagonistic to love for the mother and remains bound throughout life to some aspects of idealization and excitation.

Identification with the ideal father fulfills different tasks in a baby girl or boy. Classical psychoanalysis attributes importance to a boy's identificatory love as part of the acquisition of male characteristics, but it is different for a girl. Benjamin considers that penis envy, as Freud sees it, is an element of any child's desire to identify itself, while still pre-Oedipal, with the father: he is the real representative of the outside world, of independence and desire. McDougall (1997) tends to agree. Benjamin (1988) suggests that penis envy is not a girl's prerogative, but is also felt by boys, and expresses their desire to identify with the father as a liberator, who helps – and allows – them to separate from the mother and recognize their own wishes. A girl, like a boy, in her anxiety about separation from the mother, seeks a reference figure to guarantee and represent her shift from maternal dependence: this is the father, whose difference is symbolized by the fact that his genitals are different from the mother's, and by his own separation from her.

The girl's pre-Oedipal identificatory love for her father is a basic experience for her sexual development as an adult and for a grasp of the characteristics of sexuality and male desire essential for the development of her own sexuality and desire. A girl child therefore sees her "ideal father" as a sort of first love, a paradigm of idealized identificatory love that can serve as a model for loves to come (Benjamin, 1995).

In the pre-Oedipal phase children of both sexes want to be recognized by their father and to share his subjectivity, will and desire. Identificatory love is a preparation for the subsequent Oedipal phase when the girl affectively invests her father and wants to be one with him as a *love object*. We must therefore keep a distinction between *pre-Oedipal identificatory love* and *Oedipal object love*. They arc, however, linked in the development of the girl child's sexuality and personality.

Identificatory love, since it is pre-Oedipal, is an emotional experience stored in the implicit memory, where it cannot be repressed. It is therefore a driving force for the unrepressed infantile unconscious. The later, Oedipal object love, stored in the explicit, autobiographic memory, is repressed and can be brought to the surface more easily in analysis.

Psychoanalysis right now views the Oedipal stage as the peak of a process starting in the pre-Oedipal phase and involving a series of identifications with both parents. In the Oedipal phase a child accepts the difference (between him/her and the parents and between the parents) and grasps its sexual significance. The child has also to accept – with the trauma it may cause – outside reality that makes the child feel excluded and jealous, and is anyway beyond his or her control. Working through this experience is one step towards maturity, as it implies acceptance of reality, however painful, and towards independence.

The absence of the father at this stage can be devastating for the development of the child's sexuality and personality. The father may be physically absent or psychologically absent – distant, indifferent and unable to understand his child. Frustration at the lack of identificatory love will inevitably have effects in the subsequent Oedipal phase. The girl or boy will have trouble achieving separation and dis-identification from the mother, with the risk of an impact on their sense of independence and gender identity.

A boy's failure to detach his identity from his mother will make a homosexual object choice more likely, and the organization of perverse parts of the personality. Many authors (Stoller, 1975; Limentani, 1979, 1991; Isay, 1987; McDougall, 1989; see Mancia, 1994) hold the opinion that an absent father facilitates the development of homosexuality in a male and of perversions such as transvestism and trans-sexualism. In a richly detailed publication, Tomassini (1992) suggested that the perverse structure is organized in the pre-Oedipal phase, and comes about because the person has never "naturally" reached the Oedipal phase. Perversion, according to various theories (Quinodoz, 1992; Tomassini, 1992), is the consequence of an inability to work through the processes of separation and primary dis-identification (Greenson, 1968). This might be because these processes date from very early in the primary relation with the mother.

Today we recognize that these processes are part of the unrepressed unconscious, which contains presymbolic and preverbal experiences that cannot be recollected or worked on at a conscious level. We also know that the father is essential for fostering and ensuring dis-identification from the mother in the pre-Oedipal phase.

For a girl child the absence of the father and frustration at the impossibility of identificatory love may lead her, as an adult, to *idealize* the male figure, in the belief that a man, viewed as an "idol", can enable her to reach that love and that identificatory world that she never enjoyed as a baby. These women seek relations offering this type of love, and their willingness to idealize men leaves them open to frustration and humiliation which sometimes, however, unconsciously satisfies their masochism. Often their relations are dominated by anger, insecurity and unreliability which have characterized their frustration at not having had the chance of identificatory love.

In a girl child this lack of love will prevent the development of the Oedipus phase and will facilitate what Halberstadt-Freud (1998), for example, called the Electra complex, metaphorically referring to the development of a woman decided at birth by the *ambivalence* linking the child and her mother. This analyst believes that femininity is not the result of penis envy or a lack of castration anxiety. In addition, the theory of the zone shifting from the clitoris to the vagina and the object shifting from the mother to the father is not backed by firm clinical evidence.

The problem of the development of sexuality – particularly for females – is that a girl, unlike a boy, adds a heterosexual object choice (her father) to the homosexual object already present (her mother). Halberstadt-Freud also wonders what connection there is between female discomfort and the question of a daughter's relation with her mother and with the processes of identification, dis-identification and separation during a woman's development.

Undoubtedly a mother and daughter have closer bonds than a mother and son. According to the myth, Electra was a lonely, unhappy woman who accused her mother of neglecting her; she hated her and planned to have her killed. She is, in other words, the prototype of the woman with several internal mothers, one loved, one hated, one desired, one criticized and one feared (McDougall, 1997). Electra idealized her father Agamemnon even though she knew he had killed Clytemnestra's first husband and sons and would have sacrificed Iphigenia for the sake of a favorable wind. This is why the Electra complex is better suited than the Oedipus complex to describe a girl's combination of love and hate for her mother, and her idealization of her father.

For a girl, separation and dis-identification from the mother are not the same as for a boy, for whom this process is essential for the development of his gender identity. For the girl the process is anyway only *partial*, and runs parallel to the primary identification with the father. If separation is radical, or is not achieved, the girl has pathological problems establishing her female gender identity. The mid-way result is a state of *ambivalence* since the girl cannot develop open feelings of hostility towards her mother because she needs her and depends on her, but at the same time she is silently angry, with hostile fantasies that she carefully hides, at her mother, who will end up as a threatening, persecutory internal object.

Halberstadt-Freud therefore maintains there is no shift in object from the mother to the father as both are invested in parallel; and since the mother is an obstacle to her daughter's relationship with her father, there is a split between a "bad" internal mother who is frustrating, and a "good", idealized internal father. This explains why an Electra complex is perhaps a more appropriate term for a girl than an Oedipus complex.

That daughters never completely dis-identify from their mothers is proved by the fact that they turn to their mothers as an example, as their identification object, and adviser whenever they have to tackle "feminine" tasks. As Joyce McDougall (1997) noted, a woman's unconscious body image, too, reflects the significance her mother transmitted.

Naturally there is always the risk that something intervenes to disrupt these delicate processes of identification and separation and the woman remains trapped in a *symbiotic illusion* with her mother: she is the victim of a pathological fantasy in which mother and daughter are bound by an exclusive, idealized love for each other that splits off the negative aspects and projects them onto the external father. In such cases the Oedipal path and its emotions and feelings is blocked, and the girl cannot develop her own independence and separate identity. This does not prevent her being heterosexual – unlike a boy in whom this symbiotic illusion with his mother can lead to homosexuality and various perversions.

To conclude on this topic, dis-identification and separation from the mother is necessary for a boy but is usually fairly straightforward and complete, influencing his choice of heterosexual object; for a girl, however, separation from the mother is harder, more gradual, and never complete. She has to achieve the separation from her mother while still keeping up an identificatory but competitive relationship (Chodorow, 1994). She remains identified with her mother while in parallel she identifies with her father. A daughter makes less absolute demands on her father than a son, and her idealization of the father is aimed at achieving the "perfect state" that takes her back to her first "identificatory love" in the pre-Oedipal phase.

★ ★ ★

Two brief clinical examples will help illustrate these theories.

The case of S.

S. is a 30-year-old married woman who came to me for analysis because for many years she had been suffering from frigidity and vaginismus. She had never masturbated and had never had an orgasm. Her relations in general with her husband and at work were problematic. At the start of analysis she was six months pregnant.

In the transference S. brought to the surface feels of intense envy for me/her mother, who she wants to control completely, without ever separating from her. She identifies with the child she is carrying and becomes an omnipotent fetus herself, claiming control of my space and time. The inevitable frustrations produced by analysis cause anger and a desire for retaliation that S. projects onto me. In an early dream, *she transforms the mother/analyst into a wild beast out to kill her, but she whips out a knife and stabs it in the neck and back.*

Her envy is directed at me who, like her mother, has everything and depends on no one, while she is a defenseless baby threatened with abandon. She has an anxious dream where *she risks being drowned in a city in Israel* [analysts are all Jewish!] *by an ancient-looking man who won't let her go to the toilet more than once a day.*

For a long time during analysis, her fantasies were dominated by confusion between milk, blood and feces. She identifies with her unborn child and, full of resentment and anger, shares with him her desire for atonement for the wrongs she had suffered as a baby at the hands of her mother who she was convinced wanted her dead. Her sole weapon in this task was to deliver monotonous complaints in a slow, low voice, like missiles aimed at anesthetizing my thought and analytical creativity, represented as a nipple-penis. In one of these interminable sessions, she told me her mother had an in-turned nipple and her milk was sour; as a baby she risked dying.

On the basis of these dreams and the "musical" content of her transference, which conveyed her resentment and complaints in the form of urgent projective identification towards me, I offered S. some reconstructive interpretations about a small girl traumatized by an aggressive, insensitive mother who had aroused resentment in her daughter that could not be worked through but had found an outlet in the complaints and boredom shared with me in our sessions.

As the time approached for any separation, S. became especially annoying. She responded to one of my attempts to interpret this behavior:

It is with you that I am boring, not with other people: My mother is a terrible bore too. Children cannot be bores because they are children. I am more sorry, though, about the fact that you are going away and leaving me alone. I always wonder why people are bores. It is my only weapon: boredom is lethal.

She acts out the same kind of boring, petulant attack continuously at home too, making relations with her husband unpleasant and difficult. This obviously cools their ardor and makes their sex life miserable, a mere meeting of two people with no real interest, hostile and impotent.

After several years of analysis, with constant work of interpretation, constructive in the here and now of the session and reconstructive too, S. dreams

She is with her first man, but he disappears. The place is squalid and there is a shop window full of handbags. She wants to buy a new bag but the ones on display are all old-fashioned. The shop is closed but she manages to get in, sure she will find a nice new bag.

The associations regard her sexuality, and are delivered in a monotonous, complaining voice. But this dream seems to show a split between a part that is capable of love, allied with the analyst who boosts her hopes of a better sexuality (the new handbag), and a hostile, resentful narcissistic part that makes the man disappear, sullying sexuality by calling it old-fashioned, and harking back to her vaginismus (the shop is closed).

After about six years of four-times-weekly analysis, S. has managed to lower her defensive projective identification with me in the transference and with her family. This has made relations at home smoother, with her husband and mother. Her sexuality has also undergone a significant transformation. She no longer suffers episodes of vaginismus and has achieved orgasm several times. Her mental growth during analysis has always run parallel to improvements in her sexuality, confirming the close links between changes in the relations between the intrapsychic and intersubjective dimensions of internal objects and sexuality, seen as a process of reciprocal repair and exchange.

The case of P.

P., a woman of 40 years, asked for analysis to tackle a state of confusion and general dissatisfaction. Her sex life consisted – apart from occasional, unsatisfactory casual relations – only of clitoral masturbation, which she often felt compelled to do. P. had a younger sister. Her mother was a very beautiful woman, highly competitive with her daughters. Her father, frequently absent, left the daughters to be dominated by the mother figure. Her emotions in the transference were immediately dominated by intense jealousy and envy, reliving the feelings that had marked her relations with her mother and sister, both of whom she considered beautiful and successful.

She confused her sexuality with dirty, squalid, smelly things that made her ashamed. She confused her vagina and her anus. In one session she confessed: "I think making love is a dirty business, like defecating. I remember my mother thought the anus and the genitalia were the same – she confused them."

The sadistic-anal attack on the maternal breast-nipple brought on intense persecutory feelings which came out in the analytical relation often in the form of violently aggressive, anxious, destructive dreams. Outside the transference she acted these feelings out by attacking her various partners and used masturbation as the sole defense against the danger set up by the penis, a persecutory object. She also used masturbation as a frequent defense against the depressive anxiety induced by separation from the analyst.

Her attacks on the penis, turning it into a megalomaniac object (as defense against the primary envy of her mother's breast), are illustrated well in this scrap of a dream that same night: *there was a person blowing up a balloon which ended up the shape of an enormous penis, and finally burst. In another dream she entered a room with a man with one leg. There were other men in the room. They uncovered their genitals and she touched the man's penis, which became huge.* Associating, she says: "I always thought sodomy was better. At least that gives you the impression of being a male, not like when you are penetrated from the front."

This young woman had infantile, narcissistic and destructive parts of her personality which had stopped her having a good relationship with the maternal breast. Projective modalities prevailed over introjection, and she never managed to introject a good penis that could repair the damage done, in fantasy, to her mother's body. As a consequence her own sexual development was deeply disturbed. Her envious attacks transformed the penis into a sadistic, dangerous object. Her prevalently sadistic-anal feelings had turned her sexuality into a dirty, shameful, unacceptable experience. Masturbation was the only activity that enabled her to act out her envious attacks and to deal with the depressive anxiety of separation, providing a defense against the penis, which she felt was so dangerous.

In this patient too, cutting down infantile omnipotence, reducing splitting and projective identification, and helping introjection prevail in analysis meant her personality could mature and reduced the danger she believed the penis presented. This enabled her to achieve a more satisfactory sexual life, marriage and children.

After seven years of analysis, however, and despite her apparently normal sex life, this patient still preferred clitoral masturbation and continued doing it, although it was no longer her sole outlet. This gives an idea of the extent to which certain infantile narcissistic modalities linked to an unrepressed unconscious, making them impossible to recollect and sometimes impossible to work through, can resist analysis and live alongside more mature aspects of the personality.

11

On happiness

Happiness has fascinated thinkers since antiquity. The Greeks believed it was linked to luck. *Fero*, the Latin root of *fortuna*, the Italian word for luck, means to bear, suggesting some event that is brought from outside. It might seem that the Greek philosophers, linking happiness to luck, ruled out the possibility that this state of mind came from inside, from our inner mental world, rather than from outside. Plotinus, however, does say that happiness is always enjoyed in the present because it is a timeless "state", deep in our innermost recesses.

The Greeks maintained, however, that no outside circumstance could guarantee happiness unless a person was able to cultivate a "sense of measure", meaning one had to be able to manage the parts of the personality that generated unhappiness because of greed or destructiveness (Natoli, 1994).

Wisdom, as a popular saying has it, is knowing how to enjoy what you have without suffering because of what you lack. But Leopardi (1991) teaches that humans cannot enjoy happiness because they cannot be happy for ever. Here this "bard" of human unhappiness brings us back to Freud and the picture that emerges from that extraordinary publication *On Transience* (1915e) in which he analyzes the reasons why the young poet Rainer Maria Rilke, could not enjoy a beautiful flower-bedecked meadow while they were walking together in the mountains: the poet could not tolerate having to mourn the transience of beauty, because beauty cannot last for ever.

Humankind – and we are back to Leopardi (1991) again – once it has tasted happiness want to be happy for ever. But happiness is short-lasting so people are inevitably unhappy because they cannot tolerate this transience. The problem reflects the "separation" from a state that has been enjoyed as an "extension" of the self, an enlargement of one's own world.

This is a feeling that presumes a sort of merging with the world, an immersion in everything so as not to feel the pain of separation.

In analytical terms it goes back to a child's earliest experience as he or she blends confusedly with the mother, feeling totally at one with her, enjoying infinite pleasure. This sort of extension is based on a relationship with someone else, and individuals can live happily when their mind is fully occupied with the object by which they are willing to let themselves be invested (Natoli, 1994).

Happiness is also connected to *revelation*, in the sense that it enables individuals to manifest themselves in the fullness of their self; to *death*, as it is essential and symbolic; to *ecstasy*, when time is erased and there is no past or future, like an everlasting present that enables people to live completely; to *love*, where happiness is found in relations (Buber, 1987). To our eyes as analysts, happiness always brings to mind the child's earliest experience, stored in implicit memory, when the child was at one with the mother.

But happiness need not dissolve altogether in the intensity of the moment. It should define a life. As Natoli (1994) so perceptively notes, it is true that moments of eternity can make a life happy but it takes a life that is already happy on the whole to recognize and make the best of these moments. Happiness, in this existential view, can come about only through work on oneself, through research and conquest; this might imply lengthy self-research. Natoli (1994) said that happiness does not end with the immediate experience of fullness. The more we allow ourselves to be taken in by the immediate satisfaction, abandoning ourselves to it, the more happiness becomes a danger for people, risking making them forget the complexity of existence. Natoli also notes that the domain of happiness is broader than a moment, with a more complex profile. If happiness starts with the experience of a moment it is something to be earned then lost – something that time consumes. If, on the other hand, we consider it a characteristic of a whole life, then it becomes something that accumulates, that – paradoxically – contradicts the moment gained as life proceeds, with the ability to make the most of all the possibilities it offers.

This line of thought is very close to the psychoanalytical belief I have elaborated in this book. Freud (1930) showed interest in the relationship between the pleasure principle and happiness in an important work, entitled *Civilization and its Discontents*. He notes that humans in general seek happiness both passively – as absence of pain – and actively, as the achievement of pleasure in its full, true sense. But people's very constitution – their innate mixture of life and death instincts – means they find it easier to be unhappy than happy.

It is no wonder . . . if a man thinks himself happy merely to have escaped unhappiness or to have survived his suffering, and if in general the task of avoiding suffering pushes that of obtaining pleasure into the background.

(Freud, 1930: 77)

Humans seek pleasure anyway and sexual enjoyment gives particularly intense pleasure. Freud notes, however, that this is always limited by the possibility of losing the love object, which may turn happiness into unhappiness; it is also limited by prohibition and the risk of narcissistic hurt from the love object itself, or from taboos, laws or customs intended to rein in mankind's desires. Freud notes that "heterosexual genital love, which has remained exempt from outlawry is itself restricted by further limitations, in the shape of insistence upon legitimacy and monogamy" (1930: 104–105). Freud therefore sees the goal defined by the pleasure principle – achieving happiness from sexual pleasure – as virtually unattainable with all these limitations.

Nevertheless, humans cannot give up all hope of attaining happiness, either by directly seeking pleasure or by evading unpleasantness. Freud concludes that happiness is a problem of the individual libidinal economy: it is absolutely subjective. He also notes that there are many routes to happiness when it is humanly attainable, but none of them are really sure.

Here we have all Freud's pessimism and also his wise resignation, but wait! He then makes things even worse by raising one last problem – last but certainly not least: the unconscious sense of guilt resulting from an ancestral emotional ambivalence towards the father. This is a major obstacle on the human path towards happiness. Civilization's progress has paid a heavy price in loss of happiness, and the guilt feeling is the cause of humanity's unhappiness. Freud argues that most people do not hold work in high esteem as a means of achieving happiness.

★ ★ ★

What has psychoanalysis today to say about happiness? First of all we must return to the difference between pleasure and happiness. The first involves the body and is not a lasting experience, while the second is a lifestyle that can last. In *Civilization and its Discontents* Freud (1930), as we mentioned before, considers happiness a subjective question of individual libidinal satisfaction but above all a knowledge of oneself, meaning awareness of one's own way of living in the world. This is a highly significant idea that does not merely view happiness as an episode of relative euphoria likely to last at most a morning, but as a dialectic, relational state of mind, cut short in its risk of maniac outpouring but lasting; it reflects work on oneself, an awareness that enables individuals to manage the negative, destructive, narcissistic parts of their personality, which are a source of suffering and unhappiness for themselves and for others, and to put them to work for the rational, mature part that is capable of converting frustration and suffering, putting it to good use as a tool for self-awareness and growth.

* * *

Experience in psychoanalysis teaches us that infancy is the critical moment when human happiness seems threatened most. Once more, this takes us back to the time when the child's mind and personality were getting organized, in the earliest relations with his or her mother and surroundings. A child's mental development depends on three main factors: first, wishes, which are the motivational basis for any mental function; second, internal equipment, i.e. the genetic "dowry" – biological and psychological – a child receives from the parents; third, the environment, and particularly the mother, who should be able to tolerate and work on the child's anxiety and minimize the trauma implicit in the first human relations.

A child's wishes are total and omnipotent and can never be fully satisfied by even the best of mothers. The gap between the wish and its satisfaction does in fact color the adult's mental and emotional fate. Add in the risks of frustration and suffering, incomprehension, physical and mental violence, abuse – sometimes sexual – an environment that is ethically, psychologically and esthetically shabby, and we have the grounds for severe attachment problems (Bowlby, 1969), and difficulties in the mother–child "reflexive" processes (Fonagy and Target, 1997). These may well be sufficient to affect the organization of the self (Stern, 1985) and give rise to pathological defenses such as splitting, projective identification, denial, and idealization which will later lay the ground for relational pathologies in the adult. This is where human unhappiness starts.

These early experiences may be stored in the implicit memory, in an unconscious, non-verbalizable form, as part of an unrepressed unconscious that will influence individuals throughout their lives; as they unconsciously relive the suffering of those old traumatic experiences, they will be unable to achieve the happiness they consciously desire. This unhappiness can lead to forms of violence, perversion and addiction.

As a psychoanalyst, I tend to see happiness as the outcome of work to boost one's self-awareness and the mind's ability to transform defenses built up in infancy, that are the "negative components" of the personality, conferring competitivity, greed, envy and jealousy, persecutory anxieties, and inability to establish normal relations with the world. These are the ingredients of mental pain and human unhappiness. From this angle happiness looks like a *view of the world*, that accommodates the ability to put up with diversity, frustration, disappointment and dissonance, while at the same time fueling the person's creativity; a *lifestyle* that has achieved a good affective, emotional and cognitive balance with the world; an acceptable depressive capacity that not only enables a person to tolerate frustrations, disappointments and grief and protects from depression, but also ensures coherence with our own moral values which take us back to the internal representations of our parents and the surroundings where we grew up (our own internal Super-Ego and ideal law). If we cannot achieve this coherence and be faithful to our own moral values, the unconscious guilt feeling will make us unhappy. This is therefore a metaphor of beating down the tyranny of the Super-Ego in favor of the democratic ego ideal that helps an individual strengthen his own identity.

This is not an ephemeral moment of elation that blows over in a flash. It is the attainment of lasting self-awareness and self-dominion that enables us to transform the negative and suffering we have in us and creatively manage our destructive inner demon. What comes to mind is the unhappy lives of Francis Bacon or Van Gogh or so many other sad writers and artists who probably achieved only a moment of happiness when they managed to represent their suffering and mental pain in significant, esthetically moving artistic form.

This brings us to the conclusion that all this is the aim of every analysis: to help patients manage their negative parts better since these are a source of unhappiness, and to transform their internal figures so these are more tolerant and creative. The problem is not so much to free patients of a neurotic or psychotic symptom but to help them establish a different way of living, seeing outside reality through transformation of their own psychic reality.

In an issue of *Psiche* in 1998 dedicated to happiness, various Italian authors set out their thoughts on a topic dear to poets and lovers, as Chianese (1998) put it, but which does not at first sight seem a logical part of the psychoanalytic vocabulary. It is worth looking at what some of them had to say. Chianese (1998) maintained that happiness involves accepting not only the "necessary events" of life, but also the unpredictable "chance" happenings, so as to grasp reality not as a repetition but as a gift. He says there are different forms of happiness, depending on age, and the changes our minds and bodies undergo. All these forms, however, rest on the timelessness of the unconscious.

A theological concept of the mind was set out by Orsucci (1998) who traced the word *felicitas* (happiness) back to the Indo-European root fe whose main meaning relates to fertility and prosperity. He recalls, through Socrates, humans' need for a constant relationship with their inner demon, to ensure esthetic cohesion between the internal world and outside reality.

One of Freud's letters gave Riccardo Lombardi (1998) the idea of tracing happiness to the body and the charm of the illusion of how primary processes work, dominated by a binary logic pleasure/unpleasure, and the hallucinatory satisfaction of a wish.

Staying closer to psychoanalytical experience, Luciana Bon de Matte (1998) suggested that feelings of happiness can appear after long, hard work on conflicts, anxiety and mental suffering. She therefore concludes that

> the sole form of real, lasting happiness comes from within, triggered by confidence in ourselves, in our own possibilities, in a serene certainty that sooner or later we shall achieve what we most want. And anyway, does it matter if we don't, because accepting reality will make us equally serene and will be equally satisfying, as we shall have done everything possible to make sure things go the way we want.
>
> (Bon de Matte, 1998, our translation)

★ ★ ★

From my own reflections and those of the other analysts I have cited, it is clear that for an analyst happiness implies relatively limited anthropological expectations. In my mind it all basically boils down to keeping one's internal objects stable, meaning one's affective representations, and putting up with the inevitable conflicts among these psychic objects. This may seem a long way from the ideal of today's consumer-oriented society, which would have us all happy all the time, and looks on unhappiness as a defeat and a loser.

The pleasure and happiness that come from the feeling of internal stability is often underestimated: from our own independent thoughts, from enjoying the beauties of nature, of a work of art or a piece of music. These experiences can give pleasure that comes close to happiness in the sense that they help stabilize our internal world. But they can also threaten our stability. There are some forms of modern art or music intended to provoke "negative" emotions and upset our internal world. Then our pleasure must come from the work required to resist the provocation and re-establish the internal stability that has been temporarily thrown off balance, or lost.

These ideas may seem too simple and limited in comparison with the ideals of happiness man has built up over the centuries, especially in the western world. Nevertheless I remain convinced that happiness can come only from self-knowledge. Seneca had his character Tieste put the idea clearly: "Unhappy is the king who, sadly known to everyone, dies unknown to himself."

12

On mental pain

Tang Xianzu, an eighteenth-century Chinese writer, has the ghost of a young woman who had committed suicide put this question:

If the garden is so lush with flowers,
Why is it so full of pain?

And her mother, remembering her, recalls:

So ardent was her desire
So deep her pain.

These two images offer a good starting point for discussing mental pain in its various forms; its relationship with desire (as the mother's memory of her daughter suggests), the human mind's responses as it defends itself and adapts to pain, and finally, the particular type of suffering that surfaces in the analytical relation.

When I talk of mental pain I am referring to unconscious psychic suffering that leaks out into consciousness and invests one's whole being. It is human beings' companion from their earliest relations, developing in parallel as children structure their internal world and their representations, until thought takes form. For these ontogenetic reasons, therefore, mental suffering is intrinsic to humankind and therefore demands a prime position in any psychoanalytical theory of the mind. But mental pain can also arise from physical suffering, which reactivates old memories of deprivation and pain in the conscious and unconscious mind.

Philosophers have spent time and effort on pain since antiquity.[1] Aeschylus, a Greek tragedy writer, had grasped the main problem of common mortals: they were not immune from suffering and had to consider it the price – however dear – of living.

No one can remain neutral in the face of pain, which is a constant companion in life. But suffering is the way to self-awareness. If one does not perish because of pain, one grows. It is such a radical experience that suffering generates wisdom and knowledge (Natoli, 1986). The ancient Greeks had a phrase for it: *pathei mathos* (by suffering, you learn).

Even if only the person suffering feels pain, it spreads by identification through the world, so others feel involved too. Individual suffering is therefore a form of projection of the self into total suffering: each individual pain can be traced to a "cosmology" of pain, like a bridge linking the individual with the world around him.

Natoli (1986) believes pain involves a dual solitude: subjective solitude obliges the sufferer to withdraw from the world, and objective solitude restricts his space in the world. This solitude is individual but is regulated by "social conventions" through which it can show its face to the world, distinguishing those who do from those who do not suffer.

Contemporary philosophy admits two faces of pain too: pain generates knowledge, but knowledge can cause pain. This is one aspect of philosophy that brings it closer to psychoanalysis and the contribution this discipline has made to understanding human suffering and self-knowledge.[2]

★ ★ ★

Psychoanalytical studies have shown that to understand the processes leading to the development of a state of mind dominated by pain and anxiety, we have to follow the child from birth, through the most formative steps of his or her development, when the child's mental representations arising from the first contacts with the mother convey a vast amount of affects; these have to be transformed through different stages of significance – iconic, plastic, musical, with toys, etc. – in the transitional area of play, until the child reaches the uniquely human level of language.

Melanie Klein (1932) already outlined the gradual stages of development in the 1930s, making an enormous contribution to our knowledge of the infant's mind. She was the first to guess that from birth the infant has a dyadic relation with the mother, while the father – even if absent – plays an important part as a mental representation of the mother herself.

Klein sustains that newborn babies already suffer an anxiety due to innate sadism linked to fear of fragmentation of the self, which leads them to merge themselves totally with their mother, on whom their survival depends. We can define this state as *symbiotic* or *con-fused* (from its root "fused" in one). In the early months of life babies then start to project their anxieties and fears onto the mother, who will have to contain, work through and return them, tamed, to the child. Then is when the child enters what Klein called the paranoid–schizoid position, dominated by persecutory anxiety.

Separation from the mother at weaning, around the sixth month, shifts children into the *depressive position*, while they work through their grief at the separation. But cross-cultural studies in Africa (Antinucci et al., 1988) indicate that it is not only weaning that creates infantile depression, but also the mother's renewed availability for sexual relations with the father. This puts the African baby into a state of depression that can manifest itself in stopping playing and in slowing of linguistic development; there is also an increase in morbidity and mortality. Klein had already guessed at this painful early Oedipal situation in 1928.

This line of ontogenetic thought suggests various types of mental suffering a child inevitably encounters. There is the symbiotic or *con-fused* mental pain, when its survival is threatened, for instance because its mother is not able to feed it adequately, or cannot look after it properly because she is insensitive, or lacks *rêverie*; there is *persecutory pain*, which threatens the integrity and identity of the self; and there is *depressive pain*, which arises from the threat to the child's love objects and its early jealousy at being left out of the parental couple. These types of pain reach a peak when children start to be left on their own, and suffer anxiety at the idea of definitive separation.

Since Klein's times the development of the infant's mind has been further clarified by findings from experimental psychology and mother–child observational data. At birth, babies' psychic organization appears to rest on three pillars: their *needs and wishes*,[3] which underlie their relations with the mother; their environment, and particularly their mother, who must be capable of enough *rêverie* to grasp and work through her child's anxieties, smoothing them out and returning them to the child for introjection; then there is children's *internal equipment* or the genetically transmitted functional state of the mind which enables children to tolerate – or not – the frustrations that reality and their surroundings put in their way, and then to work through the mental suffering they will inevitably encounter in their first significant relationships.

The child's wish is omnipotent and all-embracing; the child demands exclusive possession of the object – the mother – and wants to merge in one with her. The child's wish knows no bounds, so it is a constant source of frustration that causes children distress. It is their first experience of pain, and there is no way they can be spared it since no mother, however good, can ever satisfy their wishes fully. But it is here, in their tolerance of pain, that children's innate capacities come into play, enabling them to transform the suffering and use it as a tool for affective and cognitive maturation; if children are not able to do this, their primary pain may have devastating effects, inducing the organization of defenses that will give rise to relational pathology right through adult life.

As analysts and physicians, but also as human beings, we have to bear in mind that even in the best of cases there is a gap between the wish and its fulfillment, and from birth onwards a person's affective and cognitive fate hangs on the size of this gap – the person's mental life in general. The arrival of Oedipal sentiments, either early – in the child's first year – or later, when aged 3–5 years, will cause the child to feel jealousy, exclusion, solitude and mortification, all of which will induce mental pain, leading to resentment, hostility and ambivalence towards the parents.

Then comes the additional trauma that may accompany children's ontogenesis, in relation to their surroundings and their emotional, cultural and moral level as they grow. They may suffer *macrotrauma* such as early abandon or the loss of one or both parents, or their separation; other highly traumatic experiences may arise that will have immense weight, causing pain and anxiety, and leading to pathological defenses and voids that are hard to fill.

This raises the specter of the failure of the attachment system (Bowlby, 1969), of the reflexive functions (Fonagy and Target, 1997), and of affective "tuning" (Stern, 1985). These are all highly motivational in human behavior and their failure leads to loss of direction, fear of fragmentation of the self, and mental suffering that becomes chronic and obliges the child's ego to set up highly pathological systems of defense and adaptation.

Physical and psychological violence is also highly traumatic to children, especially if repeated, as is sexual abuse – coming to light increasingly frequently in today's society – and exposure to promiscuous, perverse, violent and corrupt behavioral models; the social, cultural, psychological, moral and even esthetic shabbiness of our environment merely adds to the damage. These complicated family and environmental traumas induce mental suffering that runs through children's whole personality, obliging them to compensate with extreme "negative" feelings to defend themselves, and influence the affective and cognitive dimensions of their development. (I am referring here to psychotic, borderline, autistic and psychosomatic solutions.)

Out of these processes an individual may develop various types of mental pain. One of the most widespread is *persecutory pain*, dominated by parts of the self laden with anger, resentment, hate and ambivalence; projected onto outside reality these set up persecutory objects that torment a person with fear and anxiety, obliging him or her to take refuge in delusion, with

213

substitutive, autarchic internal objects that are delusions in the sense that they are increasingly far removed from reality.

The various forms of pain that children encounter in their first relationships, arising from highly significant emotional experiences, are "archived" while the infant is still preverbal and presymbolic in *implicit memory*, becoming essential parts of an *unrepressed unconscious* that will influence the person's affective, emotional, cognitive and even sexual life as an adult.

Clearly, therefore, the affects coloring children's earliest relations can accompany them throughout their development: creativity and learning, and even play (just think how an autistic child is unable to play and create: Flegenheimer, 1989), to say nothing of all their systems of meaning, starting from language. The affects of the primary relation are also decisive for acquiring a unique, separate identity. But separation is fundamental to acquiring identity, and is one of the most dramatic causes of *depressive mental pain*, which can give rise to anger, resentment, ambivalence and hate.

The ontogenetic paradox involves mental pain with this constellation of affects; it arises from the anxiety of separation from the mother, who, however, is indispensable for children to grow, detaching their identity from her, and achieve their separate adult identity, including gender identity. This area of maturation flourishes on mental pain since when it is tolerated, worked through and transformed, it enables children to achieve the symbolization that makes it easier to tolerate the absence of objects, and fosters the development of thought.

Nevertheless, in some cases this pain is the result of such severe trauma – for instance, parental abandon, their inability to satisfy even the child's most elementary needs, or even violence and abuse – that is impossible to think about it and work it through, let alone accept and transform it. We wonder whether it is in fact ever possible to repair some internal representations of bad, inadequate, violent or deadly parents and environment. It is easier for the patient to gradually set up a range of defenses, amounting to what we call a *negative personality*. This may be the extreme defense against traumas and violence suffered in infancy. The child will introject morally degrading, corrupt and perverse models, which will give rise to feelings such as envy, excessive competitivity, greed, amoral, violent and destructive behavior, aggressiveness towards oneself and others, depression, substance dependence, relational perversity and sexual perversion.

The negative personality, however, may also grow up when children are unable to work through their grief at separation, the pain of the attachment difficulties, and frustration and humiliation that their wishes are not fulfilled. The negative sentiments arising from this depressive pain are therefore masked in the desire for the other, which the child manifests in a con-fused fashion, wanting to merge in one with the object.

214

Mental suffering, therefore, is not primary – linked to an instinct (think of Freud's death instinct introduced in 1920) – but secondary to anxiety caused by early relational traumas such as separation from the parents, their inadequacy or violence, and lack of affection, together with frustration because the infant is unable to work through the anxiety these primary events have caused.

This discussion of psychic causality helps explain the frequently close relation between mental pain and some psychopathologies. One of these involves the organization of psychotic parts of the personality that refuse to adapt properly to reality, and form the scaffolding of a "negative personality" on the lines of destructive narcissism (Rosenfeld, 1987) that invades, seduces, dominates and destroys the healthier parts of the personality. These psychotic parts, with their burden of anxiety, may be projected out into the world, creating persecutory objects that justify the patient's aggression – in his or her eyes. Alternatively, they may be projected into the body, setting up psychosomatic disorders and sowing the somatic nucleus of hypochondriac delusion (Rosenfeld, 1987; Mancia, 1994). They can turn into a desire for revenge on the violent internal parents, justifying suicide attempts, violence and sexual perversion as part of the effort to make the other party feel the suffering the patient had felt as a child.

Pain in the analytical relation

If we shift now to the analytical relation, we can see how this whole process is recognized and lived in the encounter, through retranscription of the memory, made possible and activated by the transference (Freud's *Nachträglichkeit*). There may be specific approaches in the transference, such as *enactments* or how patients communicate (their tone of voice and volume, the rhythm and musicality of their language, making up what I call the "musical dimension" of the transference), to bring their earliest experiences and the defenses stored in their implicit memory into the relation, even if these cannot actually be recalled.

By definition the transference involves patients reliving early experiences, sometimes traumatic, buried in their memory, but without necessarily bringing to light the recollection as such. The transference serves to project onto the analyst, in the present tense of the relation, the patient's affects, fantasies, defenses and internal figures. Bringing past trauma to the surface in the present, however, may arouse despair in the patient, a pain that cannot really be felt or even thought because it refers to such old experiences, stored in the non-symbolic, non-verbal implicit memory, and never transformed over time.

215

We must add here the unreliability of the interiorized parental figures, or even severe trauma they may have caused. The sense of despair in such cases may be avoided by pathological defenses that, however, stop the patient living a normal relational life. If one cannot find the courage to live pain and transform it, however, one can never claim to experience and enjoy pleasure. Mental pain is therefore a basic step in the maturation of any personality: it is an essential experience intended to retrieve and restore the parental figures damaged during the child's development, which were lived as *trauma-objects*, the unconscious cause of suffering.

Wilfred Bion (1962), whose contribution to our understanding of mental pain is substantial, stresses the close connection between this experience and thought, since any operation of mental growth involving symbolization and thought development is painful. This may seem obvious to an analyst but experience suggests that the process of organizing and structuring thought is unquestionably painful, certainly as it is lived during analysis, when the patient starts to relive emotional experiences in a new light, finally grasping their real meaning.

In this light, thought becomes the most effective antidote to mental pain, as it enables one to work it through. If the development of thought and symbolization finds obstacles in its way, mental pain may easily turn into physical pain, in the form of psychosomatic and hypochondriac disorders, as if individuals who cannot symbolically transform mental pain were obliged to projectively identify it with their own body organs, setting up organic suffering and taking the painful soma as the object of their hypochondriac delusion.

Betty Joseph (1981) also mentions extreme mental pain arising when patients emerge from the state of confusion due to their projective identification in the analyst. When patients regain these parts, the contents of their mind, split off and projected and in fact never really lived and felt, surface once more inside them, and start to "prick [their] psychic skin from inside" – to borrow her fine metaphor. It is the most psychotic or perverse parts of the personality that perturb most. The mental suffering caused by this painful analytical operation of retrieving parts of the self lays the foundations for working through the pain and gaining greater understanding of one's own identity.

One thing is clear, however: one can talk about this mental pain only within an analytical relation. Mental pain is an experience accompanying the whole analytical path; it is always present in the encounter, even in a single session, when the distance and "affective temperature" between the patient and analyst shift, or when patients start to emerge from projecting their self into the analyst or onto objects in their outside reality.

Feelings in the transference, therefore, oscillate continuously as the retrieved affective memory brings to the surface old traumas and suffering. This may happen in particular when the patient is really alone or just separated from the analyst. At these times the patient's mind projects backwards in time, towards the paranoid-schizoid position; for example many of the dreams patients describe in moments of separation are dominated by strong persecutory figures, as if the human mind could not tolerate the absence of the object, and had to make up for it by creating one in its dreams. This is a persecutory object probably because the patients, in their resentment at the separation, identify their most hostile and aggressive parts in it, as a bad citizen of their unconscious.

Apart from retrieval of the memory, though, old traumas dating from the child's preverbal and presymbolic time can surface in the transference as "enactments" or in dreams as representations that take the patient back reconstructively to the most significant stages in the formation of the personality. This enables the patient to think about traumatic events and experiences that could not be thought about when they originated, even though they still cannot actually be recalled.

Every separation involves different degrees of mental suffering, that analysts must feel on their own skin in the countertransference if they are to contain and influence it and offer the patient a chance to consign it to his or her own mind in order to emerge from the state of confusion and anxiety that the patient is suffering. Undoubtedly acceptance of the feelings of depression at separation marks one of the most significant moments in any analysis because this is when patients start to realize they can no longer evade the pain but must face up to it, accepting the analyst's help to build up their thoughts so as to control the suffering and keep it at the necessary distance.

This is the secret of transforming the pain into an experience that fosters knowledge. However, as working through mental suffering becomes the king-pin around which the whole process of analysis revolves, it raises the question of the analyst's own distress. The analyst has obviously to be able to work through the suffering the patient projects onto him or her, like the mother who has to tolerate and contain her child's anxiety, smoothing it out before sending it back for introjection.

Bion (1962) maintains that analysts must obligatorily suffer because they must absorb their patient's mental representation of pain, but I insist they must nevertheless always maintain their ability to work things through and their analytical approach, which are the only tools they have to help the patient transform his or her distress. This means not only keeping affective contact but also maintaining enough distance to contain their patient's anger, attacks and seduction, understanding and interpreting them without

217

their own thoughts becoming paralyzed: this can easily happen when the patient tries, as an extreme defense against his or her own suffering, to knock out the analyst's ability to think and driving the analyst to come out of his or her mental "internal setting" and act.

In this profession, every analyst will meet patients who find it impossible to bear pain. They rely on very primitive mechanisms to spare their mind suffering: they clam up, becoming immobile, sometime sarcastic and apparently insensitive, with fits of anxiety that may last the whole session and end up canceling out all the emotions felt in analysis. These are attempts at putting feelings and suffering to sleep, as it were, but they also have the effect of erasing the pleasure of working together, striving to give meaning to the patient's emotions and pain.

The fact that this pain is inevitable may drive these patients to despair in their efforts to avoid it. This makes their mental and relational life poorer, not only within the analytical relationship but also outside it. In some cases the patient may act out these feelings in the real world, especially during separations, by self-destructive gestures such as suicide attempts, to "blackmail" the analyst and make him or her feel guilty and responsible for the patient's death.

In her fine book, Tonia Cancrini (2003) deals with pain and guilt. In some moving chapters, partly autobiographical, she talks about separation, pain and death. Some clinical "snapshots" illustrate her thinking and show how separation in analysis is a fundamental event in a complex emotional situation where anxiety about loss and death has to be tackled, but at the same time recognition of and love for the other party.

We are in fact vulnerable and exposed to suffering in any relationship involving our affections. Our feelings of love and distress waiver between the poles of love and loss. But why is pain inevitable? Partly it comes from the severity of the loss and from the affective investment we have made in the object of love, and partly from the fragility of the self, the lack – or at least excessive fragility – of the "psychic skin" to contain and work through the loss.

"*Infandum, regina, jubes renovare dolorem*". With this quotation from Virgil (*Aeneid*, Book IV) Cancrini introduces her idea that working through pain involves constructing a new internal object, as happens when one rebuilds an emotional bond. Virgil is talking about the love that accompanies pain. If we turn this round and apply it to the analytical relationship, we cannot fail to grasp that analysis can end only when the patient has managed to build a stable, reassuring internal object, an ideal structure to cast light on the patient's ego and enable him or her to tackle the various tasks life sets: moments of joy and satisfaction, moments of loss, sadness and mental pain.

Notes

Introduction: beyond Freud

1 For further details of Roger Money-Kyrle's work, see Mancia (2004b).
2 For further information on Bion's opinions, see the book by Grinberg, Sor and Tabak de Bianchedi (1972).

1 Memory between neuroscience and psychoanalysis

1 In Italy, a meeting in Palermo in 1982 on "Memory and oblivion" marked an important stage in the debate on the role of the memory in psychoanalysis. Of particular interest were the papers by F. Riolo, L. Sarno, F. Siracusano, A. Costa, C. Neri and F. Corrao.
2 The concept of the unconscious proposed by some post-Kleinian authors, first of all Bion (1967), and others of different schools (see Rothstein, 1985), belongs to the unrepressed unconscious, based on the relational model. Klein (1958) and some of her pupils (Segal, Rosenfeld) described the unconscious as a mixture of instinctual and relational features, dominated by the death instinct that governs the child's relation with its mother, giving rise to splitting and projective identification, two fundamental processes in Klein's concept of the unconscious.

2 Implicit memory and unrepressed unconscious

1 For further discussion of the depressive capacity as opposed to depression as a disease, see Fédida (2002).
2 This expression is not strictly a part of the concept of the unrepressed unconscious, which by definition is not known, therefore cannot be thought (after all, it is unconscious!).
3 For a fuller discussion of enactment, see Filippini and Ponzi (1993).

3 Therapeutic (f)actors in the theater of memory

1 Part of this chapter was published in my article, Mancia (2003a) "Dream actors in the theatre of memory: their role in the psychoanalytic process". *International Journal of Psychoanalysis*, 84: 945–952.
2 Translator's note: Literally "black bunches". The singular form of the noun is *mazzo*. The vulgar expression including the word *mazzo* in the sense of backside might be translated as "I'll do your arse".
3 For a definition of the processes of construction and reconstruction see the chapter on "Memory, construction and reconstruction" in Mancia (1990).

5 The dream: between neuroscience and psychoanalysis

1 This chapter was in part published in Mancia (2005) The dream between neuroscience and psychoanalysis. *Archiv für Neurologie und Psychiatrie*, 156(8): 471–479.
2 One objection might be that Freudian repression is unconscious whereas repressing by "forgetting" is conscious. Anderson et al. (2004) might therefore be referring more to this conscious model than to true repression. However, in a footnote to their article, Anderson et al. (2004) observe that some authors (Erdelyi, 2001) sustain that the strict distinction between unconscious and conscious repression was in fact a distortion of Freud's theory, upheld by Anna Freud. Freud himself used the term to indicate either an unconscious or a conscious process.
3 For my definition of the work of *construction* and *reconstruction*, see Mancia (1990).

6 The dream: a window onto the transference

1 Part of this chapter was published, in Italian, in Mancia (2000a). Il sogno: una finestra aperta sul transfert. *Rivista di Psicoanalisi*, 46: 255–268.
2 Although in *Screen Memories* Freud (1899) questioned whether we actually have recollections *of* our infancy, rather than *about* it.
3 Elsewhere (Mancia, 1990) I have shown that Freud tended to use construction and reconstruction interchangeably, as synonyms.

7 Further historical/critical and clinical reflections on narcissism

1 Cervantes in the seventeenth century described fragility as a feature of the schizophrenic personality very well, in his short story "El licenciado Vidriera" which was brilliantly analyzed by Cesare Segre (1990). The madness of the *Licenciado* (a holder of a sort of degree) consisted in the fact that he thought he was made of glass. He had lost his mother's affection early in life and all his projects and activities focused solely on himself, so he avoided any investment of libido or affection, a situation Segre acutely links to narcissism. "El licenciado Vidriera" is also interesting on account of another aspect of narcissism and psychosis: the fact that there is a healthier part of the personality on which to base oneself and use as an ally in the therapeutic encounter. The *Licenciado* was in fact considered a bit of a wise man by the other townspeople, who turned to him for advice. This was the healthy part that enabled him to shake off the psychosis and even to get his degree in law at the University of Salamanca.

2 Freud adds the term "amentia", used by Meynert in this sense.

3 In Italian there is an etymological relation between the words for hatred, anger and boredom. Hatred – as in "odious" in English – comes from the Latin *odium* which in turn is related to the Greek *odyssomai* that means to be grieved and full of wrath (Waugh, 1979).

8 Being with the patient: four clinical cases

1 This case was reported in Mancia (2006a). Implicit memory and early unrepressed unconscious: Their role in the therapeutic process (How the neurosciences can contribute to psychoanalysis). *International Journal of Psychoanalysis*, 87: 83–103.

10 Sexuality, such sweet folly

1 The idea of bisexuality has a long history. Fliess mentioned it first to Freud and later, through Svoboda, who was analyzed by Freud, it reached Otto Weininger who wrote about it in *Sex and Character*, disconcerting Fliess and arousing his resentment, leading eventually to his detachment from Freud.

12 On mental pain

1 Natoli (1986) offers an exemplary exegesis of the ancients' philosophy on pain. I cite him amply here and readers who want to go further into the question are advised to read his work.

2   When I had already finished writing this chapter, Dr. Manuela Fleming sent me her book *Dor Sem Nome: Pensar o Sofrimento* (*Pain without Name: Thinking the Sufferance*, 2003) which discusses bodily and mental pain, the psychic experience of negativity, loss and absence. Her opinions fit in well with my own.

3   Hegel made the first distinction between need and wish in "Phänomenologie des Geistes".

References

Abraham, K. (1908). Die psychosexuellen Differenzen der Hysterie und der Dementia precox. *Zentralblatt für Nervenheilkunde*, 19: 521–533. Also in *Selected Papers on Psycho-Analysis*. London: Hogarth Press, 1973.

Abraham, K. (1919). Über eine besondere Form des neurotischen Widerstandes gegen die psychoanalytische Methodik. *Internationale Zeitschrift (ärztliche) Psychoanalyse*, 5(3): 173–180. Also in *Selected Papers on Psycho-Analysis*. London: Hogarth Press, 1973.

Adolphs, R., Damasio, H., Tranel, D., Cooper, G., and Damasio, A.R. (2000). A role for somatosensory cortices in the visual recognition of emotion as revealed by three-dimensional lesion mapping. *Journal of Neuroscience*, 20(7): 2683–2690.

Agosti, S. (1996). Linguistica e psicoanalisi del poetico. *Il Verri*, 41: 27–37.

Agosti, S. (2002). *Forme e funzioni della parola letteraria.* Venice: University of Ca' Foscari Press, pp. 41–49.

Ammaniti, M. and Stern, D. (1992). *Attaccamento e psicoanalisi*. Rome: Laterza.

Anderson, M.C., Ochsner, K.N., Kuhl, B., Cooper, J., Robertson, E., Gabrieli, S.W., Glover, G.H. and Gabrieli, J.D.E. (2004). Neural systems underlying the suppression of unwanted memories. *Science*, 3(5655): 232–237.

Antinucci, F., Fiore, B., and Pisani, L. (1988). Psychologie de la petite enfance en Afrique. In P. Coppo (ed.) *Médecine traditionnelle, psichiatrie et psychologie en Afrique*. Rome: Il Pensiero Scientifico.

Antrobus, J. (1983). REM and NREM sleep reports: comparison of world frequencies by cognitive classes. *Psychophysiology*, 5: 562–568.

Antrobus, J. (1986). Dreaming: cortical activation and perceptual thresholds. *Journal of Mind and Behavior*, 7: 193–212.

Antrobus, J., Ehrlichman, H., Wiener, M. and Sollma, H. (1983). The REM report and the EEG: cognitive processes associated with cerebral hemispheres. In W. Koella (ed.) *Sleep*. Basel: Karger, pp. 49–51.

Arrigoni, M.P. and Barbieri, G.L. (1998). *Narrazione e psicoanalisi*. Milan: Cortina.

Aserinsky, E. and Kleitman, N. (1953). Regularly occurring periods of eye motility, and concomitant phenomena during sleep. *Science*, 118: 273–274.

Atkinson, R.C. and Shiffrin, R.M. (1971). Il controllo della memoria a breve termine. *Le Scienze*, 39: 76–84.

Avenanti, A. and Aglioti, S.M. (2006). The sensorimotor side of empathy for pain. In M. Mancia (ed.) *Psychoanalysis and Neuroscience*. Milan: Springer.

Balint, M. (1937). Early developmental states of the ego: primary object love. *International Journal of Psychoanalysis*, 30: 265–273, 1949.

Barale, F. and Ferro, A. (1987). Sofferenza mentale dell'analista e sogni di controtransfert. *Rivista di Psicoanalisi*, 33: 219–233.

Baranger, M. and Baranger, W. (1961–1962). La situación analítica como campo dinámico. In W. Baranger and M. Baranger, *Problemas del campo psicoanalítico*. Buenos Aires: Kargieman, 1969, pp. 129–164.

Bastide, R. (1975). *Le sacré sauvage*, préface de H. Desroche, Stock, 1997.

Batini, C., Moruzzi, G., Palestini, M., Rossi, G.F. and Zanchetti, A. (1959). Effects of complete pontine transection on the sleep–wakefulness rhythm: the midpontine pretrigeminal preparation. *Archives Italiennes de Biologie*, 96: 1–12.

Benjamin, J. (1988). *The Bond of Love*. New York: Pantheon.

Benjamin, J. (1995). *Like Subjects, Love Objects: Essays on Recognition and Sexual Difference*. New Haven, CT: Yale University Press.

Bertini, M. and Violani, C. (1984). Cerebral hemisphere, REM sleep and dreaming. In M. Bosinelli and P. Cicogna (eds) *Psychology of Dreaming*. Bologna: Clueb, pp. 131–135.

Berto, G. (1964). *Il male oscuro*. Milan: Rizzoli.

Bick, E. (1968). The experience of the skin in early object-relations. *International Journal of Psychoanalysis*, 45: 558–566.

Bion, W.R. (1957). Differentiation of the psychotic from the non-psychotic personalities. *International Journal of Psychoanalysis*, 38: 266–275.

Bion, W.R. (1962). *Learning from Experience*. London: Heinemann.

Bion, W.R. (1965). *Trasformations*. London: Heinemann.

Bion, W.R. (1967). *Second Thoughts (Selected Papers on Psychoanalysis)*. London: Heinemann.

Bion, W.R. (1970). *Attention and Interpretation: A Scientific Approach to Insight in Psycho-Analysis and Groups*. London: Tavistock.

Bion, W.R. (1975). *A Memoir of the Future*. Book One: *The Dream*. Rio de Janeiro: Imago.

Bischof, M. and Bassetti, C.L. (2004). Total dream loss: a distinct neuro-psychological dysfunction after bilateral PCA stroke. *Annals of Neurology*, 56: 583–586.

Bliss, T.V.P. and Lömo, T. (1973). Long-lasting potentiation of synaptic transmission in the dentate area of the anaesthetized rabbit following stimulation of the perforant path. *Journal de Physiologie*, 232: 331–356.

Bollas, C. (1987). *The Shadow of the Object: Psychoanalysis of the Unthought Known*. New York: Columbia University Press.

Bolognini, S. (1994). Transference: erotised, erotic, loving, affectionate. *International Journal of Psychoanalysis*, 75: 73–86.

Bolognini, S. (2002). *Psychoanalytic Empathy*. London: Free Association Books.

Bonaccorsi, M. (1980). *La psicoterapia analitica del bambino organico*. Milan: Emme Edizioni.

Bon de Matte, L. (1998). Felicità, una difficile conquista. *Psiche*, 2: 89–96.

Borges, J.L. (1949). *L'Aleph*. Milan: Feltrinelli, 1961.

Bosinelli, M. (1991). Il processo di addormentamento. In M. Bosinelli and P. Cicogna (eds) *Sogni: figli d'un cervello ozioso*. Turin: Bollati Boringhieri, pp. 249–270.

Bosinelli, M. and Franzini, C. (1986). Psicofisiologia del sonno. In L. Stegagno (ed.) *Problemi di psicofisiologia*. Turin: Boringhieri.

Bosinelli, M., Cicogna, P. and Molinari, S. (1974). The tonic-phasic model and the feeling of self-participation in different stages of sleep. *International of Journal of Psychology*, 1: 35–65.

Botella, C. and Botella, S. (2001). *La Figurabilité psychique*, Coll. Champs Psychanalytiques. Lausanne: Delachaux et Niestlé SA.

Bowlby, J. (1969). *Attachment and Loss*. London: Hogarth Press.

Braun, A.R., Balkin, T.J., Wesenten, N.J., Carson, R.E., Varga, M., Baldwin, P. et al. (1997). Regional cerebral blood flow through the sleep-wake cycle. *Brain*, 120: 1173–97.

Braun, A.R., Balkin, T.J., Wesenten, N.J., Carson, R.E., Varga, M., Baldwin, P. et al. (1998). Dissociated pattern of activity in visual cortices and their projections during human rapid eye movement sleep. *Science*, 279: 91–95.

Bremer, F. (1935). "Cerveau isolé" et physiologie du sommeil. *Comptes Rendus Société de Biologie*, Paris, 118: 1235–1241.

Bria, P. (1975). Introduzione a Matte-Blanco, I. *L'inconscio come insiemi infiniti*. Turin: Einaudi, 1981.

Buber, M. (1987). *Confessioni estatiche*. Milan: Adelphi.

Cancrini, T. (2003). *Un tempo per il dolore: Eros, dolore e colpa*. Turin: Bollati Boringhieri.

Canestri, J. (1993). Allarme d'incendio: alcune considerazioni sull'amore di transfert. In E.S. Person, A. Hagelin and P. Fonagy (eds) *L'amore di transfert*. Milan: Cortina, 1994, pp. 131–148.

Cavallero, C. (1991). Recenti sviluppi dello studio sperimentale sul sogno: l'approccio cognitivista. In M. Bosinelli and P. Cicogna (eds) *Sogni: figli d'un cervello ozioso*. Turin: Bollati Boringhieri, pp. 354–71.

Cesio, F. (1993). La tragedia edipica nel processo psicoanalitico: l'amore di trasfert. In E.S. Person, A. Hagelin and P. Fonagy (eds) *L'amore di transfert.* Milan: Cortina, 1994, pp. 115–130.

Chasseguet-Smirgel, J. (1964). *La Sexualité féminine.* Paris: Payot.

Cheour, M., Martynova, O., Naatanen, R., Erkkola, R., Sillanpaa, M., Kero, P., (2002). Speech sounds learned by sleeping newborns. *Nature,* 415: 599–600.

Chianese, D. (1998). Del destino e della felicità. *Psiche,* 2: 19–26.

Chodorow, N. (1994). *Femininities, Masculinities, Sexualities.* Lexington, KY: Kentucky University Press.

Chomsky, N. (2002). *On Nature and Language.* Cambridge: Cambridge University Press.

Ciani, N. (ed.) (1983). *Il narcisismo: appunti teorici e clinici.* Rome: Borla.

Cima, A. (1984). *Ipotesi d'amore.* Milan: Garzanti.

Cipolotti, L., Shallice, T., Chan, D., Fox, N., Scahill, R., Harrison, G., Stevens, J. and Rudge, P. (2001). Long-term retrograde amnesia . . . the crucial role of the hippocampus. *Neuropsychologia,* 39: 151–172.

Condon, W.S. and Sander, L.W. (1974). Neonate movement is synchronized with adult speech: international participation and language acquisition. *Science,* 182: 99–101.

Cooper, A.M. (2005). Will neurobiology influence psychoanalysis? In E.L. Auchincloss (ed.) *The Quiet Revolution in American Psychoanalysis: Selected Papers of Arnold M. Cooper.* Hove, UK: Brunner-Routledge, pp. 81–94.

Cordeau, J.P. and Mancia, M. (1959). Evidence of an electroencephalographic synchronization mechanism originating in the lower brain stem. *Electroencephalography Clinical Neurophysiology,* 11: 551–564.

Corrao, F. (1982). Memoria e oblio. *Rivista di Psicoanalisi,* 3: 342–345.

Costa, A. (1982). Oblio e memoria dell'altro. *Rivista di Psicoanalisi,* 3: 329–337.

Dalle Luche, R. (2002). Sotto il segno di Edipo: destini di un mito nel Novecento. Introduction to A. Tatossian (1988). *Edipo in Kakania. Kafka, Musil e Freud.* Turin: Bollati Boringhieri, 2002, pp. 7–46.

Damasio, A. (1994). *Descartes' Error: Emotion, Reason, and the Human Brain.* New York: G.P. Putnam.

Damasio, A.R. (2000). *The Feeling of What Happens.* New York: Harcourt Brace.

Damasio, A.R. (2003). *Looking for Spinoza: Joy, Sorrow, and the Feeling Brain.* New York: Harcourt Brace.

Dapretto, M., Davies, M.S. and Pfeifer, J.H. (2005). Understanding emotions in others: mirror neuron dysfunction in children with autism spectrum disorders. *Nature Neuroscience,* 4 December (on line).

Darwin, C. (1872). *The Expression of the Emotions in Man and Animals.* Chicago, IL: University of Chicago Press, 1965.

Davis, J.T. (2001). Revising psychoanalytic interpretations of the past: an examination of declarative and non-declarative memory processes. *International Journal of Psychoanalysis*, 82: 449–462.

De Casper, A.J. and Fifer, W.P. (1980). Of human bonding: newborns prefer their mothers' voices. *Science*, 208: 1174–1176.

Deleuze, G. and Guattari, F. (1972). *L'Anti-Œdipe*. Paris: Minuit.

De Masi, F. (2000). The unconscious and psychosis: some considerations on the psychoanalytic theory of psychosis. *International Journal of Psychoanalysis*, 81: 1–20.

Dement, W.C. (1965). Does rapid eye movements sleep have a function? In M. Jouvet (ed.) *Aspects anatomo-fonctionnels de la physiologie du sômmeil: a symposium*. Paris: CNRS (Centre National de la Recherche Scientifique), pp. 567–604.

Dement, W.C. and Kleitman, N. (1957). The relation of the eye movements during sleep to dream activity: an objective method for the study of dreaming. *Experimental Psychology*, 53: 339–346.

Dement, W.C. and Wolpert, E. (1958). Interrelation in the manifest content of dreams occurring on the same night. *Journal of Nervous and Mental Disease*, 126: 568–578.

Dennet, D.C. (1991). *Consciousness Explained*. Boston, MA: Little, Brown.

De Simone, G. (1994). *La conclusione dell'analisi: Teoria e tecnica*. Rome: Borla.

Di Benedetto, A. (2000). *Prima della parola: L'ascolto psicoanalitico del non detto attraverso le forme dell'arte*. Milan: F. Angeli.

Di Benedetto, A. (2003). *L'ascolto musicale in psicoanalisi: Un "modo" per contattare il pre-verbale*. Seminari Multipli di Bologna, 27 September.

Di Chiara, G. (2003). *Curare con la psicoanalisi*. Milan: Cortina.

Di Giorgio, A.M. (1929). Persistenza, nell'animale spinale, di asimmetrie posturali e motorie di origine cerebellare. *Archivio di Fisiologia*, 27: 519–542.

Durkheim, E. (1912). *Les Formes élémentaires de la vie religieuse*. Paris: Alcan.

Eco, U. (1981). *Voce Simbolo*. In *Enciclopedia*, vol. 12. Turin: Einaudi, pp. 877–915.

Edelman, G.M. (1992). *Bright Air, Brilliant Fire: On the Matter of the Mind*. New York: Basic Books.

Edelman, G.M. and Tononi, G. (2000). *Un universo di coscienza: come la materia diventa immaginazione [A Universe of Consciousness: How Matter becomes Imagination]*. Turin: Einaudi.

Eickhoff, F.W. (1993). Una rilettura di "Osservazioni sull'amore di transfert". In E.S. Person, A. Hagelin and P. Fonagy (eds) *Amore di transfert*. Milan: Cortina, 1994, pp. 17–39.

Eliade, M. (1946). *Traité d'histoire des religions*. Paris: Payot.

Erdelyi, M.H. (2001). Defense processes can be conscious or unconscious. *The American Psychologist*, 56: 761–762

Erikson, E.H. (1974). *Dimensions of a New Identity: The 1973 Jefferson Lectures in the Humanities*. New York: W.W. Norton.

Faggi, V. (2001). Resine. *Nuova Serie*, 89: 103–104.

Fairbairn, W.R.D. (1952). *Psychoanalytic Studies of the Personality*. London: Tavistock.

Farroni, T., Csibra, G., Simion, F. and Johnson, M.H. (2002). Eye contact detection in humans from birth. *Proceedings of the National Academy of Sciences USA*, 99: 9602–9605.

Fast, I. (1984). *Gender Identity: A Differentiation Model*. Hillsdale, NJ: The Analytic Press.

Federn, P. (1925). Il narcisismo nella struttura dell'Io. In P. Federn (1952) *Psicosi e psicologia dell'Io*. Turin: Boringhieri, 1976.

Fédida, P. (2002). *Des bienfaits de la dépression: eloge de la psychothérapie*. Paris: Odile Jacob.

Ferenczi, S. (1909). L'interpretazione scientifica dei sogni. In *Opere (1908–1912)*. Vol. 1. Milan: Cortina, 1989, pp. 59–77.

Ferro, A. (1999). *Psychoanalysis as Therapy and Story Telling*. London: Routledge.

Ferro, A. (2002). *Seeds of Illness, Seeds of Recovery*. London: Routledge.

Fessard, A. (1954). Mechanisms of nervous integration and conscious experience. In J.F. Delafresnaye (ed.) *Brain Mechanisms and Consciousness*. Springfield, IL: C.C. Thomas.

Filippini, S. and Ponzi, M. (1993). Enactment. *Rivista di Psicoanalisi*, 39: 501–506.

Flegenheimer, F.A. (1989). Barriera autistica e creatività artistica. Paper presented at the Psychoanalytic Center, Milan.

Fleming, M. (2003). *Dor sem nome: pensar o sofrimento*. Porto: Edições Afrontamento.

Fogassi, L., Ferrari, P.F., Gesierich, B., Rozzi, S., Chersi, F. and Rizzolatti, G. (2005). Parietal lobe: from action organization to intention understanding. *Science*, 308(5722): 622–667.

Fonagy, P. (1999). Memory and therapeutic action. *International Journal of Psychoanalysis*, 80: 215–223.

Fonagy, P. and Target, M. (1997). Attachment and reflective function: their role of self-organization. *Development and Psychopathology*, 9: 679–700.

Foulkes, D. (1985). *Dreaming: A Cognitive-Psychological Approach*. Hillsdale, NJ: Erlbaum.

Freeman-Sharpe, E. (1937). *Dream Analysis*. London: Hogarth Press, 1961.

Freud, S. (1887–1904). *The Complete Letters of Sigmund Freud to Wilhelm Fliess 1887–1904*. Edited by J.M. Masson. Cambridge, MA: Belknap Press of Harvard University Press.

Freud, S. (1895). *Project for a Scientific Psychology. SE 1*.

Freud, S. (1899). *Screen Memories. SE 2.*

Freud, S. (1900). *The Interpretation of Dreams. SE 4–5.*

Freud, S. (1901). *Fragment of an Analysis of a Case of Hysteria. SE 7.*

Freud, S. (1905). *Three Essays on the Theory of Sexuality. SE 7.*

Freud, S. (1910). *Leonardo da Vinci and a Memory of his Childhood. SE 11.*

Freud, S. (1911). *Psycho-Analytic Notes on an Autobiographical Account of a Case of Paranoia (Dementia Paranoides). SE 12.*

Freud, S. (1912). A note on the unconscious in psycho-analysis. *SE 12.*

Freud, S. (1912–1913). *Totem and Taboo and Other Works:* List of Writings by Freud Dealing with Social Anthropology, Mythology and the History of Religion. *SE 13.*

Freud, S. (1914a). *On Narcissism: An Introduction. SE 14.*

Freud, S. (1914b). *Remembering, Repeating, and Working-Through (Further Recommendations on the Technique of Psycho-Analysis, II). SE 12.*

Freud, S. (1914c). *Observations on Transference-Love (Further Recommendations on the Technique of Psycho-Analysis, III). SE 12.*

Freud, S. (1915a). *Repression. SE 14.*

Freud, S. (1915b). *The Unconscious. SE 14.*

Freud, S. (1915c). *Instincts and their Vicissitudes. SE 14.*

Freud, S. (1915d). *Mourning and Melancholia. SE 14.*

Freud, S. (1915e). *On Transience. SE 14.*

Freud, S. (1920). *Beyond the Pleasure Principle. SE 18.*

Freud, S. (1922). *The Ego and the Id. SE 19.*

Freud, S. (1923a). *The Infantile Genital Organization: An Interpolation into the Theory of Sexuality. SE 19.*

Freud, S. (1923b). *Neurosis and Psychosis. SE 19.*

Freud, S. (1924a). *The Economic Problem of Masochism. SE 19.*

Freud, S. (1924b). *The Dissolution of the Oedipus Complex. SE 19.*

Freud, S. (1924c). *A Note upon the "Mystic Writing-Pad". SE 19.*

Freud, S. (1930). *Civilization and its Discontents. SE 21.*

Freud, S. (1931). *Female Sexuality. SE 21.*

Freud, S. (1932). *New Introductory Lectures on Psycho-Analysis. SE 22.*

Freud, S. (1937a). *Analysis Terminable and Interminable. SE 23.*

Freud, S. (1937b). *Constructions in Analysis. SE 23.*

Freud, S. (1938). *An Outline of Psycho-Analysis. SE 23.*

Fromm, E. (1951). *The Forgotten Language.* New York: Holt.

Fuster, J.M. (1997) *The Prefrontal Cortex. Anatomy, Physiology, and Neuropsychology of the Frontal Lobe.* Philadelphia, PA: Lippincott-Raven.

Gabrieli, J.D.E., Fleishman, D.A., Keane, M.M., Reminger, S.L. and Morrell, F. (1995). Double dissociation between memory systems underlying explicit and implicit memory in the human brain. *Psychological Science,* 6: 76–82.

Gaddini, E. (1969). On imitation. *International Journal of Psychoanalysis*, 50: 475–484.

Gaddini, E. (1977). Note su alcuni fenomeni del processo analitico. In *Scritti, 1953–1985*. Milan: Cortina, 1989.

Gaddini, E. (1981). Note sul problema mente-corpo. *Rivista di Psicoanalisi*, 1: 3–29.

Gainotti, G. (2006). Unconscious emotional memories and the right hemisphere. In M. Mancia (ed.) *Psychoanalysis and Neuroscience*. Milan: Springer.

Gallese, V. (2001). The "shared manifold" hypothesis: from mirror neurons to empathy. *Journal of Consciousness Studies*, 8(5–7): 33–50.

Geschwind, N. (1965). Disconnection syndromes in animals and man. *Brain*, 88: 237–274 and 585–644.

Giaconia, G. and Racalbuto, A. (1997). Il circolo vizioso trauma-fantasma-trauma. *Rivista di Psicoanalisi*, 43: 541–558.

Gill, M.M. (1982). *Analysis of Transference, Vol. I: Theory and Technique*. New York: International Universities Press.

Gill, M.M. (1993). Prospettiva intrasoggettiva e prospettiva intersoggettiva: "Osservazioni sull'amore di transfert". In E.S. Person, A. Hagelin and P. Fonagy (eds) *L'amore di transfert*. Milan: Cortina, 1994, pp. 99–114.

Goldman-Rakic, P.S., Scalaidhe, S.P.O. and Chafee, M.V. (2000). Domain specificity in cognitive systems. In M.S. Gazzaniga (ed.) *The New Cognitive Neurosciences*. Cambridge, MA: MIT Press, pp. 733–742.

Gombrich, E.H. (1959). *Art and Illusion: A Study in the Psychology of Pictorial Representation*. Washington, DC: Trustees of the National Gallery of Art.

Green, A. (1982). *Narcissisme de vie, narcissisme de mort*. Paris: Minuit.

Green, A. (1990). *Le complèxe de castration*. Paris: Presses Universitaires de France.

Green, A. (1993). *Le Travail du négatif*. Paris: Minuit.

Greenson, R.R. (1965). The working alliance and the transference neurosis. *Psychoanalytic Quarterly*, 34: 155–181.

Greenson, R.R. (1968). Dis-identifying from mother: its special importance for the boy. *International Journal of Psychoanalysis*, 49: 370–374.

Grinberg, L. (1962). On a specific aspect of countertransference due to the patient's projective identification. *International Journal of Psychoanalysis*, 43: 436–440.

Grinberg, L., Sor, D. and Tabak De Bianchedi, E. (1972). *Introduzione al pensiero di Bion*. Rome: Armando, 1975.

Grünbaum, A. (1993). *Validation in the Clinical Theory of Psychoanalysis*. Madison, WI: International Universities Press.

Halberstadt-Freud, H.C. (1998). Electra versus Oedipus: femininity reconsidered. *International Journal of Psychoanalysis*, 79: 41–56.

Hegel, G.W.F. (1807). *System der Wissenschaft. Erster Teil, die Phänomenologie des Geistes*. Bamberg und Würzburg.

Heimann, P. (1950). On counter-transference. *International Journal of Psychoanalysis*, 31: 81–84.

Heimann, P. (1952) Preliminary notes on some defence mechanisms in paranoid states. *International Journal of Psychoanalysis*, 33: 208–213.

Hernandez, M. (1993). Nota su una nota a piè di pagina in "Osservazioni sull'amore di transfert". In E.S. Person, A. Hagelin and P. Fonagy (eds) *L'amore di transfert*. Milan: Cortina, 1994, pp. 81–86.

Hobson, J.A. (2002). *Dreaming*. Oxford: Oxford University Press.

Hobson, J.A. and McCarley, R.W. (1977). The brain as a dream generator: an activation synthesis hypothesis of the dream process. *American Journal of Psychiatry*, 134: 1335–1348.

Hobson, J.A., Stickgold, R. and Pace-Schott, E. (1998). The neuropsychology of REM sleep dreaming. *NeuroReport*, 9: R1–R14.

Hobson, J.A., Pace-Schott, E.F. and Stickgold, R. (2003). Dreaming and the brain: toward a cognitive neuroscience of conscious states. In E.F. Pace-Schott, M. Solms, M. Blagrove and S. Harnad (eds) *Sleep and Dreaming: Scientific Advances and Reconsiderations*. Cambridge: Cambridge University Press, pp. 1–50.

Holmes, J. (2000). Memory and therapeutic action, Letter to the Editor. *International Journal of Psychoanalysis*, 81: 353–355.

Huber, R., Ghilardi, M.F., Massimini, M. and Tononi, G. (2004). Local sleep and learning. *Nature*, 430(6995): 27–28.

Iacoboni, M., Woods, R.P., Brass, M., Bekkering, H., Mazziotta, J.C. and Rizzolatti, G. (1999). Cortical mechanisms of human imitation. *Science*, 286: 2526–2528.

Imbasciati, A. (1998). *Nascita e costruzione della mente*. Turin: UTET.

Isay, R. (1987). Fathers and their homosexually inclined sons in childhood. *Psychoanalytic Study of the Child*, 42: 275–293.

Jaques, E. (1970). *Work, Creativity, and Social Justice*. London: Heinemann.

Jasper, K. (1964). *Psicopatologia generale*. Rome: Il Pensiero Scientifico.

Jones, E. (1927). The early development of female sexuality. *International Journal of Psychoanalysis*, 8: 459–472.

Joseph, B. (1981). Defence mechanism and phantasy in the psychoanalytic process. In M. Feldman and E. Bott Spillius (eds) *Psychic Equilibrium and Psychic Change: Selected Papers of Betty Joseph*. London: Routledge, 1989, pp. 116–126.

Joseph, B. (1985). Transference: the total situation. *International Journal of Psychoanalysis*, 66: 447–454.

Joseph, B. (1989). *Psychic Equilibrium and Psychic Change*. London: Routledge.

Joseph, B. (1993). Sul lavoro di transfert: alcune osservazioni attuali. In

E.S. Person, A. Hagelin and P. Fonagy (eds) *Amore di transfert*. Milan: Cortina, 1994, pp. 87–98.

Joseph, R. (1996). *Neuropsychiatry, Neuropsychology and Clinical Neuroscience*. Baltimore, MD: Williams and Williams.

Jouvet, M. (1962). Recherches sur les structures nerveuses et les mécanismes responsables des différentes phases du sommeil physiologique. *Archives Italiennes de Biologie*, 100: 125–206.

Kafka, F. (1954). *Diari: 1910–1923*. Milan: Mondadori, 1977.

Kafka, F. (1975). *Lettere*. Milan: Mondadori, 1988.

Kafka, F. (1976–1984). *Oeuvres complètes*. Paris: Gallimard.

Kafka, F. (1980). *Hochzeitsvorbereitungen auf dem Lande und andere Prosa aus dem Nachlass*. Frankfurt a.M: Fischer.

Kafka, F. (1997). *The Castle*. London: Penguin.

Kandel, E.R. (1998). A new intellectual framework for psychiatry. *American Journal of Psychiatry*, 155: 457–469.

Kandel, E.R. (1999). Biology and the future of psychoanalysis: a new intellectual framework for psychiatry revisited. *American Journal of Psychiatry*, 156: 505–524.

Kandel, E.R. (2001). The molecular biology of memory storage: a dialogue between genes and synapses. *Science*, 294: 1030–1038.

Kandel, E.R., Schwartz, J.H. and Jessell, T.M. (1994) *Principles of Neural Science*. East Norwalk, CT: Appleton and Lange.

Kant, I. (1781). *Critique of Pure Reason*. Trans. N. Kemp Smith. London: Macmillan, 1929.

Karten, Y.J.C., Olariu, A. and Cameron, N.A. (2005). Stress in early life inhibits neurogenesis in adulthood. *Trends in Neurosciences*, 28: 171–172.

Kernberg, O.F. (1984). *Severe Personality Disorders: Psychotherapeutic Strategies*. New Haven, CT: Yale University Press.

Kihlstrom, J.E. (1987). The cognitive unconscious. *Science*, 237: 1445–1452.

Klein, M. (1928). Early stages of the Oedipus conflict. In *Love, Guilt and Reparation and Other Works 1921–1945*. London: Hogarth Press, 1975, pp. 186–198.

Klein, M. (1930). The importance of symbol-formation in the development of the ego. In *Love, Guilt and Reparation and Other Works 1921–1945*. London: Hogarth Press, 1975, pp. 219–232.

Klein, M. (1932). *The Psycho-analysis of Children*. London: Hogarth Press, 1975.

Klein, M. (1946). Notes on some schizoid mechanisms. In *Envy and Gratitude and Other Works 1946–1963*. London: Hogarth Press, 1975, pp. 1–24.

Klein, M. (1958). On the development of mental functioning. *International Journal of Psychoanalysis*, 39: 84–90.

Kohut, H. (1971). *The Analysis of the Self*. New York: International Universities Press.

Kohut, H. (1978a). Forms and transformations of narcissim. In *The Search for the Self*. Vols 1 and 2. New York: International Universities Press.

Kohut, H. (1978b). *The Search for the Self*. Vols 1 and 2. New York: International Universities Press.

Kolata, G. (1984). Studying learning in the womb. *Science*, 225: 302–303.

Kornhuber, H.H. (1973). Neural control of input into long term memory: limbic system and amnesic syndrome in man. In H.P. Zippel (ed.) *Memory and Transfer of Information*. New York: Plenum Press, pp. 1–22.

Lacan, J. (1966). *Ecrits*. Vols 1 and 2. Paris: Seuil.

Langer, S. (1942). *Philosophy in a New Key*. New York: Mentor.

Lashley, K. (1950). The problem of serial order in behavior. In L.A. Jeffers (ed.) *Cerebral Mechanisms in Behavior*. New York: Wiley

Ledoux, J. (1996). *The Emotional Brain*. New York: Simon and Schuster.

Le Goff, J. (1977). *Storia e memoria*. Turin: Einaudi.

Lehmann, D. and Koukkou, M. (2006). Brain's experience-dependent plasticity, state-dependent recall, and creation of subjectivity of mental functions. In M. Mancia (ed.) *Psychoanalysis and Neuroscience*. Milan: Springer.

Lehtonen, J. (2006). In search of the early mental organization of the infant: contributions from the neurophysiology of nursing. In M. Mancia (ed.) *Psychoanalysis and Neuroscience*. Milan: Springer.

Leopardi, G. (1991). *Zibaldone di pensieri*, 3 vols. Milan: Garzanti.

Leuzinger-Bohleber, M. and Pfeifer, R. (2006). Recollecting the past in the presence: memory in the dialogue between psychoanalysis and cognitive science. In M. Mancia (ed.) *Psychoanalysis and Neuroscience*. Milan: Springer.

Lévi-Strauss, C. (1964). *Le Cru et le cuit*. Paris: Librairie Plon.

Limentani, A. (1979). The significance of transexualism in relation to some basic psychoanalytic concepts. *International Review of Psychoanalysis*, 6: 139–153.

Limentani, A. (1991). Neglected fathers in the aetiology and treatment of sexual deviations. *International Journal of Psychoanalysis*, 72: 573–584.

Llinas, R. and Ribary, U. (1993). Coherent 40Hz oscillation characterizes dream state in humans. *Proceedings of the National Academy of Sciences USA*, 90: 2078–2081.

Loewald, H.W. (1960). On the therapeutic action of psycho-analysis. *International Journal of Psychoanalysis*, 41: 16–33.

Lombardi, R. (1998). Felicità e corporeità. *Psiche*, 2: 75–88.

Longhin, L. and Mancia, M. (1998). *Temi e problemi in psicoanalisi*. Turin: Bollati Boringhieri.

Longhin, L. and Mancia, M. (2001). *Sentieri della mente: Filosofia, letteratura, arte e musica in dialogo con la psicoanalisi*. Turin: Bollati Boringhieri.

Luria, A.R. (1973). *Un mondo perduto e ritrovato*. Rome: Riuniti, 1991.

McDougall, J. (1989). The dead father: on early psychic trauma and its relation to disturbance in sexual identity and in creative activity. *International Journal of Psychoanalysis*, 70: 205–219.

McDougall, J. (1997). *The Many Faces of Eros: A Psychoanalytic Exploration of Human Sexuality*. New York: W.W. Norton.

McEwen, B.S. and Sapolsky, R.M. (1995). Stress and cognitive function. *Current Opinion in Neurobiology*, 5: 205–216.

McGaugh, J.L. (2002). Memory consolidation and the amygdala: a systems perspective. *Trend in Neurosciences*, 9: 456–461.

Mancia, M. (1974). Sleep and instinct: an interdisciplinary approach. In P. Levin and K.P. Koella (eds) *Sleep 1974*. Munich: Karger, 1975.

Mancia, M. (1975). Sonno, sogno e istinti: un approccio interdisciplinare. *Archivio di Psicologia, Neurologia e Psichiatria*, 34: 176–203.

Mancia, M. (1976). Sommeil, rêve et instincts: une approche interdisciplinaire, *Revue Française de Psychanalyse*, 1:31–58.

Mancia, M. (1980a). *Neurofisiologia e vita mentale*. Bologna: Zanichelli.

Mancia, M. (1980b). Neurofisiologia e psicoanalisi di fronte al problema della vita psichica fetale. Introduction to A. Rascovsky. *La vita psichica nel feto*. Milan: Il Formichiere, 1980.

Mancia, M. (1981). On the beginning of mental life in the foetus. *International Journal of Psychoanalysis*, 62: 351–357.

Mancia, M. (1982). Voce "Cervello". *Enciclopedia Sistematica, XV*. Turin: Einaudi, pp. 64–80.

Mancia, M. (1983). Archaeology of Freudian thought and the history of neurophysiology. *International Journal of Psychoanalysis*, 10: 185–192.

Mancia, M. (1985). Nascita della psicoanalisi nel contesto scientifico neurologico e psichiatrico dell'Europa di fine Ottocento. In A.M. Accerboni (ed.) *La cultura psicoanalitica*. Atti del Convegno di Trieste, 5–8 December 1985, Trieste: Studio Tesi, 1987, pp. 231–244.

Mancia, M. (1987). *Il sogno come religione della mente*. Rome: Laterza.

Mancia, M. (1988). The dream as religion of the mind. *International Journal of Psychoanalysis*, 69: 419–426.

Mancia, M. (1989). Vita prenatale e organizzazione della mente. In M. Ammaniti (ed.) *La nascita del Sé*. Rome: Laterza, pp. 129–137.

Mancia, M. (1990). *In the Gaze of Narcissus*. London: Karnac, 1993.

Mancia, M. (1991). Costruire e ricostruire nel transfert. In M. Ammaniti and D.N. Stern (eds) *Rappresentazioni e narrazioni*. Rome: Laterza, pp. 201–211.

Mancia, M. (1994). *From Oedipus to Dream*. London: Karnac.

Mancia, M. (1995). *Percorsi: Riflessioni sulla psicoanalisi contemporanea*. Turin: Bollati Boringhieri.

Mancia, M. (1996a). Imitazione, rappresentazione, identificazione: loro ruolo nello sviluppo e nel transfert. *Rivista di Psicoanalisi*, 2: 225–247.

Mancia, M. (1996b). *Sonno e sogno*. Rome: Laterza (2nd edn, 2006).

Mancia, M. (1998a). *Breve storia del sogno.*Venice: Marsilio.

Mancia, M. (1998b). *Coscienza sogno memoria.* Rome: Borla.

Mancia, M. (2000a). Il sogno: una finestra aperta sul transfert. *Rivista di Psicoanalisi*, 46: 225–268.

Mancia, M. (2000b). Sulle molte dimensioni della memoria: neuroscienze e psicoanalisi a confronto. *Psiche*, 2: 181–193.

Mancia, M. (2002). Wittgenstein's personality and his relations with Freud's thought. *International Journal of Psychoanalysis*, 83: 161–177.

Mancia, M. (2003a). Dream actors in the theatre of memory: their role in the psychoanalytic process. *International Journal of Psychoanalysis*, 84: 945–952.

Mancia, M. (2003b). Il sonno della memoria genera mostri. *Rivista di Psicoanalisi*, 49: 691–708.

Mancia, M. (2003c). Implicit memory and unrepressed unconscious: their role in creativity and transference. *Israel Psychoanalytic Journal*, 3: 331–349.

Mancia, M. (2004a). *Il sogno e la sua storia.*Venice: Marsilio.

Mancia, M. (2004b). Una lettura critica dell'opera di Roger Money-Kyrle. *Rivista di Psicoanalisi*, 50: 513–529.

Mancia, M. (2004c). Coscienza e inconscio, sogno e memoria: possibili contaminazioni tra neuroscienze e psicoanalisi. *Psiche*, 1: 75–89.

Mancia, M. (2005). The dream between neuroscience and psychoanalysis. *Archiv für Neurologie und Psychiatrie*, 156(8): 471–479.

Mancia, M. (2006a). Implicit memory and early unrepressed unconscious: their role in the therapeutic process (how the neurosciences can contribute to psychoanalysis). *International Journal of Psychoanalysis*, 87: 83–103.

Mancia, M. (2006b). Implicit memory and unrepressed unconscious: how they surface in the transference and in the dream. In M. Mancia (ed.) *Psychoanalysis and Neuroscience*. Milan: Springer.

Mancia, M. (2006c). How the neuroscience can contribute to psychoanalysis. Introduction to M. Mancia (ed.) *Psychoanalysis and Neuroscience*. Milan: Springer.

Mancia, M. and Smirne, S. (1985). *Il sonno e i suoi disturbi*. Milan: Cortina.

Manfredi Turillazzi, S. and Ferro, A. (1990). "Introduzione all'edizione italiana". In W. Baranger and M. Baranger, *La situazione psicoanalitica come campo bipersonale*, Milan: Cortina, pp.VII–XVI.

Maquet, P., Péters, J.-M., Aerts, J., Delfiore, G., Degueldre, C., Luxen, A. and Franck, G. (1996). Functional neuroanatomy of human rapid-eye-movement sleep and dreaming. *Nature*, 383: 163–166.

Maquet, P., Laureys, S., Peigneux, P., Fuchs, S., Petiau, C., Phillips, C., (2000). Experience-dependent changes in cerebral activation during human REM sleep. *Nature Neuroscience*, 3: 831–836.

Markowitsch, H.J. (2000). The anatomical bases of memory. In M.S. Gazzaniga (ed.) *The New Cognitive Neurosciences*. Cambridge, MA: MIT Press, pp. 781–795.

Massimini, M., Ferrarelli, F., Huber, R., Esser, S.K., Singh, H. and Tononi, G. (2005). Breakdown of cortical effective connectivity during sleep. *Science*, 309: 2228–2232.

Matte-Blanco, I. (1975). *The Unconscious as Infinite Sets: An Essay in Bi-logic*. London: Duckworth.

Maulsby, R.L. (1971). An illustration of emotionally evoked theta rhythm in infancy: hedonic hypersynchrony. *Electroencephalography and Clinical Neurophysiology*, 31: 157–165.

Mehler, J., Bertoncini, J., Barriere, M. and Jassik-Gerschenfeld, D. (1978). Infant recognition of mother's voice. *Perception*, 7: 491–497.

Meltzer, D. (1966). The relation of anal masturbation to projective identification. *International Journal of Psychoanalysis*, 47: 335–342.

Meltzer, D. (1978). *The Kleinian Development*. Roland Harris Educational Trust Library, Vol. 8. Perthshire: Clunie Press.

Meltzer, D. (1980). *Sexual States of Mind*. Perthshire: Clunie Press.

Meltzer, D. (1984). *Dream Life: A Re-Examination of the Psycho-Analytical Theory and Technique*. Perthshire: Clunie Press.

Meltzer, D. (1986). *Studies in Extended Metapsychology*. Perthshire: Clunie Press.

Meltzer, D. (1988). *The Apprehension of Beauty: The Role of Aesthetic Conflict in Development, Violence and Art*. Perthshire: Clunie Press.

Meltzer, D. (1992). *The Claustrum: An Investigation of Claustrophobic Phenomena*. Roland Harris Educational Trust. Perthshire Clunie Press.

Meltzoff, A.N. (1995). What infant memory tells us about infantile amnesia: long-term recall and deferred imitation. *Journal of Experimental Child Psychology*, 59: 497–515.

Michnick Golinkoff, R. and Hirsh-Pasek, K. (2000). *How Babies Talk: The Magic and Mystery of Languague in the First Three Years of Life*. New York: Plume Books.

Miller, E.K., Li, L. and Desimone, R. (1993). Activity of neurons in anterior inferior temporal cortex during a short term memory task. *Journal of Neuroscience*, 13: 1460–1478.

Mishkin, M. (1978). Memory in monkeys severely impaired by combined but not separated removal of amygdala and hyppocampus. *Nature*, 273: 297–298.

Molinari, S. and Foulkes, D. (1969). Tonic and phasic events during sleep: psychological correlates and implications. *Perceptual and Motor Skills*, 29: 343–368.

Money-Kyrle, R. (1930). *The Meaning of Sacrifice*. London: Hogarth Press.

Money-Kyrle, R. (1938). *Superstition and Society*. London: Hogarth Press and the Institute of Psycho-Analysis.

Money-Kyrle, R. (1951). *Psychoanalysis and Politics.* London: Duckworth.

Money-Kyrle, R. (1961). *Man's Picture of his Worlds.* London: Duckworth.

Money-Kyrle, R. (1978). *The Collected Papers of Roger Money-Kyrle.* Perthshire: Clunie Press.

Moruzzi, G. (1969). Sleep and instinctive behavior. *Archives Italiennes de Biologie,* 107: 175–216.

Moruzzi, G. (1972). The sleep-waking cycle. *Ergebnisse der Physiologie,* 64: 1–165.

Moruzzi, G. and Magoun, H.W. (1949). Brain stem reticular formation and activation of the EEG. *Electroencephalography and Clinical Neurophysiology,* 1: 455–473.

Murray, E.A. (2000). Memory for objects in nonhuman primates. In M.S. Gazzaniga (ed.) *The New Cognitive Neurosciences.* Cambridge, MA: MIT Press, pp. 753–763.

Musil, R. (1957). *Der Mann ohne Eigenschafter.* Berlin: Rowohltverlag.

Nadel, L. and Moscovitch, M. (2001). The hippocampal complex and long-term memory revisited. *Trends of Cognitive Sciences,* 5(6): 228–230.

Natoli, S. (1986). *L'esperienza del dolore: Le forme del patire nella cultura occidentale.* Milan: Feltrinelli.

Neri, C. (1982). Ricordi di ciò di cui non si è fatta esperienza. *Rivista di Psicoanalisi,* 3: 338–341.

Newcombe, N. and Fox, N.A. (1994). Infantile amnesia: through a glass darkly. *Child Development,* 65: 31–40.

Nielsen, T.A. (2003). A review of mentation in REM and NREM sleep: "Covert" REM sleep as a possible reconciliation of two opposing models. In E.F. Pace-Schott, M. Solms, M. Blagrove and S. Harnad (eds) *Sleep and Dreaming: Scientific Advances and Reconsiderations.* Cambridge: Cambridge University Press, pp. 59–74.

Nissim-Momigliano, L. and Robutti, A. (eds) (1992). *L'esperienza condivisa.* Milan: Cortina.

Ogden, J.H. (1999). "The music of what happens" in poetry and psychoanalysis. *International Journal of Psychoanalysis,* 80: 979–994.

Ogden, J.H. (2001). *Conversations at the Frontier of Dreaming.* Northvale, NJ: Jason Aronson.

Ognibene, A. (1999). La spinta di Eros dalle rappresentazioni al linguaggio. In A. Bimbi (ed.) *Eros e Psiche.* Tirrenia (Pisa): Edizioni del Cerro, pp. 27–37.

Orsucci, F. (1998). Felicità ed ecologia profonda. *Psiche,* 2: 35–46.

Osaka, N. (2006). Human anterior cingulate cortex and affective pain induced by mimic words: a functional magnetic resonance imaging study. In M. Mancia (ed.) *Psychoanalysis and Neuroscience.* Milan: Springer.

Osaka, N., Osaka, M., Morishita, M., Kondo, H. and Fukuyama, H. (2004).

A word expressing affective pain activates the anterior cingulate cortex in the human brain: an fMRI study. *Behavioural Brain Research*, 153: 123–127.

Pally, R. (1999). Memory: brain systems that link past, present and future. *International Journal of Psychoanalysis*, 78: 1223–1234.

Palmisano, A. (2000). I processi di memoria, tra neuroscienze e psicoanalisi. *Psiche*, 2: 195–208.

Panksepp, J. (2001). The long-term psychobiological consequences of infant emotions: prescriptions for the twenty-first century. *Neuro-Psychoanalysis*, 2: 149–178.

Paré, D., Collins, D.R. and Pelletier, G. (2002). Amygdala oscillations and the consolidation of emotional memories. *Trends in Cognitive Sciences*, 7: 306–314.

Pavlov, I. (1915). Donnée sur la physiologie du sommeil. *Comptes Rendus Société de Biologie*, 79: 1070–1084, 1916.

Perner, J. and Ruffman, T. (1995). Episodic memory and autonoetic consciousness: developmental evidence and a theory of childhood amnesia. *Journal of Experimental Child Psychology*, 59: 516–548.

Phelps, E.A. (2004). Human emotion and memory: interactions of the amygdala and hippocampal complex. *Current Opinion in Neurobiology*, 14: 198–202.

Pieron, H. (1913). *Le problème physiologique du sommeil*. Paris: Masson.

Piontelli, A. (2006). On the onset of human fetal behavior. In M. Mancia (ed.) *Psychoanalysis and Neuroscience*. Milan: Springer.

Pribram, K.H. (1969). La neurofisiologia della memoria. *Le Scienze*, 2: 28–39.

Quinodoz, J.-M. (1992). Homosexualité et angoisse de séparation. 52ème Congrès des Psychanalystes de Langue Française des Pays Romans. *Bulletin de la Société Psychanalytique de Paris*, 23: 87–93.

Quinodoz, J.-M. (2001). *Dreams that Turn over a Page: Paradoxical Dreams in Psychoanalysis*. London: Brunner-Routledge.

Rascovsky, A. (1977). *El psiquismo fetal*. Buenos Aires: Paidos.

Resnik, S. (1982). Psicosi, gruppi, istituzioni. *Quaderni di psicoterapia di gruppo 2*. Rome: Borla.

Resnik, S. (1999). *Temps des glaciations*. Ramonville Saint'Ague, France: Editions Erès.

Resnik, S. (2002). *Il teatro del sogno*. Turin: Bollati Boringhieri.

Riolo, F. (1982). Memoria e coscienza. *Rivista di Psicoanalisi*, 3: 287–301.

Rizzolatti, G., Fogassi, L. and Gallese, V. (2001). Neurophysiological mechanisms underlying the understanding and imitation of action. *Nature Reviews Neuroscience*, 2: 661–670.

Rose, S. (1992). *The Making to Memory: From Molecules to Mind*. London: Bantam Press.

Rosenfeld, H.A. (1965). *Psychotic States: A Psychoanalytic Approach*. London: Hogarth Press.

Rosenfeld, H.A. (1987). *Impasse and Interpretation*. London: Tavistock.

Rothstein, A. (1985). *Models of the Mind: Their Relationship to Clinical Work*. New York: International Univiersities Press.

Rovee-Collier, C. (1993). The capacity for long-term memory in infancy. *Current Directions in Psychological Science*, 2: 130–135.

Russo, L. (1998). *L'indifferenza dell'anima*. Rome: Borla.

Sakai, K.L. (2005). Language acquisition and brain development. *Science*, 310: 815–819.

Sandler, J. and Sandler, A.M. (1987). The past unconsciouss, the present unconscious and the vicissitudes of guilt. *International Journal of Psychoanalysis*, 68: 331–341.

Sandler, J., Dare, C. and Holder, A. (1973). *The Basis of the Psychoanalytic Process*. Plymouth, UK: Clarke, Doble & Brendon.

Sarno, L. (1982). Sulla reminiscenza. *Rivista di Psicoanalisi*, 3: 302–319.

Sassanelli, G. (1982). *Le basi narcisistiche della personalità*. Turin: Boringhieri.

Sassanelli, G. (1989). *L'io e lo specchio*. Rome: Astrolabio.

Saussure, F. de (1916). *Cours de linguistique générale*. Edition critique préparée par Tullio De Mauro. Paris: Payot, 1972.

Scalzone, F. (2000). Note storico-critiche sul concetto di "memoria" in Freud. *Psiche*, 2: 21–37.

Scalzone, F. (2005) Notes for a dialogue between psychoanalysis and neuroscience. *International Journal of Psychoanalysis*, 86: 1405–1423.

Schacter, D.L. (1995). Implicit memory: a new frontier for cognitive neuro-science. In M.S. Gazzaniga (ed.) *The Cognitive Neurosciences*. Cambridge, MA: MIT Press, pp. 815–824.

Schacter, D.L. (1996). *Searching for Memory: The Brain, the Mind, and the Past*. New York: Basic Books.

Schacter, D.L. and Curran, T. (2000). Memory without remembering and remembering without memory: implicit and false memories. In M.S. Gazzaniga (ed.) *The Cognitive Neurosciences*. Cambridge, MA: MIT Press, pp. 829–840.

Schacter, R. (1993). Cinque letture di "Osservazioni sull'amore di transfert". In E.S. Person, A. Hagelin and P. Fonagy (eds) *L'amore di transfert*. Milan: Cortina, 1994, pp. 59–79.

Schafer, R. (1983). *The Analytic Attitude*. New York: Basic Books.

Segal, H. (1957). Notes on symbol-formation. *International Journal of Psychoanalysis*, 38: 391–397.

Segre, C. (1990). La struttura schizofrenica del "Licenciado Vidriera" di Cervantes. In *Fuori del mondo: i modelli nella follia e nelle immagini dell'aldilà*. Turin: Einaudi, pp. 121–132.

Semenza, C. (2001). Types of memory in psychoanalysis. Paper presented at the Congress on *Neuroscientific and Psychoanalytic Perspectives on Memory*. New York, 20–22 April.

Semenza, C., Costantini, M.V. and Mariani, F. (2000). Memoria, cognitivismo e psicoanalisi. *Psiche*, 2: 209–220.

Semi, A.A. (2003). *La coscienza in psicoanalisi*. Milan: Cortina.

Sergerie, K. and Armony, J. (2006). Interaction between emotion and cognition: a neurobiological perspective. In M. Mancia (ed.) *Psychoanalysis and Neuroscience*. Milan: Springer.

Sherrington, C. (1906). *The Integrative Action of the Nervous System*. Cambridge: Cambridge University Press, 1952.

Shevrin, H. (2001). A psychoanalytic view of memory in the light of recent cognitive neuroscience research. Paper presented at the Congress on *Neuroscientific and Psychoanalytic Perspectives on Memory*. New York, 20–22 April.

Siegel, S.J. (1999). *The Developing Mind*. New York: Guilford Press.

Singer, T., Seymour, B., O'Doherty, J., Kaube, H., Dolan, R.J. and Frith, C.D. (2004). Empathy for pain involves the affective but not sensory components of pain. *Science*, 303: 1157–1164.

Siracusano, F. (1982). Il messaggio nascosto nell'oblio. *Rivista di Psicoanalisi*, 28: 320–328.

Solms, M. (1995). New findings on the neurological organization of dreaming: implications for psychoanalysis. *Psychoanalytic Quarterly*, 44: 43–67.

Solms, M. (1999). Dreaming and REM sleep are controlled by different brain mechanisms. Paper presented at the Annual Meeting of the American Academy for the Advancement of Science, Anaheim, CA, 25 March.

Solms, M. (2001). A neuro-psychoanalytic hypothesis. Paper presented at the Congress on *Neuroscientific and Psychoanalytic Perspectives on Memory*. New York, 20–22 April.

Solms, M. (2003). Dreaming and REM sleep are controlled by different brain mechanisms. In E.F. Pace-Schott, M. Solms, M. Blagrove and S. Harnad (eds) *Sleep and Dreaming: Scientific Advances and Reconsiderations*. Cambridge: Cambridge University Press, pp. 51–58.

Solms, M. and Turnbull, O. (2002). *The Brain and the Inner World*. New York: Other Press.

Spector Person, E., Hagelin, A. and Fonagy, P. (1993). *On Freud's Observations on Tranference-Love*. New Haven, CT: Yale University Press.

Sperry, R.W. (1974). Lateral specialization in the surgically separated hemispheres. In F.D. Smith and F.G. Worden (eds) *The Neurosciences: Third Study Program*. Cambridge, MA: MIT Press.

Speziale-Bagliacca, R. (2002). *Freud messo a fuoco: passando dai padri alle madri*. Turin: Bollati Boringhieri.

Squire, L.R. (1994). Declarative and nondeclarative memory: multiple brain system supporting learning and memory. In D.L. Schacter and E. Tulvin (eds) *Memory Systems*. Cambridge, MA: MIT Press, pp. 203–232.

Squire, L.R. and Knowlton, B.J. (2000). The medial temporal lobe, the hippocampus, and the memory systems of the brain. In M.S. Gazzaniga (ed.), *The New Cognitive Neurosciences*. Cambridge, MA: MIT Press, pp.765–779.

Squire, L.R. et al. (1993). The structure and organization of memory. *Annual Review Psychology*, 44: 453–495.

Steiner, J. (1989). The aim of psychoanalysis. *Psychoanalytic Psychotherapy*, 4: 109–120.

Steiner, J. (1993). *Psychic Retreats: Pathological Organisations in Psychotic, Neurotic and Borderline Patients*. London: Routledge.

Sterman, M.B. and Clemente, C.D. (1962). Forebrain inhibitory mechanisms: cortical synchronization induced by basal forebrain stimulation. *Experimental Neurology*, 6: 91–102.

Stern, D.N. (1985). *The Interpersonal World of the Infant*. New York: Basic Books.

Stern, D.N. (1993). Agire e ricordare nell'amore di transfert e nell'amore infantile. In E.S. Person, A. Hagelin and P. Fonagy (eds) *L'amore di transfert*. Milan: Cortina, 1994, pp. 157–170.

Stern, D.N., Danfer, L.W., Nahum, J.P., Harrison, A.M., Lyons-Ruth, K., Morgan, A.C., Bruschweiler-Stern, N. and Tronick, E.Z. (1998). Non-interpretative mechanisms in psychoanalytic therapy: the "something more" than interpretation. *International Journal of Psychoanalysis*, 79: 903–921.

Stickgold, R., Malia, A., Maguire, D., Roddenberry, D. and O'Connor, M. (2000). Replaying the game: hypnagogic images in normals and amnesics. *Science*, 290: 350.

Stoller, R.J. (1975). *Perversion: The Erotic Form of Hatred*. New York: Pantheon.

Svevo, I. (1976). *La coscienza di Zeno*. Bologna: Dall'Oglio Editore.

Tatossian, A. (1988). *Edipo in Kakania. Kafka, Musil e Freud*. Turin: Bollati Boringhieri, 2002.

Tinbergen, N. (1951). *The Study of the Instinct*. Oxford: Oxford University Press.

Tomassini, M. (1992). Désidentification primaire, angoisse de séparation et formation de la structure perverse. 52ème Congrès des Psychanalystes de Langue Française des Pays Romans. *Bulletin de la Société Psychanalytique de Paris*, 23: 1–48.

Vallard, G. (1983). La neuropsicologia della memoria a breve termine. *Le Scienze*, 31(184): 34–55.

Warrington, E.K. and Weiskrantz, L. (1974). The effect of prior learning on subsequent retention in amnesic patients. *Neuropsychologia*, 12: 419–428.

Waugh, M. (1979). Some psychoanalytic observations on boredom. *International Journal of Psychoanalysis*, 60(4): 515:528.

Weininger, O. (1906). *Sex & Character*. London: William Heinemann.

Winnicott, D.W. (1956). On transference. *International Journal of Psychoanalysis*, 37: 386–388.

Winnicott, D.W. (1958). The capacity to be alone. In *The Maturational Processes and the Facilitating Environment: Studies in the Theory of Emotional Development*. London: Hogarth Press and the Institute of Psycho-Analysis, 1965, pp. 29–36.

Winnicott, D.W. (1965). The theory of the parent–infant relationship. *International Journal of Psychoanalysis*, 41: 585–595.

Winnicott, D.W. (1967). The location of cultural experience. *International Journal of Psychoanalysis*, 48: 368–372.

Winnicott, D.W. (1971). *Playing and Reality*. London: Tavistock.

Wolpert, E.A. and Trosman, H. (1958). Studies in psychophysiology of dreams. I. Experimental evocation of sequential dream episodes. *American Association Archives of Neurology and Psychiatry*, 79: 603–606.

Zapparoli, G. (1979). *La paura e la noia*. Milan: Il Saggiatore.

Index

abandonment 152, 153, 157, 177, 184
Abraham, Karl 7, 116, 118, 127
acting out 68, 131, 167, 170;
    masturbation 128; mental pain 218;
    sexual 176
activation-synthesis hypothesis 91–2
addiction 206
Adolphs, R. 18
Aeschylus 210
affectionate transference 178–9
aggression 16, 152, 214, 215
alpha function 13, 52, 98
Alzheimer's disease 34
ameba metaphor 115, 116
amnesia 36, 64; infantile 43; semantic
    34
amorous transference 178, 179, 181,
    184
amygdala 17–19, 29, 33–4, 35, 46, 92
anal masturbation 77, 107, 128
anal penetration 67, 69, 70, 77
analysts: archaeology metaphor 42–3;
    levels of reality 167–8; mental pain
    216–18; negative personality 142;
    psychotic/borderline patients 124–5;
    transference love 169–70, 171–9;
    unrepressed unconscious 167
analytic relationship: Bion 12–13;
    Kleinian school 8; memory 45, 46;
    pain 215–18; unrepressed
    unconscious 64
analytical third party 54
Anderson, M.C. 47, 93, 220n2

anger: clinical cases 152, 157, 158–9,
    161, 162, 163; mental pain 213, 214;
    musical dimension of transference 60
Antrobus, J. 90, 91
anxiety 66–7, 72, 74, 77, 78, 157;
    castration 3, 133, 134; depressive 145,
    201; Klein 211–12; loss and death
    218; mental pain 212, 215; narcissistic
    personality 133, 135, 136;
    persecutory 192, 193, 212; psychotic
    120; separation 123, 132, 180–1
aphasia 34
archaeology metaphor 42–3
art 29, 55–8, 62, 171
arts 169–70
Aserinsky, E. 88
Atkinson, R.C. 31–2
attachment system 122, 128, 213
attention 38, 48–9
autism 59, 213, 214
auto-erotic satisfaction 116, 118
autobiographic memory 45, 47, 58, 59,
    64, 66; brain structures 36; dreams
    96; repression 6, 7; retranscription of
    166

Balint, M. 118
Baranger, Madeleine 10
Baranger, Willy 10
Bassetti, C.L. 48, 94
Bastide, Roger 83
Benjamin, J. 195
Berlusconi, Silvio 139

243

object' 113; unrepressed unconscious 29
mother-child relationship: Bion 13–14; Klein 7–8, 118–20, 194, 211–12; memory 32–3; neuroscience 17; reflexive processes 206; Winnicott 15–16, 194
MTL *see* medial temporal lobe
music 29, 53, 54, 57–8, 86
'musical dimension' of the transference 20, 29, 54–5, 59–60, 62, 65, 166, 215
Musil, Robert 2, 3, 4
myth 84, 85

Nachträglichkeit 20–1, 96, 99–100, 102, 164; mental pain 215; reconstruction 44–5; transference love 169, 170, 186
Nadel, L. 36
narcissism 6, 10, 113, 115–43; clinical cases 129–41, 142–3, 152, 159; Freud 115–19, 141; Klein 8, 116, 118–20, 121; malignant 124, 142; 'negative personality' 120, 121–8, 141–2, 215; normal vs pathological 121; primary 116, 117, 118; secondary 116, 117; transference love 173
narcissistic identification 116
Natoli, S. 204, 211, 221n1
'negative personality' 120, 121–8, 141–2, 158, 206–7, 213, 214–15
neglect 154, 161
neurons: Alzheimer's patients 34; consciousness 25; emotions 17–18; Freud 39–40; memory fields 35; synapses 36–8
neurophysiology 21, 22–3, 79, 81, 88, 89
neuropsychoanalysis xiv–xv
neuropsychology: dreams 79, 93; memory 33–6, 46–7; repression 93
neuroscience xiv–xv, 16–27; consciousness 23–5; dreams 21–2, 79, 88–94, 105; emotions and memory 17–20; empathy and shared affects 22–3; language development 26–7; memory 33–8, 46–50; prenatal life

25–6; the unconscious 20–1, 24–5, 49–50; *see also* brain
neurosis: Bion 125–6; erotic transference 177; Kafka 4; narcissistic 6, 118
normality 11

object relations: dreams 85, 97, 103, 104, 105; erotic transference 178; idealized object 121; Klein 9; narcissism 10, 116, 117, 118, 119–20, 141; negativity 122; pathological defenses 123; psychotic/borderline patients 124; transference love 173; trauma-objects 122, 128
Oedipal phase 40, 190, 192, 194, 196, 197, 213
Oedipus complex 2–5, 6, 7–9, 119, 177–8, 190–1
Ogden, J.H. 54
Ognibene, Adele 59
omnipotence 10, 124, 141, 206
omniscience 10, 124
orbito-frontal cortex 19
Orsucci, F. 208

pain 22, 118, 207, 210–18
Panksepp, J. 18
paranoia 115
paranoid-schizoid position 7–8, 74, 106, 119, 124, 212, 217
parietal cortex 92
Parmigianino 55, *56*
Pasolini, Pier Paolo 5
Pavlov, I. 88
penis envy 191, 192–4, 195
persecutory phenomena 152, 158, 159, 201; anxiety 192, 193, 212; dreams 106, 217; mental pain 212–13
personality: mental pain 216; 'negative' 120, 121–8, 141–2, 158, 206–7, 213, 214–15
personality disorders 49
perversion 196, 206, 214, 215
PET *see* positron emission tomography
philosophy 211
Pieron, Henry 88
play 15, 171, 214